SELF-CONTROL AND SELF-MODIFICATION OF EMOTIONAL BEHAVIOR

ADVANCES IN THE STUDY OF COMMUNICATION AND AFFECT

Volume 1 • NONVERBAL COMMUNICATION
Edited by Lester Krames, Patricia Pliner, and Thomas Alloway

Volume 2 • NONVERBAL COMMUNICATION OF AGGRESSION
Edited by Patricia Pliner, Lester Krames, and Thomas Alloway

Volume 3 • ATTACHMENT BEHAVIOR
Edited by Thomas Alloway, Patricia Pliner, and Lester Krames

Volume 4 • AGGRESSION, DOMINANCE, AND INDIVIDUAL SPACING
Edited by Lester Krames, Patricia Pliner, and Thomas Alloway

Volume 5 • PERCEPTION OF EMOTION IN SELF AND OTHERS
Edited by Patricia Pliner, Kirk R. Blankstein, and Irwin M. Spigel

Volume 6 • ASSESSMENT AND MODIFICATION OF EMOTIONAL BEHAVIOR
Edited by Kirk R. Blankstein, Patricia Pliner, and Janet Polivy

Volume 7 • SELF-CONTROL AND SELF-MODIFICATION OF EMOTIONAL BEHAVIOR
Edited by Kirk R. Blankstein and Janet Polivy

Volume 8 • AGING AND COGNITIVE PROCESSES
Edited by F. I. M. Craik and Sandra Trehub

A Continuation Order Plan is available for this series. A continuation order will bring delivery of each new volume immediately upon publication. Volumes are billed only upon actual shipment. For further information please contact the publisher.

ADVANCES IN THE STUDY OF COMMUNICATION AND AFFECT

Volume 7

SELF-CONTROL AND SELF-MODIFICATION OF EMOTIONAL BEHAVIOR

Edited by

Kirk R. Blankstein and Janet Polivy

Erindale College
University of Toronto
Mississauga, Ontario, Canada

PLENUM PRESS · NEW YORK AND LONDON

Library of Congress Cataloging in Publication Data

Main entry under title:

Self-control and self-modification of emotional behavior.

(Advances in the study of communication and affect; v.7)
Includes bibliographical references and index.
1. Emotions. 2. Behavior modification. I. Blankstein, Kirk R. II. Polivy, Janet. III. Series. [DNLM: 1. Emotions. 2. Behavior therapy. WI AD8801 v. 7 / WM 425 S465]
BF561.S44 1982 152.4 82-10234
ISBN 0-306-40945-3

A Division of Plenum Publishing Corporation
233 Spring Street, New York, N.Y. 10013

Printed in the United States of America

Contributors

JACQUELINE AVARD
Department of Psychology, University of Montreal, Montreal, Quebec, Canada

LAURENCE H. BERGER
Department of Psychology, University of Montana, Missoula, Montana

KIRK R. BLANKSTEIN
Department of Psychology, Erindale College, University of Toronto, Mississauga, Ontario, Canada

RICHARD R. BOOTZIN
Department of Psychology, Northwestern University, Evanston, Illinois

D. BALFOUR JEFFREY
Department of Psychology, University of Montana, Missoula, Montana

JANET POLIVY
Department of Psychology, Erindale College, University of Toronto, Mississauga, Ontario, Canada

GERALD M. ROSEN
Clinical Psychologist, Private Practice, Seattle, Washington

ETHEL ROSKIES
Department of Psychology, University of Montreal, Montreal, Quebec, Canada

RICHARD SCHULZ
Institute on Aging, Portland State University, Portland, Oregon

GARY E. SCHWARTZ
Department of Psychology, Yale University, New Haven, Connecticut

LINDA C. SOBELL
Clinical Institute, Addiction Research Foundation, 33 Russell Street, Toronto, Ontario, Canada

MARK B. SOBELL
Clinical Institute, Addiction Research Foundation, 33 Russell Street, Toronto, Ontario, Canada

G. TERENCE WILSON
Department of Psychology, Rutgers University, New Brunswick, New Jersey

Contents

CHAPTER 1

Emotions, Self-Control, and Self-Modification
An Introduction

Kirk R. Blankstein and Janet Polivy

Department of Psychology
Erindale College
University of Toronto
Mississauga, Ontario, Canada

Personality theorists, behavioral scientists, and clinicians have long been concerned about how people control and modify the way they feel and how they exercise personal control over other behaviors that have emotional correlates and consequences. Therapists often attempt not only to resolve current distress, but to help the person to develop self-control over his or her emotions and potential problem behaviors to avoid future distress.

Self-Control and Self-Modification: Working Definitions

Although examination of the scientific literature suggests some definitional confusion about what is meant by *self-control* and the notion is referred to by a variety of connotatively similar terms, we will attempt to avoid this terminological babel. In our working definition, we use the term *self-control* to mean a person's influence over and regulation of his or her own psychological, behavioral, and physical processes. The person who exercises self-control is able to regulate her or his own behavior—emotions, actions, and desires—by emitting responses to inhibit, maintain, or change behavior in a desired direction. People often make active or deliberate efforts, using more-or-less formal strategies, to change or modify the ways in which they control their feelings and behavior. We use the term *self-modification* to designate personal efforts toward such modification and control that are initiated and implemented without the active assistance or monitoring of a therapist or significant others. Thus, the goal of self-modification is the development of improved self-control.

Perspectives on Self-Control and Self-Modification

How do we conceptualize self-controlled behavior? What basic strategies do people use to regulate emotional behavior, and what problems are typically encountered? How do we go about modifying an individual's self-regulated behavior (or lack of it), and what is the most effective and efficient way to do this? How do we effect generalization and maintenance of the changes? What actions can the person take to influence his or her own internal and external behavior?

Freud's ideas about self-control were probably the first in modern literature that significantly influenced scientists and most laypersons as well. To explain the individuals' ability to predict and control their own behavior, psychoanalytic writers have posited within the organism some kind of internal agent that makes deliberate decisions relating to the individuals' controlled behavior. The mechanisms of cognitive control proposed by Freud and the ego analysts (unconscious "defense mechanisms"; "ego strength" or "ego controls") have been the focus of much research. Phenomenological and humanistic writers such as Rogers and Maslow have also theorized about human beings' ability to control their personal world. These writers have emphasized freedom and self-direction, and they posit an inherent ability to actualize potential ("self-actualization"). Behaviorists, especially Skinner, have objected to the "explanations" of self-control behavior proposed by these writers, regarding them as simply a relabeling of the phenomena. The theories and interventions proposed by the psychoanalysts and humanists have also been criticized as being not testable, difficult to apply, or not generally applicable because they focus only on a limited range of emotions and behaviors.

In the past 20 years, behavioral conceptualizations of self-control have been added to and modified at a rapid pace. The earliest behavioral view was Skinner's: an individual engages in self-control when she or he arranges the environment so that only certain controlling stimuli are present. One of the oldest, and most often cited, examples of this type of self-control was reported by Homer in the travels of Odysseus (Kanfer & Phillips, 1970). To manage the bewitching effects of the Sirens, Odysseus ordered his oarsmen to fill their ears with beeswax. He commanded his men to tie him to the mast and ordered them not to release him under any circumstances. The key to Odysseus's success was in his recognition that self-control is integrally bound up with knowledge of and control over current environmental factors. Thus, in this view, behavior is a function of the environment, but the environment itself is controlled by the organism.

Recent social-learning theory conceptualizations (e.g., Bandura, 1977b) emphasize reciprocal as opposed to environmental determinism. Thus, the phenomenon of self-control is made up of an infinite and complex chain of interdependent behavior–environment influences, and the individual is viewed not as a passive product of environmental influence, but rather as an active participant in arranging and regulating his or her own behavior. Expansion of the Skinnerian model has generated renewed interest and concern with "private," "cognitive" events: the acquisition of, maintenance of, persistence in, and capacity for self-directed behavior change are assumed to be determined largely by cognitive mechanisms. Bandura (1977a) has now assigned a central role to self-efficacy–a personal belief in one's ability to cope successfully with a threatening situation–in mediating the behavior changes evidenced as a result of psychological treatments. Behavioral conceptualizations such as Bandura's have had a tremendous impact on clinical intervention strategies: self-control treatment "packages" based on these conceptualizations are being developed at a rapid pace and are being evaluated with myriad target behaviors and populations.

Cognitive activity is often available to self-control when external circumstances are not. Recent years have witnessed the development of cognitive therapies. These diverse procedures are based on the theoretical premise that faulty cognitions underlie emotional and behavioral disturbance. In contrast to the traditional emphasis on behavioral intervention, the cognitive therapies seek to change these faulty cognitions, (primarily) through cognitive means. Thus, the task of therapy is to identify maladaptive or faulty thought patterns and to replace them with more adaptive cognitions. These self-statements or "internal dialogues" emphasize "both perceived and actual personal control, mastery, and coping ability in the face of threatening circumstances" (Wilson, 1979, p. 176).[1]

[1]It has been suggested that behavior therapy has "gone cognitive" with a "marriage" of the behavioral and cognitive therapies. The emergence of this "cognitive connection" led Wilson (1978) to consider the possibility of a "paradigm shift." The cognitive-behavioral integration has met some resistance from more traditional behaviorists, and some cognitive theorists have

Many other conceptualizations of self-regulatory processes and research findings are relevant to attempts to understand and modify self-control. Most of the classical theories of emotion emphasize that aspects of personal control play an important role in determining how one feels. Lazarus (e.g., 1977) relates his theory of emotion to problems of stress and coping skills. He distinguishes between coping responses directed toward altering the environment and those serving to regulate the individual's emotional state, which are thus "self-control" responses.

Social psychological research on attributions, expectations, self-perceptions, attitudes, and beliefs is also relevant. For example, "attribution theory" (Thibault & Kelley, 1959) has generated considerable interest in the hypothesis that changes in behavior that the individuals attribute to their own efforts are more long-lasting than changes they attribute to external forces or agents. Jones and Berglas (1978) have used an attribution theory framework to describe what they call "self-handicapping strategies." The self-handicapper is the person who reaches out for impediments, exaggerates handicaps, and embraces any factor (e.g., alcohol, the "sick role") that reduces personal responsibility for mediocrity and that enhances personal responsibility for success. Seligman and his associates (e.g., Seligman, 1975) have conducted research demonstrating the emotional, motivational, and cognitive effects of uncontrollability ("learned helplessness"). Presumably, when the environment precludes the exertion of efficacious self-modification or self-control (i.e., when there is no response that the individual can make to influence his or her feelings or available behaviors), negative feelings and behavioral deficits are the result.

People differ in the degree to which they believe that they have the ability to control (and the extent to which they feel personally responsible for) what happens to them. According to Rotter (1966), such perceptions involve a dimension of "perceived locus of control" (also called *internal–external control of reinforcement*). Individual differences in this internal–external control dimension have been measured by a questionnaire that has yielded many correlates. Naturally, the degree to which one feels able to control the environment should be related to one's perceived self-control.

More recently, Rosenbaum (1980) developed a self-report measure, based on a cognitive-behavioral conceptualization of self-control methods. He found that highly self-controlled subjects tolerate the pain of a cold pressor longer than subjects who have low self-control. Janis (1980) has written about the related issue concerning different personality characteristics or

---

protested the shotgun wedding. It is clear, however, that the differentiation among conceptual approaches has become less distinct. It seems just as clear that manipulation of "self-talk" may be implicated in successful emotional control and behavior change.

predispositional attributes that lead clients, carrying out a difficult course of action, to react differently to a helping relationship intended to bolster self-control. Thus, individual differences in a sort of general predisposition to benefit from self-control programs apparently result both from "ability" differences and from characterological responses to self-control "aids."

Current research on biofeedback from a physiological perspective has also expanded our understanding of human self-regulation and its application to emotional control and behavior change (e.g., Yates, 1980). Schwartz (1977) has described how stressful transactions with the environment can disrupt physiological regulatory processes. Recently, Carver and Scheier (1981) applied the concepts of control theory (cybernetics) to behavioral self-regulation.

There is also an emerging literature on commonsense beliefs about self-control and on naturally occurring episodes of self-controlled behaviors. Many of us "know" that a "drink" (of alcohol) is relaxing, that coffee will perk us up, and that we should "count to 10" before acting in anger, but are there any assessments of the common stock of knowledge about self-control strategies? Rippere (e.g., 1977) has been exploring what people already know about managing depression and how they apply their knowledge in getting through their daily lives ("What's the thing to do when you're feeling depressed?"). She has argued that to ignore the canon of commonsense beliefs about depression and antidepressive behavior is to risk the possibility of "grossly oversimplifying our own 'expert' views of what we are dealing with" (p. 473). She has suggested that the clinician often neglects to ask patients about their own views about an emotional problem and their own ways of managing it and has argued that "lack of interest in patients' self-management techniques is unfortunate, because it means a loss of potentially useful information about people's ways of coping" (p. 467).

Self-control or modification of mood through the use of mood-altering drugs may well be the most common form of self-control of emotional behavior. Not only does common knowledge assert that alcohol is a sedative, the so-called tension reduction hypothesis of alcohol consumption may well be the most widely researched explanation for the use and/or the abuse of alcohol (e.g., Cappell & Herman, 1972). Although self-medication with recognized mood-altering drugs like tranquilizers or hallucinogens is condemned for abuse, few objections have been raised to self-control or modification of mood with drugs like caffeine and nicotine. The publicity on the health hazards of cigarettes and on the irritability caused by excessive caffeine consumption somehow ignores the use of nicotine and caffeine to regulate affect. Kozlowski and his colleagues (Kozlowski, Jarvik, & Gritz, 1975; Koslowski, 1976) have demonstrated that people modulate their intake of coffee and cigarettes on the basis of the drug dosage (caffeine and nicotine) supplied by each unit (cup of coffee or cigarette), increasing the intake of "weak" units (low-caffeine coffee or low-nicotine cigarettes) and decreasing their intake of "strong" ones.

Although scant attention has been paid to the individuals in the general population who undertake self-initiated programs to control emotional and other problem behavior, the naturally occurring episode of self-controlled behavior is a common and sometimes dramatically successful experience (even when we disregard "self-medication" with mood-altering drugs). Schachter (1981) finds that many more people successfully change behaviors like eating and smoking than any "outcome" study reports. Perri and Richards (e.g., 1977) have been assessing the factors and methods that are crucial to success in these naturally occurring episodes. Successful self-controllers rated themselves as more committed to personal change, and they used a greater number of strategies and for longer periods of time, than did their unsuccessful peers.

Given the current clinical interest in procedures that increase the client's capacity for self-control, the common assumption that self-regulation is a learnable skill, and a trend toward placing increased amounts of responsibility on the client, it is not surprising that self-control treatment programs are now being commercially packaged as self-help manuals and are being disseminated to the general public (e.g., Watson & Tharp, 1981). A basic question is: How useful are these programs and remedies?

Self-Control and Self-Modification of Emotional Behavior

This book provides a sampling of theoretical perspectives and research activity related to self-control and the self-modification of emotional behavior. Some of the chapters are broad-based and theoretical; others focus on specific research problems and applications. Although there is some bias toward behaviorally oriented approaches to self-control, the orientation of most of the authors in this volume is multitheoretical and empirical. Several of the authors attempt to build a bridge between competing perspectives, and chapters dealing with basic research are interwoven with presentations of more clinical concern. Intervention strategies range from classic, "tried-and-true" behavioral techniques to new, multifaceted, experimental approaches. The authors also focus on a variety of populations, ranging from children and normal college students, to adults with serious emotional or behavioral problems, to the aged in institutions. The target behaviors include complex blends of positive and negative emotions, depression and loneliness, anxiety and problem drinking, eating habits, social skills, self-defeating thoughts, and the rushed, aggressive, competitive, achievement-oriented lifestyle called Type A behavior.

Gary E. Schwartz, our first contributing author, reviews the psychophysiology of emotion from a systems perspective and argues persuasively that emotional self-control requires "an integrated and organized regulation of multiple psychobiological processes." He believes that lack of attention to feedback from the body or to negative affect can cause a "disregulation" between brain and body (disease). Schwartz reviews research on emotion within the framework of cerebral laterality and poses a series of questions about the implications of the findings for issues of self-regulation (e.g., does the modification of Type A behavior produce greater hemispheric integration and correspondence between subjective experience and physiological activity?). Schwartz indicates many other directions for future research. For example, he suggests that biofeedback-oriented self-monitoring can be used to increase the ability to label emotional states correctly, and he speculates about the clinical utility of teaching people to self-regulate complex blends of emotion. In his opinion, research is also needed to obtain a more complete measure of the spectrum of emotions experienced before, during, and following self-regulation strategies (such as relaxation training) in order to provide a better prediction of who will respond in what ways to different methods.

In the next chapter, D. Balfour Jeffrey and Laurence H. Berger discuss the clinical implications for behavior change of their "self-environmental systems model." Their main point is that a combined systems–learning theory provides a broader conceptual framework for understanding a wide range of emotional and social behaviors. Jeffrey and Berger provide an organizing framework from a systems theory perspective for a variety of behavioral change techniques. They suggest that the framework, called *SERTS,* provides a convenient checklist of principles and procedures to be used in assessing and modifying breakdowns in regulated behavior. Finally, they provide examples of applications of the model to specific clinical and social problems.

Richard Schulz presents a comprehensive overview and critique of classical theories of emotion as they apply to the social-psychological and biological changes associated with growing old. He asks questions such as "Do central nervous system and end organ changes have any functional significance with respect to the experience of emotion?" His basic premise is that "aging is characterized by many losses, the combined impact of which is to induce feelings of lack of control and helplessness." Schulz describes fieldwork in which these mood states were altered as a consequence of interventions designed to increase aged individuals' level of competence and ability to control and predict their environment. He also outlines several controversial policy implications of his conclusion that expectations for controlling outcomes are determined largely by the individual's reference group.

Loneliness is a common and distressing problem (cf. Peplau & Perlman, 1979) but one that has received little empirical research. The major focus of Richard R. Bootzin's chapter is on a skill deficit approach to loneliness and its implications for prevention and treatment. His analysis distinguishes between the loneliness produced by social isolation and that produced by emotional isolation. Bootzin describes a multimodal intervention package that includes a systematic focus on strategies ranging from social skills to efficacy expectations or a sense of control. He summarizes a pilot project designed to determine whether the development of skills to cope with aloneness would be "protective" at a time of environmental changes and the disruption of social networks. The strategy, if supported by empirical outcome research, may be a useful addition to the armamentarium of self-control interventions.

The next two chapters, by G. Terence Wilson and by Mark B. Sobell and Linda C. Sobell, deal with drinking behavior, but each has a different focus. Wilson addresses the issue of whether alcohol use actually reduces tension in social as well as problem drinkers (as the tension reduction hypothesis posits), and Sobell and Sobell ask whether or not problem drinkers can learn to be "controlled" drinkers.

Individuals employ many different strategies in their attempts to control negative emotional states. Some of these personal strategies are successful, while others can be inefficient, ineffective, and even maladaptive. Wilson points out that the belief that alcohol reduces tension is steeped in folklore and clinical tradition. In fact, many interventions for problem drinking are based on the assumption that people learn to drink to excess as a way of coping with emotional problems. Wilson reviews critically the evidence for this tension reduction hypothesis. In a style reminiscent of the classical conclusions about the effects of psychotherapy, he argues that the useful question to ask would be "under what conditions, at which doses, in whom, and on what measures does alcohol reduce anxiety?"

Another learned expectation, held by many professionals, by Alcoholics Anonymous, and by the general public, is the belief that alcoholics, once treated, must remain abstinent because alcohol problems are largely beyond the individual's control. In Chapter 7, Sobell and Sobell review evidence indicating that self-regulation of drinking is within the individual's capacity, and more importantly, they address the issues of "determining when, for whom, and by what methods nonproblem drinking might be an appropriate treatment goal." The Sobells' viewpoint is consistent with Wilson's conclusion regarding the role of cognitive mediation in the tension reduction issue: they suggest that cognitive factors are related to non-problem-drinking outcomes.

Type A behavior has been found to be related to the incidence of coronary heart disease. In a previous volume in this series, Glass (1980) suggested that the coronary-prone behavior pattern can be characterized as a coping response to environmental stressors that threaten an individual's sense of control. In the present volume, Ethel Roskies and Jacqueline Avard describe the conceptual, methodological, and practical issues involved in designing and carrying out a multimodal, self-control intervention program with Type A healthy managers. A particularly important emphasis in this package is on the building in of strategies for generalizing and maintaining treatment benefits. In addition to "booster" sessions, participants are furnished with a model of self-induced change.

Numerous "self-help" books offering broad-based and specialized programs for self-induced change are now available to the general public. These self-modification manuals are often promoted as effective treatments that can be totally self-administered. Although many academically based and highly respected clinicians are jumping on the bandwagon "to give psychology away to the people," other clinicians eschew the rapid proliferation of these do-it-yourself programs. For example, in a critical review of one manual, Shtasel (1980) lamented as follows: "Why must we insist on 'self-help' for all of our emotional ills? Why do we spend years training experts? Is it going to be by-pass surgery by the numbers next?" (p. 26). In our final chapter, Gerald M. Rosen puts the self-help zeitgeist into historical perspective and assesses the status of current self-help programs (including his own excursions into the self-help arena). Although self-help programs may have potential for helping individuals, he notes that there are few data indicating the effectiveness of these self-control packages and expresses concern about the risks faced by consumers who use untested self-help programs.

The contributions herein provide a contemporary cross section of psychological theory and research on self-control and emotion. The attempts to "bridge the gap" between different conceptual approaches improves our perspective on the issue of the interface between self and environment (cf. Stuart, 1977). If our contributions are representative, then it is clear that research and theory on self-control have "gone cognitive" with psychology in general. However, even if cognition turns out to be a final common pathway, most of the contributors assume that the most effective way to understand and modify self-controlled behavior is to focus on all aspects of the individual's cognitive-behavioral repertoire. Although there is reason to be optimistic, we are still far from knowing which specific "guidance blueprints" will determine stable and effective self-regulation skills (cf. Thoresen & Mahoney, 1974). In fact, the authors raise more questions than they answer. For example, those concerned with modification identify a number of critical problems and highlight numerous areas of concern, in addition to the usual methodological ones: the issue of self-diagnosis; the problem of commitment or compliance; problems related to the complexity of treatment regimen; issues of generalization and long-term maintenance; the issue of therapist supervision and assistance; and the concern about "what works best for whom." It is clear that more controlled research is an essential ingredient for the further refinement of self-regulation theory and intervention methods. In addition to the intellectual stimulation provided by these present contributions, it is hoped that they will stimulate further research inquiry on self-control and emotion.

References

Bandura, A. Self-efficacy: Toward a unifying theory of behavioral change. *Psychological Review,* 1977, *84,* 191–215. (a)

Bandura, A. *Social learning theory.* Englewood Cliffs, N.J.: Prentice-Hall, 1977. (b)

Cappell, H., & Herman, C. P. Alcohol and tension reduction: A review. *Quarterly Journal of Studies on Alcohol,* 1972, *33,* 33–64.

Carver, C. S., & Scheier, M. F. *Attention and self-regulation: A control–theory approach to human behavior.* New York: Springer-Verlag, 1981.

Glass, D. C. Stress, behavior patterns, and coronary disease. In K. R. Blankstein, P. Pliner, & J. Polivy (Eds.), *Advances in the study of communication and affect, Vol. 6: Assessment and modification of emotional behavior.* New York: Plenum Press, 1980.

Janis, I. Personality differences in decision making under stress. In K. R. Blankstein, P. Pliner, & J. Polivy (Eds.), *Advances in the study of communication and affect, Vol. 6: Assessment and modification of emotional behavior.* New York: Plenum Press, 1980.

Jones, E. E., & Berglas, S. Control of attributions about the self through self-handicapping strategies: The appeal of alcohol and the role of underachievement. *Personality and Social Psychology Bulletin,* 1978, *4,* 200–206.

Kanfer, F. H., & Phillips, J. S. *Learning foundations of behavior therapy.* New York: Wiley, 1970.

Kozlowski, L. T. Effect of caffeine on coffee drinking. *Nature,* 1976, *264,* 354–355.

Kozlowski, L. T., Jarvik, M. E., & Gritz, E. R. Nicotine regulation and cigarette smoking. *Technical Pharmacology and Therapeutics,* 1975, *17,* 93–97

Lazarus, R. S. Psychological stress and coping in adaptation and illness. In Z. J. Lipowski, D. R. Lipsitt, & P. C. Whyrow (Eds.), *Psychosomatic medicine: Current trends and clinical applications.* New York: Oxford University Press, 1977.

Peplau, L. A., & Perlman, D. Blueprint for a social psychological theory of loneliness, In M. Cook & G. Wilson (Eds.), *Love and attraction.* Oxford, England: Pergamon Press, 1979.

Perri, M. G., & Richard, C. S. An investigation of naturally occurring episodes of self-controlled behaviors. *Journal of Counseling Psychology,* 1977, *24,* 178–183.

Rippere, V. Commonsense beliefs about depression and antidepressive behavior: A study of social consensus. *Behaviour Research and Therapy,* 1977, *15,* 465–473.

Rosenbaum, M. A schedule for assessing self-control behaviors: Preliminary feelings. *Behavior Therapy,* 1980, *11,* 109–121.

Rotter, J. B. Generalized expectancies for internal versus external control of reinforcement, *Psychological Monographs,* 1966, *80*(1).

Schacter, S. *Recidivism and self-cure of smoking and obesity.* Paper presented at the Addiction Research Foundation Research Conference, May 1981.

Schwartz, G. E. Biofeedback and the self-management of disregulation disorders. In R. B. Stuart (Ed.), *Behavioral self-management: Strategies, techniques and outcomes.* New York: Brunner/Mazel, 1977.

Seligman,M. E. P. *Helplessness—On depression, development, and death.* San Francisco: W. N. Freeman, 1975.

Shtasel, T. F. Review of *Control your depression. The Behavior Therapist,* 1980, *3*(2), 25–27.

Stuart, R. B. (Ed.). *Behavioral self-management: Strategies, techniques and outcomes.* New York: Brunner/Mazel, 1977.

Thibaut, J. W., & Kelley, H. H. *The social psychology of groups.* New York: Wiley, 1959.

Thoresen, C. E., & Mahoney, M. J. *Behavioral self-control.* New York: Holt, Rinehart & Winston, 1974.

Watson, D. L., & Tharp, R. G. *Self-directed behavior: Self-modification for personal adjustment,* (3rd ed.). Monterey, Calif.: Brooks/Cole, 1981.

Wilson, G. T. Cognitive behavior therapy: Paradigm shift or passing phase? In J. P. Foreyt & D. P. Rathyen (Eds.), *Cognitive behavior therapy: Research and application.* New York: Plenum Press, 1978.

Wilson, G. T. Perceived control and the theory and practice of behavior therapy. In L. C. Perlmuter & R. A. Monty (Eds.), *Choice and perceived control.* Hillsdale, N.J.: Lawrence Erlbaum, 1979.

Yates, A. J. *Biofeedback and the modification of behavior.* New York: Plenum Press, 1980.

CHAPTER 2

Physiological Patterning and Emotion

Implications for the Self-Regulation of Emotion

Gary E. Schwartz

Department of Psychology
Yale University
New Haven, Connecticut

Introduction

The purpose of this chapter is to review some of our recent research on the psychophysiology of emotion from a systems perspective and to consider some of its implications for the self-regulation of emotion. We will emphasize the general concepts of response patterning and emergent property. The basic premise underlying this chapter is that the term *emotion* is used to refer to a complex pattern (combination) of psychobiological processes, where no single process (or part) equals the whole emotion. Rather, in systems terms (Miller, 1978), emotion *emerges* out of the unique interaction of the parts that comprise the entire response complex. In systems terms, therefore, the whole is "greater" than the sum of its parts, yet is dependent on the interaction of its parts for its unique properties. It follows that the self-regulation of emotion, if it is to be complete, requires that multiple processes be regulated in an integrated and organized fashion. Regulating a part of the emotion complex should only partially mimic the complete emotional response and experience.

The history of emotion is replete with examples of the importance of response patterning and interactions of psychobiological processes in the emergence of emotion. For example, the James–Lange (James, 1884) theory of emotion posited that emotions emerge from peripheral feedback emanating from patterns of bodily responses. According to this theory, emotional experiences accompany rather than precede behavior as a function of patterned feedback from the muscles and glands. This theory was criticized by Cannon (1932) on various grounds, including the observation that the viscera were too sluggish to account for the rapid experience of different emotions. Although Cannon seriously questioned the role of the autonomic (not skeletal) nervous system as being fundamental to the subjective experience of different emotions, Cannon did not believe that the autonomic nervous system was therefore diffuse and unpatterned. Although various theorists subsequently interpreted Cannon as implying that the numerous organs controlled by the autonomic nervous system responded primarily in terms of general arousal, this was not Cannon's belief. Cannon was well aware that there were psychobiological differences among fight, flight, sexual behavior, hunger and thirst, and so forth. He recognized that there were unique, integrated blends or patterns of physiological responses that were carefully controlled via homeostatic, self-regulatory mechanisms.

One of the most influential theories of emotion in psychology has been the Schacter–Singer (1962) theory. This theory posits that physiological activity summates into general arousal. The arousal affects the intensity with which a person experiences different emotions. The selection of which emotion is experienced is presumably made by cognitive mechanisms that are superimposed and that interact with the person's general level of physiological arousal. It should be pointed out that in systems terms, the Schacter–Singer theory is (at a higher level) actually a "pattern" theory, in the sense that a *combination* of cognitive and physiological processes is hypothesized to determine the particular emotional experience. Neither component is sufficient by itself to produce a complete emotion.

As will be discussed in this chapter, recent psychophysiological data suggest that neither the peripheral physiological nor the higher-order cognitive processes are simply unitary. Rather, cognitive and physiological levels of processes each consist of components. Furthermore, each component can interact, both within and between the levels of processing and can contribute to the emergent experience of emotion. It follows that the experience of emotion is only one aspect of emotion. Many physiological components of emotion may only indirectly, if at all, contribute to the experience of emotion, and people can be very selective in determining which physiological cues they will process to mold their emotional experience. As will be discussed in this chapter, there are sometimes discrepancies among people's physiology, their behavior and what they experience. These discrepancies turn out to have important basic and clinical implications for psychopathology and for the self-regulation of emotion.

To pursue the question of the patterning of the different processes in emotion in a comprehensive fashion, it is necessary to consider the patterning of subjective experience, the patterning of the skeletal muscles, the patterning of the autonomic nervous system's responses, and, ideally, the patterning of the brain processes subserving all these components. Although I discuss each of these components sequentially in this chapter, I should note that a significant portion of our research program resulted from accidental discoveries, some of which occurred in studies that were conducted for other purposes. Hence, the true flavor of our research program reflects a balance between serendipity and theoretical–programmatic concerns.

Patterning of Subjective Experience

Because emotion is often thought of as being a unitary phenomenon, it is typically assessed in a limited manner. Research on anxiety is often conducted without any assessment of depression, and vice versa, and both areas of research are conducted without any assessment of anger and frustration, which are studied in yet other research areas. Multivariate pattern analyses of emotion are typically not performed. Emotions are often labeled as positive or as negative: they are not labeled as being positive *and* negative. By holding a univariant view of emotion, research is often conducted in a univariant manner, and the underlying pattern-nature of emotion is usually not revealed.

However, it is surprisingly easy to obtain reliable measures of patterns of the subjective experience of different emotional situations. We came to this realization by accident. In an effort to find representative emotional situations that could be used with college students to elicit relatively pure experiences of happiness, sadness, anger, and fear via imagery, we conducted an emotion-rating survey of different situations. We serendipitously uncovered striking evidence of blends of the subjective experience of different imagined emotional situations.

Following on the work of Izard (1972), we adopted his Differential Emotion Scale to rate individual emotional situations on six dimensions (Happiness, Sadness, Anger, Fear, Anxiety, and Depression–called HASAFAD for short). The complete design is described in Schwartz and Weinberger (1980). Briefly, approximately 50 Yale undergraduates were asked to list different situations that elicited in them feelings primarily of happiness, sadness, anger, fear, anxiety, and depression. The subjects were requested to give three situations for each emotion representing low, middle, and high intensities of affect. This request resulted in 18 situations per subject. Then, the 18 situations of 20 of the subjects were selected and randomly distributed among four questionnaires containing 90 items each (20 subjects times 18 items, divided by 4), and

Table 1. *Ratings on an Abbreviated DES*

Item	HAP	SAD	ANG	FEAR	ANX	DEP
Your dog dies.	1.09	4.08	2.08	1.38	1.93	3.34
Your girlfriend/boyfriend leaves you for another.	1.13	4.13	3.41	2.11	2.72	4.09
You realize that your goals are impossible to reach.	1.15	3.64	3.00	2.48	3.08	3.67

a sample of at least 50 subjects per questionnaire rated each situation on HASAFAD, using a 1 to 5 rating scale for each emotion.

We discovered that on the average, these subjects generated consistent subjective patterns of emotional experiences. As shown in Table 1, for example, in response to the item "Your dog dies," the subjects reported feeling mostly sadness and depression, whereas in response to the item "Your girlfriend/boyfriend leaves you for another," not only did the subjects report sadness and depression, but they also reported relatively high anger and anxiety as well. Both of these items could be labeled "depression items" (and/or "sadness items," which are not the same; Schwartz & Weinberger, 1980), though they clearly differ in terms of anger and anxiety as elicited by the latter situation.

Note that in response to the item "You realize that your goals are impossible to reach," the subjects reported high levels of all the negative emotions sampled by HASAFAD. It is significant that this particular situation evoked so many different negative emotions all at once, especially since this sort of realization is one that Type A individuals work hard to ignore (see Roskies, in this volume). Also, this is a general realization that is confronting a large segment of the human species at this particular point in our evolutionary history.

Is it possible that these different emotional situations are accompanied by different combinations of negative emotions expressed physiologically? Is it possible that the greater the number of conflicting negative emotions that are elicited by a given situation, the more likely it is that a person will develop stress-related physiological disorders? At the present time, the answers to these and related questions are not known.

Table 2 illustrates two items particularly relevant to Yale students. Note that in response to the item "You are accepted at Yale," the subjects report high happiness and high anxiety. Is this a happiness situation, an anxiety situation, or a combined happiness–anxiety situation? (The latter is implied by a pattern perspective on emotion.) Note that in response to the item "You have just graduated from Yale," the subjects reported happiness and anxiety, but

Table 2. Ratings on an Abbreviated DES

Item	HAP	SAD	ANG	FEAR	ANX	DEP
You are accepted at Yale.	4.18	1.14	1.04	1.96	3.04	1.09
You have just graduated Yale.	4.09	2.74	1.38	2.57	3.40	2.36

they also reported being depressed and somewhat frightened. Clearly, leaving Yale evoked more of a complex blend of emotions than coming to Yale, at least in terms of self-report.

Subtle changes in wording can have a striking effect on the nature of the patterns of emotions evoked. For example, as shown in Table 3, in response to the item "You feel loved," the subjects reported primarily high happiness—a relatively pure happiness situation for these college students. However, in response to the question "You meet someone with whom you fall in love," the subjects reported high happiness accompanied by high anxiety.

Numerous implications follow from findings such as these for basic and clinical research on emotion and the self-regulation of emotion. For example, in assessing the impact of life stresses, it might be useful to go beyond rating events such as "You are divorced" simply in terms of whether the situation is "positive" or "negative." Rather, more complete information could be obtained if the ratings of various positive *and* negative emotions were made *simultaneously* for each event (for some people, divorce may have both positive and negative consequences: Do these people develop more or fewer psychophysiological disorders than those who experience divorce as being primarily positive or primarily negative?).

With regard to the self-regulation of emotion, it is critical to examine, for example, whether relaxation training leads to decreases in anxiety, yet simultaneous increases in the awareness of frustration. For other individuals, relaxation may be boring, if not unpleasant. To better predict who will respond in what ways to different relaxation methods, and who will continue to practice various emotional self-regulation strategies, it could be fruitful to obtain a more complete measure of the spectrum of emotions experienced before, during, and following these self-regulation strategies. (See Schwartz & Weinberger, 1980, for a more detailed discussion of these issues.)

Table 3. Ratings on an Abbreviated DES

Item	HAP	SAD	ANG	FEAR	ANX	DEP
You feel loved.	4.78	1.28	1.13	1.19	1.57	1.19
You meet someone with whom you fall in love.	4.58	1.20	1.04	2.00	3.06	1.33

Facial Muscle Patterning and Emotion

Because subjects can experience different combinations of emotions, even via imagery per se, we can ask whether these differences in subjective experience are paralleled by changes in patterns of physiological responses. The human face is an ideal physiological system for examining this question, since the face is intimately involved in the expression of different emotions. Following on Darwin's (1872) theory of the biological bases of different emotional expressions, and Tomkins' (1962) extension of this theory to include the role of feedback from the face in the experience of different emotions Tomkins (1961, 1962), Ekman, Friesen, and Ellsworth (1972), and Izard (1971) have documented that there are at least six emotions expressed in the face that are commonly and consistently labeled across cultures: happiness, sadness, anger, fear, surprise, and disgust.

We can speculate what might happen if subjects were instructed to imagine and reexperience different emotional situations. Would the subjects generate subtle patterns of facial muscle tension, possibly not visible to the naked eye, yet detectable by recording muscle tension electromyographically? In a series of studies, we have found that this is the case (e.g., Schwartz, Fair, Salt, Mandel, & Klerman, 1976a, b; Schwartz, Brown, & Ahern, 1980). Parenthetically, our initial choice to study self-generated imagery was made partly for methodological reasons. The original funding for our facial electromyography (EMG) work came from the Food and Drug Administration, the goal being to evaluate whether facial electromyography could be used to assess the effects of antidepressant medication. In order to reduce possible movement artifacts from contaminating the data, we decided to use self-generated affective imagery (since our subjects hardly moved their faces when they imagined past emotional situations with their eyes closed). As it turned out, our use of affective imagery proved to be especially relevant to the question of self-regulation of emotion.

For example, in our first two studies, we found that in situations involving sadness or anger, depressed subjects generated facial EMG patterns of an equal if not greater intensity than normal subjects. However, in response to past situations that involved happiness, depressed subjects showed a marked attenuation (e.g., Schwartz *et al.*, 1976b) of their facial muscle patterns. Furthermore, when our subjects were asked to think about what they did in a "typical day," the normal subjects generated a miniature happiness pattern, whereas depressed subjects generated a miniature sadness–anger pattern. These findings raise a series of questions. Do depressed subjects generate depressive facial patterns across various situations throughout the day? Do these subtle expressions provide facial feedback to the brain and thereby contribute to the continued experience of depression? Under what conditions can the deliberate self-regulation of facial muscle patterning modify a depressed person's emotional experience?

Although facial behavior and subjective experience often covary together, there are specific circumstances in which they are discordant. People sometimes attempt to disguise their emotions, sometimes to others and sometimes to themselves. Also, people may not pay attention to or misinterpret their facial behavior. In two studies, we have found in a ward situation that depressed patients tend to report feeling more happiness than their facial behavior actually shows, whereas schizophrenic patients tend to report less happiness than their facial behavior actually shows (Brown *et al.*, 1978, 1979). Different disorders, therefore, produce a different dissociation between facial behavior and the subjective experience of emotion. These discrepancies are potentially of theoretical as well as clinical importance. Clearly, cognitive and motivational variables can influence a person's self-awareness and self-report of emotion and can thereby produce discrepancies between subjective experience and aspects of the physiology. However, as we discuss below regarding hemispheric asymmetry and emotions, a finer analysis of patterns of physiological responses may help us understand what some of these underlying psychobiological mechanisms are.

The face has the potential to express combinations of emotions, which Ekman and Friesen (1975) referred to as "blends of emotion." Are such patterns or blends elicited when subjects imagine situations that evoke conflicting emotions? In a recently completed study (Polonsky & Schwartz, unpublished) we have found that subjects who imagine situations that evoke a combination of happiness and sadness elicit moderate increases in both zygomatic and corrugator muscle activity, whereas when subjects imagine situations that evoke relatively pure happiness or pure sadness, they elicit large increases in zygomatic or corrugator muscle activity, respectively. As multivariate statistical procedures are applied to physiological data such as these, it may be possible in the future to examine in more detail the relationship between physiological and subjective blending.

Autonomic Nervous System Patterning and Emotion

If subjects self-generate patterns of facial muscle activity when they imagine different emotional situations, is it possible that they can self-generate patterns of other physiological responses? Not only could research on the patterning of other skeletal muscles be revealing and important, but research on the patterns of autonomic responses accompanying these skeletal muscle patterns could have important basic and clinical implications as well.

The classic research on autonomic nervous system patterning and emotion suffered from two methodological limitations that may have compromised the finding of large and consistent patterns. In the Ax (1953) and Schachter (1957) pioneering studies on physiological patterning in anger versus fear, subjects were exposed to two contrived situations, one used to elicit anger in the subjects, the other used to elicit fear. During the experiment, the subjects were required to sit absolutely still so as to collect the elaborate set of physiological measures. The nature of the contrived situations probably evoked a complex blend of emotions that were not measured in these studies (for example, in the situation where subjects were told that the equipment was causing problems and bogus sparks were produced at the electrode board, the subjects were probably not only frightened but also angry that they had to continue to sit still and could not rip off the electrodes and get out of there!). Furthermore, since the subjects were not allowed to move, they had to *regulate themselves,* keeping their fear and anger under control, a reaction that may have served to dampen the response amplitudes and patterns of the emotions observed (Schwartz, 1982).

We recently conducted a study to see whether subjects could voluntarily generate the kinds of blood-pressure and heart-rate patterns that Ax and Schachter had reported for anger and fear, as well as to see if we could extend their findings to happiness, sadness, and relaxation (Schwartz, Weinberger, & Singer, 1981). Thirty-two students with training in acting were asked (1) to imagine walking up and down a step, expressing, nonverbally, either happiness, sadness, anger, fear, control, or relaxation, and then (2) actually to walk up and down a step for about a minute, expressing, nonverbally, these different emotions. Systolic and diastolic blood pressures and heart rate were recorded following the imagery and following the overt exercise periods for each trial.

The results revealed striking cardiovascular patterning for the different emotions during both the imagery and the exercise parts of the study. Not only did we replicate the prior findings differentiating anger and fear, but we found that following the exercise, differential recovery rates occurred above and beyond the peak increases in response amplitudes. For example, although the systolic blood pressure increased on the average more than 20 mmHg for both the anger and the fear exercises, the systolic blood pressure recovered more slowly following the anger exercise than following the fear exercise. Since the subjects had been told to relax after each trial, it seems likely that these recovery effects reflected real differences in the half-lives of different emotions after they had been triggered (for example, it may take, on the average, more time to get over being angry than to get over being frightened).

These differences in recovery may have important evolutionary and psychobiological significance.

One implication of these findings is that "exercise is not exercise is not exercise." It is possible that "relaxed" jogging is accompanied by physiological (and hormonal) changes different from those accompanying "angry" jogging. The Type A person who squeezes in 20 minutes of frantic, frustrating jogging may be inadvertently accentuating his or her heart disease. This possibility could help explain why some people become subjectively and physiologically healthier after a regular program of exercise, while other people die of heart attacks in the process of attempting to become "healthy." Future research could examine facial and bodily measures of emotion in everyday behavior (using nonverbal visual scoring techniques as well as direct physiological monitoring). The facial expressions of joggers may turn out to be better predictors of their cardiovascular changes than their own self-perceptions. As Glass and colleagues (reviewed in Glass, 1977) have reported, Type A persons tend to exercise harder and push themselves longer, yet at the same time to report less fatigue, than Type B subjects.

We have hypothesized that inattention to feedback from the body can under certain conditions promote a functional neuropsychological disconnection between brain and body, causing a *disregulation* between brain and body that is evident as a biobehavioral disorder, labeled medically as a disease (Schwartz, 1979a,b). The behavior of Type A individuals who show a high cardiovascular and behavioral response to challenge may involve some variant of the disregulation process. As described below, subjects who use repressive coping styles may employ inattention processes to ignore negative affect. Thus, these coping styles may have the negative side effect of disregulating their physiological responses to emotionally provoking situations.

Clearly, current research has barely scratched the surface regarding the ability of humans to self-regulate the different patterns of physiological processes in the different emotions. In view of the potential theoretical and clinical importance of such findings, future research might profit from systematically measuring patterns of self-report and patterns of skeletal muscle activity (either directly by physiological methods or indirectly by nonverbal, visual scoring methods) in order to appropriately interpret the significance of the physiological changes occurring in different emotional states.

Denial, Dissociation, and Disregulation

If a person reports low values on scales tapping anxiety, depression, frustration, or other negative emotions, how do we know whether the person's self-perceptions are accurate or not? One way to determine accuracy is to assess whether the person's physiological responses are consistent or inconsistent with her or his subjective experience. If we use this criterion, the research on anxiety, for example, is replete with instances in which a subset of subjects who reported low anxiety ended up looking behaviorally and physiologically like subjects reporting high anxiety. Is it possible to distinguish among subjects reporting low anxiety by means of other self-report scales in order to predict this subjective–physiological dissociation?

Weinberger, Schwartz, and Davidson (1979) hypothesized that subjects who reported low anxiety and also scored low on defensiveness as measured by a second personality scale should be "true low anxious," whereas subjects who reported low anxiety but also scored high on defensiveness as measured by the second scale should be "repressors." Using the Marlow-Crowne Social Desirability Scale as an indirect measure of defensiveness (see Weinberger *et al.*, 1979, for a detailed analysis of why this scale is not a particularly good measure of social desirability, whereas it is a very good measure of defensiveness), we studied three groups of subjects (low-anxious, repressor, and high-anxious subjects) in a moderately stressful laboratory situation (a phrase association task). Heart rate, skin resistance, and frontalis muscle tension were monitored. We also scored verbal reaction times and made ratings of verbal disturbance. The data indicated, as predicted, that the repressors (who ended up reporting significantly *less* anxiety than the low-anxious subjects!) nonetheless responded behaviorally and physiologically similarly to (or more strongly than) the high-anxious subjects.

These data suggest that it is erroneous and counterproductive to take low self-reports of emotion as being indicative of low emotional reaction. Research that ignores the distinction between correct self-perception and self-deception will end up inadvertently combining these two extreme groups into a single "low" group. This error will lead to findings of inconsistent differences when all the "low" subjects are compared with subjects reporting high levels of emotion.

The self-deception issue is, of course, more complex than as presented thus far. For example, in a recent study, we have found that when repressors rate standardized emotion-eliciting items on the HASAFAD (as previously described), they report a level of intensity of the *primary* emotion evoked by the item comparable to that of true low-anxious subjects (Weinberger & Schwartz, unpublished). For example, in response to the item "You find that someone has broken into your car," both repressors and low-anxious subjects tend to report similar levels of anger. However, the groups diverge in their ratings of the other, less primary emotions on each item. For example, repressors tend to report experiencing less depression in response to the above item than do the true low-anxious subjects. These data support clinical observations that repressors tend to report experiencing relatively bland, stereotypical, less rich emotions in comparison with normal subjects.

It is possible that repressors may experience techniques like relaxation and meditation differently from true low-anxious subjects. For example, repressors may feel boredom or actual negative emotions when required to be self-reflective. A just-completed study (Polonsky & Schwartz, unpublished) indicates that repressors generate sizable increases in corrugator facial-muscle activity while they meditate, in comparison with low-anxious subjects. It is possible that a prerequisite for successfully treating clients with strong repressive tendencies may be to teach them to recognize that they are actually experiencing negative emotions that must be resolved for the sake of their health. Thus, it may be necessary first to increase a repressor's *awareness* of negative symptoms before one can appropriately reduce his or her symptoms to healthier levels.

One technique for increasing a person's self-awareness of physiological activity is to use biofeedback-oriented self-monitoring. Clinically, we have treated a number of patients with strong repressive tendencies using psychophysiological monitoring. Significant discrepancies between self-report and physiological responding are carefully highlighted in our patients' self-monitoring diaries and in the actual therapy sessions so that these discrepancies can be brought into awareness. As one patient described it, "When I first saw you, I had terrible headaches and thought my work and home life were almost perfect. Now I realize that I have been anxious and angry about things happening at work and at home, and my headaches are decreasing." Teaching a person both to experience and to self-regulate complex blends of emotion can be potentially clinically useful for certain problems, and it deserves more systematic research in the future.

Patterns of Central Nervous System Processes and Emotion

Theoretically, all of the subjective, skeletal-muscular, and autonomic processes described above involve underlying patterns of neuropsychological processes. It is extremely difficult in intact humans to tease apart what these different patterns of brain subsystems are. However, some progress is being made in this direction, especially within the framework of cerebral laterality. For example, Schwartz, Davidson, and Maer (1975) reported that in right-handed subjects, questions that involved emotional processing and experience evoked, on the average, more evidence of relative right-hemispheric activation (as inferred from lateral eye movements) than nonemotional questions.

Also, questions that involved spatial imagery evoked, on the average, more evidence of relative right-hemispheric activation than verbal questions. As would be predicted, questions that were both emotional *and* spatial evoked the most evidence of right-hemispheric involvement.

In a seminal paper, Galin (1974) has proposed that a possible mechanism for producing a dissociation between verbal processes and affective awareness may be the development of a functional disconnection syndrome between the two hemispheres. Simply stated, Galin proposed that right-handed repressors may attenuate the transfer of affective information from the right to the left hemisphere. Not only would this attenuation result in repressors' reporting less negative affect than actually triggered, but according to disregulation theory (Schwartz, 1979a,b), the negative affect itself would be relatively disregulated and would therefore be more prone to disorder.

Not surprisingly, basic research on the laterality of emotion and the application of this work to repression turn out to be more complex than originally proposed. For example, we have recently found, using eye movements (Ahern & Schwartz, 1979) and facial electromyography (Schwartz, Ahern, & Brown, 1979) as indirect measures of laterality, that positive emotions (in right-handed subjects) tend to be more involved with the left hemisphere, whereas negative emotions tend to be relatively more involved with the right hemisphere. We have suggested that these affective differences in laterality may reflect fundamental differences in approach (left-hemispheric) versus avoidance (right-hemispheric) behavior and may be organized subcortically. Therefore, the positive–negative emotion differences may be more fundamentally lateralized than the verbal–spatial cognitive differences (Ahern & Schwartz, 1979).

Using EEG measures of laterality (Davidson, Schwartz, Saron, Bennett, & Goleman, 1979), we have uncovered data suggesting that the emotion-laterality picture may be even more interesting and complex. These data suggest that the initial perception of emotional stimuli (be it positive or negative) may involve relatively more right-hemispheric processing of the primary and secondary sensory receiving areas, whereas the decisions on hedonic value regarding pleasure and pain (approach and avoidance) may in part be subcortical and may be communicated to the cortex via the frontal regions.

To the extent that this conclusion is true, we might hypothesize that repressors, who claim that things are quite good when the opposite is the case, may attempt to keep unwanted "negative" right-hemispheric information from affecting the activity of the "positive" left hemisphere. Consistent with this general interpretation, Polonsky and Schwartz (unpublished) have recently found that when repressors imagine positive and negative scenes, they show striking evidence of facial laterality in the predicted direction (greater right-sided zygomatic activity—controlled by the left hemisphere—for positive imagery, and greater left-sided corrugator activity–controlled by the right hemisphere–for negative imagery), whereas true low-anxious subjects show a relative symmetry across both sides of the face for positive and negative imagery patterns.

It appears that a general picture is slowly beginning to emerge here, one that suggests that differential communication within and between the hemispheres may reflect cognitive, skeletal-muscle, and physiological patterns in different subjects who are in different emotional states. Furthermore, as discussed in Schwartz, Ahern, and Brown (1979), the voluntary control of emotional behavior may involve neuropsychological processes different from those involved in spontaneously produced emotional behavior. Although a more accurate picture is slowly emerging, it will very likely become more elaborate, complex, and three-dimensional as data from various systems are brought to bear on the problem.

Do lateralized differences in positive versus negative emotions predict cardiovascular disregulation? Do hypertensive patients who score high on measures of defensiveness evidence lateralized differences in emotion more strongly than normotensive subjects? Is successful psychotherapy in repressors and/or in Type A individuals accompanied by a greater integration between the two hemispheres, as well as a greater correspondence between self-report and physiological activity in different emotional states?

Summary and Conclusions

We have reviewed some of our current research on psychophysiological patterning and emotion, and we have considered some of the implications of this research for basic and clinical research on the self-regulation of emotion. We have illustrated that no single subjective, physiological, or behavioral measure can be viewed as a "pure" measure of any single emotion. Furthermore, not only does a "single" emotion appear to be a complex, integrated psychobiological system involving specific patterns of subsystems, but emotions typically occur in various combinations, and subjects can vary to the extent that different response subsystems covary. Although this complexity makes research more difficult, it also makes it more rich and potentially more important.

The issue regarding the self-regulation of combinations of processes and the emergent experience of emotion is one that could profit from future research. As described in Schwartz (1977), we have conducted a pilot study suggesting that the simultaneous self-regulation of heart rate and frontalis muscle tension results in greater subjective reports of anxiety than the separate regulation of heart rate or frontalis muscle tension. The ability of biofeedback training to produce specific patterns of physiological activity (Schwartz, 1977) makes it possible to examine how various combinations of systems interact, and how the self-regulation of different emotions compares with emotions elicited by other means, such as environmental stimuli.

It seems that we need to learn more about the interaction of the cognitive processes in the perception and modulation of emotional behavior if we are going to make further progress in this general area. Is it possible that certain cognitive mechanisms used to attenuate the subjective experience of emotion may be physiologically disregulatory, whereas other cognitive mechanisms used to attenuate the subjective experience of emotion may enhance homeostasis? Can biofeedback-oriented self-monitoring be used to increase people's ability to label their emotional states correctly, and will this increased ability have neuropsychological, physiological, and subjective consequences reflective of improved health? Hopefully, by taking a multiprocess approach, future research will be able to obtain some answers to these fundamental questions about the nature of human emotion.

References

Ahern, G. L., & Schwartz, G. E. Differential lateralization for positive versus negative emotion. *Neuropsychologia,* 1979, *17,* 693–697.

Ax, A. R. The physiological differentiation between fear and anger in humans. *Psychosomatic Medicine,* 1953, *15,* 433–442.

Brown, S. L., Schwartz, G. E., & Sweeney, D. R. Dissociation of self-reported and observed pleasure in depression. *Psychosomatic Medicine,* 1978, *40,* 536–548.

Brown, S. L., Sweeney, D. R., & Schwartz, G. E. Differences between self-reported and observed pleasure in depression and schizophrenia. *Journal of Nervous and Mental Disease,* 1979, *167,* 410–415.

Cannon, W. B. *The wisdom of the body.* New York: W. W. Norton, 1932.

Darwin, C. R. *The expression of emotions in man and animals.* London: John Murray, 1872.

Davidson, R. J., Schwartz, G. E., Saron, C., Bennett, J., & Goleman, D. Frontal versus parietal EEG asymmetry during positive and negative affect. *Psychophysiology,* 1979, *16,* 202–203. (Abstract)

Ekman, P., & Friesen, W. *Unmasking the face.* Englewood Cliffs, N.J.: Prentice-Hall, 1975.

Ekman, P., Friesen, W. V., & Ellsworth, P. C. *Emotion in the human face.* New York: Pergamon, 1972.

Galin, D. Implications of left-right cerebral lateralization for psychiatry: A neurophysiological context for unconscious processes. *Archives of General Psychiatry,* 1974, *9,* 412–418.

Glass, D. C. *Behavior patterns, stress and coronary disease.* Hillsdale, N.J.: Lawrence Erlbaum, 1977.

Izard, C. *The face of emotion.* New York: Appleton-Century-Crofts, 1971.

James, W. What is an emotion? *Mind,* 1884, *9,* 188–205.

Miller, J. G. *Living systems.* New York: McGraw-Hill, 1978.

Schachter, J. Pain, fear and anger in hypertensives and normotensives. *Psychosomatic Medicine,* 1957, *19,* 17–29.

Schwartz, G. E. Biofeedback and physiological patterning in human emotion and consciousness. In J. Beatty & H. Legewie (Eds.), *Biofeedback and behavior.* New York: Plenum Press, 1977.

Schwartz, G. E. The brain as health care system. In G. Stone, N. Adler, & F. Cohen (Eds.), *Health psychology.* San Francisco: Jossey-Bass, 1979. (a)

Schwartz, G. E. Disregulation and systems theory: A biobehavioral framework for biofeedback and behavioral medicine. In N. Birbaumer & H. D. Kimmel (Eds.), *Biofeedback and self-regulation.* Hillsdale, N.J.: Lawrence Erlbaum, 1979. (b)

Schwartz, G. E. Psychophysiological patterning and emotion revisited: A systems perspective. In C. Izard (Eds.), *Measuring emotions in infants and children.* Cambridge, England: Cambridge University Press, 1982.

Schwartz, G. E., & Weinberger, D. A. Patterns of emotional responses to affective situations: Relations among happiness, sadness, anger, fear, depression, and anxiety. *Motivation and Emotion,* 1980, *4,* 175–191.

Schwartz, G. E., Davidson, R. J., & Maer, F. Right hemisphere lateralization for emotion in the human brain: Interaction with cognition. *Science,* 1975, *190,* 286–288.

Schwartz, G. E., Fair, P. L., Salt, P., Mandel, M. R., & Klerman, G. L. Facial expression and imagery in depression: An electromyographic study. *Psychosomatic Medicine,* 1976, *38,* 337–347. (a)

Schwartz, G. E., Fair, P. L., Salt, P., Mandel, M. R., & Klerman, G. L. Facial muscle patterning to affective imagery in depressed and non-depressed subjects. *Science,* 1976, *192,* 489–491. (b)

Schwartz, G. E., Ahern, G. L., & Brown, S. L. Lateralized facial muscle response to positive versus negative emotional stimuli. *Psychophysiology,* 1979, *16,* 561–571.

Schwartz, G. E., Brown, S. L., & Ahern, G. L. Facial muscle patterning and subjective experience during affective imagery: Sex differences. *Psychophysiology,* 1980, *17,* 75–82.

Schwartz, G. E., Weinberger, D. A., & Singer, J. A. Cardiovascular differentiation of happiness, sadness, anger, and fear following imagery and exercise. *Psychosomatic Medicine,* 1981, *43,* 343–364.

Tomkins, S. S. *Affect, imagery, consciousness* (2 vol.). New York: Springer, 1962.

Weinberger, D. A., Schwartz, G. E., & Davidson, R. J. Low anxious, high anxious, and repressive coping styles: Psychometric patterns and behavioral and physiological responses to stress. *Journal of Abnormal Psychology,* 1979, *88,* 368–380.

CHAPTER 3

A Self-Environmental Systems Model and Its Implications for Behavior Change

D. Balfour Jeffrey and Laurence H. Berger

Department of Psychology
University of Montana
Missoula, Montana

Psychologists who are interested in basic research and psychologists who are interested in applied research often do not communicate well; they often talk at one another rather than with one another. Such a tendency is particularly unfortunate in the field of psychology. For example, "rat runners" and "behavior therapists" have a great deal to offer one another, precisely because of their different perspectives on the same general subject matter. If the two branches of psychology were to get "divorced" on the grounds of irreconcilable differences, it would surely be the case that the applied branch would have to develop a basic science capability, for effective application is based on scientific discovery. In a similar vein, the basic science branch would have to develop an applied capability, because basic science without application is sterile and wasteful. It would be a shame to go through all that work and conflict just to end up in the same places.

This chapter is the attempt of a "behavior therapist" (Jeffrey) and a "rat runner" (Berger) to work together in applying a common theoretical framework (that of self-regulating control systems) to psychological situations of quite different kinds. This chapter is a first step by the authors to stretch their own horizons, and to increase the exposure and critique of their notions.

The first general portion of the chapter is an explanation of the common cybernetic approach as applied to behavioral systems. The second general portion describes some applications to experimental laboratory situations involving abstracted variables and hypothetical "rats." The third general portion describes applications to less abstract, more lifelike situations with a more applied focus. The fourth general portion describes applications of systems theory to the individual management of obesity and to an analysis of television food advertising.

The surface of the potential integration has only been scratched in this chapter. It is hoped that the readers will recognize the opening of a door in a wall artificially separating a common area into two realms, and that they will recognize the value of the breeze flowing through that door. No claim of Truth, Beauty, and a Little Bit of Salt is made, but the authors do maintain that an approach to psychology based on self-regulating control systems has promise for the analysis and synthesis necessary for the description and understanding of a wide range of behaviors.

Introduction to Systems Theory

Since Norbert Wiener (1948) developed his ideas about cybernetic control systems, there has been growing interest in applying such systems to be-

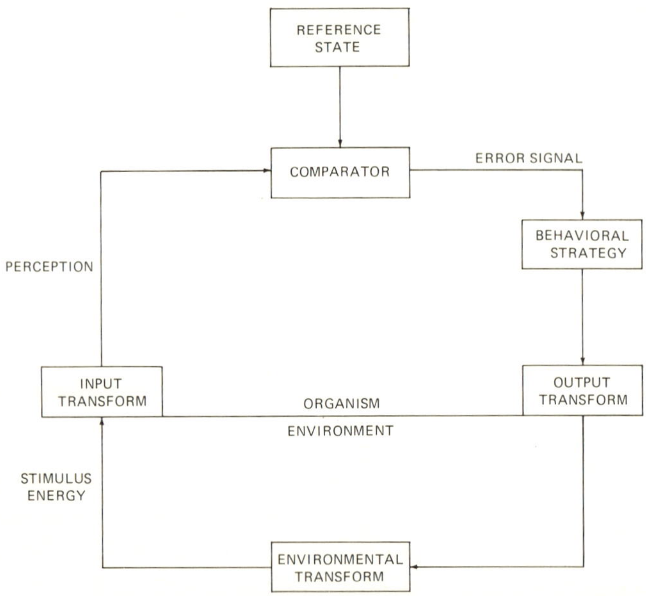

Fig. 1. Diagram of the minimum required components of a cybernetic control system.

havioral analysis (Buckley, 1968). The self-regulatory nature of cybernetic systems can give the appearance of purposiveness of behavior, an appearance shared by organismic behavior in many cases. However, control systems were designed and analyzed by engineers for engineering purposes, so when psychologists investigated the application of control systems to organismic behavior, they started with engineering notions and perspectives. Unfortunately, it is not necessarily the case that the engineering perspectives are precisely isomorphic with the perspectives required for psychological application.

Generally, a system may be thought of as an ordered network of interrelated physical or abstract variables and components. Figure 1 depicts the relationship of the components in a cybernetic system. It is a depiction based on a presentation by Powers (1973). It is a simplified schema that can be elaborated on greatly. The environmental components of the system are behavioral energy, the environmental transform, and physical stimuli. Behavioral energy is the physical energy in the environment that results directly from organismic behavior, such as the movement of muscles. The environmental transform is a description of how the environment acts on and changes behavioral energy, or, from a different perspective, it is a description of how the behavioral energy acts on and changes the environment. Physical stimuli are physical energies in the environment that impinge on the organism, some of which can be sensed by the organism.

The organismic components are the input transform, perception, the reference state, the comparator, the error signal, behavioral strategies, and the output transform. The input transform is the transduction process and the information processing of the sensory systems, which change physical stimuli into perceptions. The term *perception* is used in its most general sense and is the organismic representation of information about the state of the external environment. The reference state specifies the value of the controlled variable that the system attempts to maintain invariant. It could be thought of as a desired state, or motive, or goal without undue distortion. The comparator compares the perceived state of the environment with the reference state and determines if there is a discrepancy between the two. If there is, the comparator emits an error signal. The error signal is, in a real sense, the proximal cause of behavior and, as such, is not unlike the concept of motivation. Behavioral strategies could be considered algorithms of tactics and sequences of responses to be engaged in by the organism. The output transform is those neural and muscular processes that transduce neural energy into behavioral energy in the environment. The product of the output transform is behavior.

In order to function as a self-regulating system, these components must include a feedback loop and the feedback must be negative. A negative feedback loop means that the system will behave so as to maintain a particular state (which is defined by the reference state), and that any deviation from that state will tend to be counteracted by the behavior of the system. In contradistinction, in a positive feedback loop, any deviation from the reference state value will tend to be increased by the behavior of the system, such as in the behavior associated with a vicious circle. It is important to emphasize from the outset that a control system regulates a particular variable (the controlled variable), the value of which is specified by the reference state, so that the value of the controlled variable remains constant and in agreement with the specified reference-state value. It is that tendency to maintain the controlled variable at some constant, invariant value that is the self-regulating control system's most salient characteristic.

Some variables in the system are directly observable and subject to direct measurement. These are the environmental components. Behavior may be generally considered the process of putting physical energy into the environment, such as in vocalization or movement. Usually, the energy is mechanical and is the result of activation of the musculature, but other kinds are possible, such as chemical energy in the form of pheromones. The environmental transform is directly observable, also. Behavior does something to the environment, and the environment may transform that behavioral energy into something else. For example, in an operant situation, the environmental transform is the schedule contingencies. A behavior such as a bar press is transformed by the environmental contingencies into the delivery of a food pellet. The environmental transform may be thought of as the relationship between the physical energy that the organism puts into the environment and the physical energy that impinges on the organism from the environment as stimuli. Physical energy impinging on the animal and acting as stimuli is clearly observable and measurable.

The organismic variables of the system are not available for direct observation and measurement. Years of study of the relationship between the physical stimuli and the operation of sensory systems, psychophysical phenomena, and complex perceptions have provided some information about input transforms so that in particular cases, the relationship between physical stimulation and perceptual response is known to some degree. In a similar vein, particular characteristics of the output transform are known in some cases. However, in the usual behavioral situation, neither the input nor the output transforms are measured, nor is it possible to measure them completely or accurately. Therefore, these transforms must be regarded as being not directly observed or measured. Although organismic variables are not amenable to direct observation and measurement, they are susceptible to being deduced from the direct observation and measurement of environmental variables. The following is a discussion of the deduction processes for particular organismic variables.

Perception may be considered the internal representation by an organism of the state of the external world. It, and the input transform, have been the study of investigators in the field of sensory systems, psychophysics, and perception for some time. Perception is known not to be the same as the objective state of the world, but in most cases, perception is a reasonably accurate representation of that objective state. There are many levels of abstraction of perception, from simple perceptions (which are often called *sensations*) such as perceiving color, to perceptions with high levels of abstraction, such as perceptions of motion, relationships, and social perception. In self-regulating system analysis, an important point about perception is that it provides information that may or may not be accurate about the state of the external environment. It is the information contained in perception that is acted on by the control system. If the perceptual information accurately represents the state of the environment, the control system can behave appropriately, but if the perceptual information is not accurate, the erroneous information will lead to inappropriate behavior by the system. The techniques used to deduce perceptions on the basis of direct observation and measurement of environmental variables are so widely known that it is not necessary to deal with them here.

The reference state specifies the value of the controlled variable that the system endeavors to maintain constant and invariant. In a properly functioning control system, it is precisely that characteristic of maintaining a variable at a constant, invariant value that provides the key to revealing the reference state. The key to deducing the existence of a controlled variable and its reference state lies in finding a dependent variable that remains constant or invariant in value under conditions in which one would otherwise expect some variation.

An illustration with a simple organismic control system may help to clarify the point. Consider the body temperature of a human. Were body temperature not a controlled variable, body temperature would be expected to have a high positive correlation with the environmental temperature. The degree of control is revealed by the lack of correlation between environmental temperature and body temperature. If a person is in a chamber, the temperature of which is varied from warm to cold, the body core temperature of the person will remain close to 37°C. It is that constancy of a dependent variable (body core temperature) in the face of varying values of the independent variable (environmental temperature) that reveals the dependent variable to be controlled, and the reference state to be the maintenance of 37°C. It should be noted that other dependent variables will remain constant in value but can be rejected as controlled variables of the system under study because they would not be expected to vary under the conditions observed. In the example above, one might measure a dependent variable such as pupil size and find that it did not vary in value, but that invariance would not suggest its candidacy as a controlled variable of the system because pupil size would not be expected to vary under conditions of varying environmental temperature.

The comparator of a control system performs a specific and unchanging function: the comparison of the perceived state of the environment with the reference state. As a result, the state of the comparator does not have to be deduced from direct observations and measurements. Rather, its function is constant within the control system framework. Likewise, the error signal is posited and obeys specific rules within the control system. If organisms can be shown to behave according to the rules of the control systems, the existence of a comparator and error signals would seem to be verified functionally. However, it seems likely that the direct confirmation of these components must come from physiological investigations of brain functions and behavior, but such a confirmation for processes as complex as those involved in psychological phenomena would not be expected to be imminent.

Like the reference state, the behavioral strategy is not susceptible to direct observation or measurement but is revealed through the observation and measurement of environmental variables. Once a variable is known to be controlled and the reference state is known, the behavioral strategies of the system will be revealed by producing deviations from the reference state and observing the behaviors emitted. In the example of human temperature control above, several behavioral strategies may be revealed depending on the environmental circumstances. If a person is placed in a temperature-controlled environmental chamber and has no clothing to wear, the behavioral strategies observed will be (1) vasoconstriction and shivering in an environment colder than the reference state and (2) vasodilation and perspiring in an environment warmer than the reference state. If clothes were available in the environmental chamber, additional behavioral strategies would be revealed: putting clothes on in the cold and taking them off in the heat. If in addition a localized heat source were available in the environmental chamber, the behavioral strategies of approaching the heat source in the cold and avoiding it in the heat would be observed. Thus, behavioral strategies would be revealed by a positive correlation between the behavior exhibited and deviations from the reference state value.

In principle, the analysis of organismic behavior according to control system principles is not forbidding. Environmental variables are directly observable and measurable. Organismic variables are not directly observable or measurable but are revealed through the measurement of environmental variables. The existence of a controlled variable is revealed by a constancy of a dependent variable when such a constancy would not be expected in a passive system. The reference state value of that controlled variable is revealed by the particular value of that constancy. The behavioral strategy is revealed by the correlation of particular behavior patterns with deviations of the environmental state from the reference state. However, as in chess, the basic rules may be simple, but the application may be complex.

An organism may be expected to have many reference states controlling different variables, and some may compete with others. For example, an organism may have reference states for avoiding both hunger and thirst, and in some circumstances, reducing the discrepancy from one reference state (say, hunger) may prevent the reduction of a discrepancy—or may even increase the discrepancy—from another reference state (say, thirst). Such a situation would lead to conflict among reference states and can produce a situation difficult to analyze.

Similar complexities exist with regard to behavioral strategies. A given discrepancy from a given reference state may result in different behaviors, or the same behavior could be used to reduce the discrepancy from different reference states. An example of the first would be that a hungry animal might move about to seek food, or it might remain in a fixed position waiting for prey. The highly different behaviors would exhibit behavioral strategies of a different character, either of which could be the result of the same reference state discrepancy. An example of the second would be that an organism might move around either to seek food or to keep its body temperature up. The same behavior would be the product of the same behavioral strategy but would be related to two different reference states of two different control systems. However, a judicious control and observation of environmental variables can resolve such complexities.

It has probably occurred to the reader that some of the terminology used in this analysis has been long used in psychology, for example, such terms as *perception* and *behavioral strategies.* Some terminology is different, but the concepts are not alien to psychology. The reference state might be called a *desired state,* a *motive,* or a *goal* without doing damage to the basic concept. The error signal might well be called *motivation,* for it is the immediate cause of behavior. These conceptual similarities point out the fundamental similarities between traditional psychological approaches and the approach of control system analysis. Moreover, the two approaches share some functional similarities. For example, in the control system approach, much importance lies with the identification of invariant dependent variables. Psychologists have been labeling abstracted invariances on the basis of behavior patterns for some time (e.g., hunger, fear, love, and masochism). Given these similarities, it may be the case that control system analysis has its primary value in providing a unified and rigorous framework that encompasses the diverse perspectives already extant in the field of psychology, and that provides a relational organization for them.

Application of a Systems Theory to a Mechanical System

The application of control system analysis to a commonly understood, simple mechanical system, that of a thermostatically controlled heating system, can serve to illustrate how system functions and dysfunctions can be determined. The system variables and components are simple. Examine Figure 1 for a schematic analysis of this example. The physical stimulus is room air temperature. The input transform is a thermometer, a transducer that changes thermal energy into electrical energy. The perceptual signal is the electrical output of the thermometer. The reference state is the temperature setting of the thermostat. The system comparator is an electrical comparator that compares the electrical signals from the thermometer and the thermostat and emits an electrical signal (the error signal) if the electrical signal from the thermometer indicates a room temperature less than the temperature setting of the thermostat. The behavioral strategy is to turn the furnace on if an error signal exists. The output transform is the transduction and amplification of the electrical energy of the error signal into thermal energy through the activation of the furnace. The behavioral energy is heat released into the room environment. The environmental transform is the physics of heat transfer between the heat sources in the room and the system thermometer sensing room temperature.

If one were given the task of discovering whether a control system was operating on the room environment and, if so, what was being controlled and to what value, one would follow certain courses of action to analyze the situation. First, one would measure dependent variables in the environment, such as temperature and humidity, and, if possible, manipulate independent variables in the environment, such as adding heat and moisture to the room or removing them. One would find that the introduction of moisture to and the removal of moisture from the room air resulted in corresponding changes in humidity with a high positive correlation, that is, just as would be expected in a passive system. However, the introduction and removal of heat would not have the same results. The introduction of heat into the room—say, by lighting a fire—would result in an increase in room temperature that has a high positive correlation with the amount of heat added to the room from the fireplace, but the removal of heat from the room—say, by opening a door to the cold outside air—would not cause a drop in room temperature below a certain value; that is, there would be little or no correlation between removing heat from the room and room temperature. Such a result would not be expected in a passive system. Consequently, one would conclude that humidity and high temperatures in the room are uncontrolled, but a control system is operating with regard to minimal room remperature.

Next, one would add to the process of investigation the observation of the behaviors of the things in the room and the conditions related to the occurrence of those behaviors. One would observe that the behavior of the lighting system in the room, for example, was not correlated with room temperature, but one would observe that the behavior of the furnace was highly correlated with room temperature. By recording the room temperature and the furnace behavior, a pattern would be apparent that would reveal the reference state value of the control system, for example, the maintenance of a minimal room temperature of 68°F. Moreover, the pattern of behavior would reveal the behavioral strategy employed: turning the furnace on if the room temperature is below 68°F. Thus, by observing the environmental variables directly, one has deduced (1) what is and is not controlled, (2) the reference state, and (3) the behavioral strategy.

Because the components of the system are arranged in a series loop, all components must function properly if the system as a whole is to function properly. It is similar to a chain in that all the links must be intact if the chain is to serve its function. If any component of the system is completely nonfunctional, the system as a whole will be completely nonfunctional because no feedback loop will exist. However, if any system component is partially, but erroneously, functioning, the system as a whole may still function, but with possible distortion. The thermostatic system can illustrate some of these problems.

If the thermometer were miscalibrated so that it read 5°F lower than the actual room temperature, the system would behave so as to keep the room temperature 5°F warmer than the reference state value, the thermostat setting. Such a malfunction would be readily observable if the reference state value were known, and a test of the functioning of the perceptual system would reveal the malfunction's source. However, if the reference state value were unknown, and the usual procedures were used to determine its value, the deduced value would be 5°F above its actual value because of the perceptual malfunction. The correct reference state value could be deduced only if the perceptual malfunction were known.

If the reference state value were miscalibrated so that it was 5°F lower than it was set for, the effects would be the converse of the effects of the perceptual malfunction: the system would behave so as to keep the room temperature 5°F cooler than the reference-state-value setting. If the reference-state-value setting were known, the malfunction of the system would be readily observable. A test of the functioning of the perceptual system would reveal that it was not malfunctioning and that the thermometer was accurate, so one could conclude that the malfunction was in the reference state. If the reference state value setting were unknown, the usual procedures would reveal the actual reference state value but not the set reference-state value.

In a system as simple as the thermostatic system, most malfunctions of behavioral strategy will either open the feedback loop or make the feedback loop positive. For example, a behavioral strategy of turning the room lights on when the temperature drops below 68°F will open the feedback loop, or a behavior strategy of turning on an air-conditioning unit when the temperature drops below 68°F will cause a positive, regenerative feedback loop driving the room temperature lower and lower. A malfunction such as a 10-minute delay in responding to error signal information will reduce the effectiveness of the control system and produce wider swings in room temperature than would the normal behavioral strategy. It would also make more difficult the discovery of the reference state value. Nevertheless, appropriate manipulation of the independent variables will reveal the reference state value, and given that, the behavioral strategy can be deduced and, if necessary, corrected.

If the output transform is inadequate (e.g., the BTU output of the furnace is too low to meet the requirements of the reference state), the control system will operate properly, but the furnace will be on all the time and will never be able to raise the room temperature to the reference state value. In such a case, the general characteristic of the reference state may be deduced, but the actual reference state value cannot be deduced because it is never attained. The actual reference state value can be deduced only by manipulating independent variables, such as adding an auxiliary heat source and raising the room temperature above the reference state value, or by manipulating system variables, such as selectively heating the thermometer and changing the perception of the system. If the output transform is excessive (e.g., the BTU output of the furnace is far more than merely adequate to meet the requirements), the control system will function properly. It should be noted that the reference state value, the output transform, and the environmental transform are important in determining the effectiveness of regulation of a control system. The output transform and the environmental transform may be in conflict with one another because the output transform attempts to manipulate the environment. This conflict is particularly severe when the environmental transform is itself another control system with a conflicting reference state. If the output transform is inadequate to manipulate the environment to the degree required to match the reference state value, the control system will be overloaded and will operate constantly. Constant operation at overload will increase the likelihood of system breakdown. The overload situation can be remedied by three means: (1) changing the reference state value to a value within the capacity of the output transform to achieve; (2) increasing the power of the output transform to manipulate the environment; or (3) changing the environmental transform so that the environment is more susceptible to manipulation.

The environmental transform in this case would be the physics of the relationship between the heat entering the room and the sensing of room temperature by the thermometer. The behavior of the system would vary widely depending on the environmental transform, if the rest of the control system is performing perfectly.

Several examples will illustrate the effect of the environmental transform on system behavior. If the room is poorly insulated, much of the heat entering the room from the furnace will escape through the walls and never reach the thermometer, so the system will keep the furnace on much of the time. If the room is well insulated, little heat will escape, most of it will reach the thermometer, and the furnace will be on rarely. If the thermometer is placed in a location with little airflow (e.g., in a cubby hole in the wall and covered by a picture), there will be a long time-lag between the changing of room temperature and the sensing of it by the thermometer. Consequently, the behavior of the system will be greatly prolonged in any given state (i.e., when the furnace comes on it will stay on for a long time, and when it goes off it will stay off for a long time). As a result, room temperature will fluctuate widely around the reference state value. On the other hand, if the thermometer is located directly in front of the furnace heating duct, the furnace will never stay on for very long: as soon as the furnace comes on, the thermometer will sense the heat coming into the room and turn the furnace off immediately. As a result, the on–off cycle of the system will be quite rapid and frequent, and the control of average room temperature will be less than optimal.

It is worth noting that the environmental transform is extremely important in determining the behavior emitted by a given system operating with consistent rules. Consequently, when studying a given system operating in different situations with different environmental transforms and emitting different behavior patterns, it is quite easy to be diverted into studying the characteristics of the behavior patterns themselves and cataloging them. When that happens, one is simply correlating behavior patterns with properties of the environment, the environmental transform. Such has been a tendency of operant psychology, for the operant approach has prohibited dealing with organismic variables because they are not directly observable. It can be argued that that is only part of the appropriate interest, and that the rest of the appropriate interest is in the organismic portion of the control system, for example, the reference state and the behavioral strategies.

The application of control system analysis to a simple, mechanical thermostatic system is intended to illustrate some of the properties of such a system by means of a common and well-known control system. The simplicity of the system and the availability to direct measurement of all components of the system make such an illustration an imperfect analogy to the analysis of an organismic system. Yet, in principle, all control systems function in a similar manner and have similar properties, so that to some degree, there is a valid transfer of analysis from mechanical to organismic systems, even though organismic systems are more complex and have components not available for direct observation and measurement.

Application of Systems Theory to Simple Operant Schedules

In order to test the application of a control system analysis to organismic behavior, one of the authors (Berger) described mathematically the rules of behavior of an organism according to control system analysis, programmed these rules in a computer simulation program, and applied the program to simple, temporal operant schedules. The computer programs simulate behavior by (1) perceiving the state of the environment; (2) using that information in conjunction with information received from the environment through previous behavior, and comparing that information with a reference state; (3) selecting a behavior for emission according to a behavioral strategy; and (4) perceiving the results of that behavior, thus beginning the next cycle of a reiterative process. For purposes of simplification of the computer programs, the physical stimulus, the input transform, and perception were treated as a unit; the reference state and the comparator were treated as a unit; the behavioral strategy and the behavior emitted were treated as a unit; and the environmental transform was treated as a unit reflecting experimental contingencies. The process of developing a model of behavior is both analytic and synthetic. It is synthetic in that the model synthesizes a series of operations, rules, and variables into an ordered system, and it is analytic in that the selection of specific operations, rules, and variables is based on an analysis of the behavior of organisms and properties of organisms that seem justifiable on the basis of that behavior.

For the perceptual unit, it was assumed that the organism can perceive standard stimuli, the occurrence of events, and the passage of time. Moreover, it was assumed that the organism is capable of some more abstract perceptions, such as the probability of occurrence of events and the frequency of occurrence of events. These assumptions are not unreasonable in the light of research with animals in signal detection theory (cf. Green & Swets, 1974). All perceptions were considered accurate except for the perception of duration. Organisms' "clocks" are not precisely accurate, so the perceived duration was regarded as being distributed according to a normal distribution. The mean of the perceived distribution for any objective interval is equal to the objective interval, and the standard deviation of the distribution is a constant proportion of the mean value, in recognition of Weber's law (which states in essence that the error of perception is proportional to the magnitude of the stimulus). The relevant perceptions were considered (1) the utility value of an event's occurrence; (2) the probability of the occurrence of an event; and (3) the frequency or temporal density of the event's occurrence. The events considered were (1) receipt of reinforcement and (2) responding. Thus, six perceptual factors were considered: the three relevant perceptions for each of two events.

For the reference state, it was assumed that the organism's reference state followed the law of effect: the organism will behave so as to obtain satisfiers and avoid annoyers. For incorporation into the computer program, the law of effect was restated: the organism will behave so as to maximize the positive expected utility and minimize the negative expected utility, so that the net expected utility will be the maximum positive. It should be noted that in a situation in which no positive utility can be expected, such as avoidance situations using aversive reinforcing stimuli, the maximum positive will be the minimum negative. The net expected utility, $E(N)$, is the sum of the expected utility associated with reinforcement, $E(X)$, and the expected utility associated with responding, $E(R)$:

(1) $$E(N) = E(X) + E(R)$$

It is additive because either factor could attain a value of zero without the net expected utility's attaining a value of zero. The expected utility associated with reinforcement is the product of the utility of a single reinforcement, U_x, the probability of receipt of a reinforcement, P_x, and the frequency of receipt of reinforcement, F_x:

(2) $$E(X) = U_x * P_x * F_x$$

These factors are multiplicatively related because, if any of the factors attained a value of zero, the value of the expected utility associated with reinforcement would also attain a value of zero. The expected utility associated with responding is exactly parallel to that of the expected utility associated with reinforcement:

(3) $$E(R) = U_r * P_r * F_r$$

in which U_r is the utility of a single response, P_r is the probability of occurrence of a response, and F_r is the frequency of emission of responses. Expectations were based on the perception of previous events and experience as stored in memory in conjunction with the perception of the current state of the environment. Memory storage was a time-weighted integral, so that recent events affected memory more than events more distant in time.

For the behavioral strategy unit, it was assumed that the organism responded on a threshold basis. The organism would respond in the first interval in which the expected net utility was equal to or greater than some proportion of the most positive utility expected to be obtainable in the situation.

In the computer simulation programs, the simulated organism was assumed to have the basic schedule contingencies already learned, but the specific values of the schedules had to be gained through simulated experience. For example, in a Sidman schedule, a negative reinforcing stimulus is delivered to the subject at a given interval after the occurrence of the previous response, the response–shock interval. The receipt of reinforcement can be delayed indefinitely by continual responding at interresponse intervals (IRTs) less than the response–shock interval. The simulated organism would know that some relationship existed between the IRT and the receipt of reinforcement, but the specific values of the response–shock interval, the reinforcement magnitude, and the response cost magnitude were unknown and had to be gained through simulated experience in the situation. In essence, the simulated organism responded on the basis of its perception of the current state of the environment and its previous experience, applied these perceptions to the reference state for comparison, and chose the time of the next response according to the behavioral strategy. The process was repeated reiteratively, and as more experience was gained in the situation, the behavioral patterns became stable.

Sidman Schedule

The Sidman schedule was the first one simulated because of its amenability to mathematical expression, and it is the schedule dealt with most extensively here. Figures 2 through 5 display IRT histograms based on computer simulation data. Each figure shows the effect on behavior of varying one of the model's variables when other variables are held at constant, standard values. Figure 2 indicates that over a wide range in variation of reinforcement utility magnitude, the simulated behavior changes remarkably little. Thus, according to the model, behavior should be relatively insensitive to reinforcement magnitude variation above some minimal level. Figure 3 indicates that according to the model, an increase in response cost utility tends to increase the proportion of longer IRTs. Figure 4 indicates that according to the model, the organism's temporal uncertainty or precision of accurately perceiving time has substantial effects on behavior. Two things

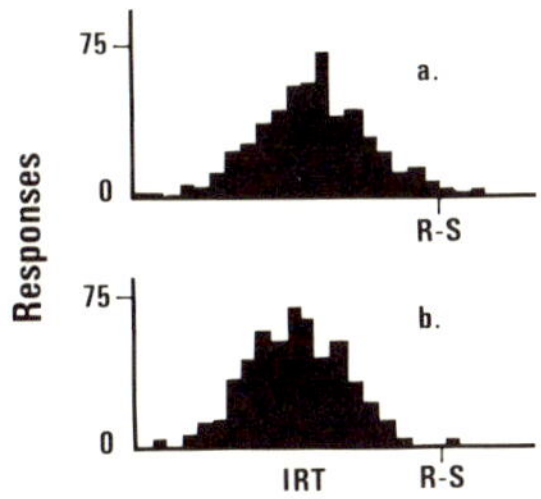

Fig. 2. Sidman schedule IRT distribution simulation: (a) small shock magnitude, (b) large shock magnitude.

are noteworthy about the simulated behavior. First, poorer temporal discrimination is associated with IRT distributions shifted toward short IRTs, while better temporal discrimination is associated with shifts toward longer IRTs. Second, even with poor temporal discrimination, few shocks are received, although the price paid is a high rate of responding. Figure 5 indicates that a variation in response threshold produces a behavioral effect. As the response threshold becomes lower (more lenient), the IRT distribution shifts toward shorter IRTs, but in a manner different from that associated with poor temporal discrimination.

For those variables that have been studied experimentally, the simulated behavior is consistent with the observed behavior. Within reasonable limits, shock strength does not have a great influence on the IRT distribution. Poor temporal-discrimination ability produces rapid responding and an IRT distribution shifted toward short IRTs, but relatively few shocks are received by the subject (Sidman, 1966). Such a consistency is encouraging, but it would have little value if it were limited to the Sidman schedule situation.

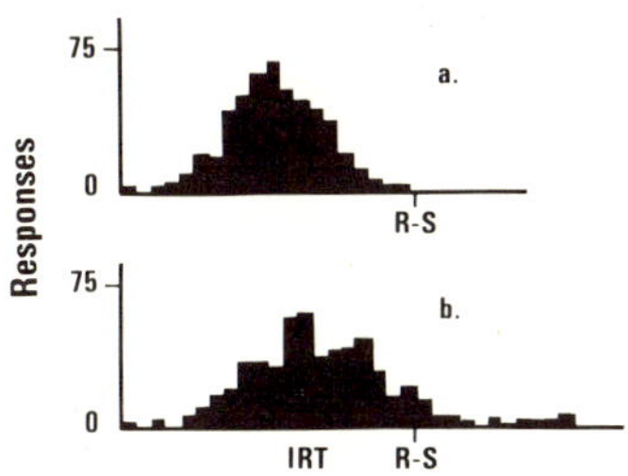

Fig. 3. Sidman schedule IRT distribution simulation: (a) small response cost utility, (b) large response cost utility.

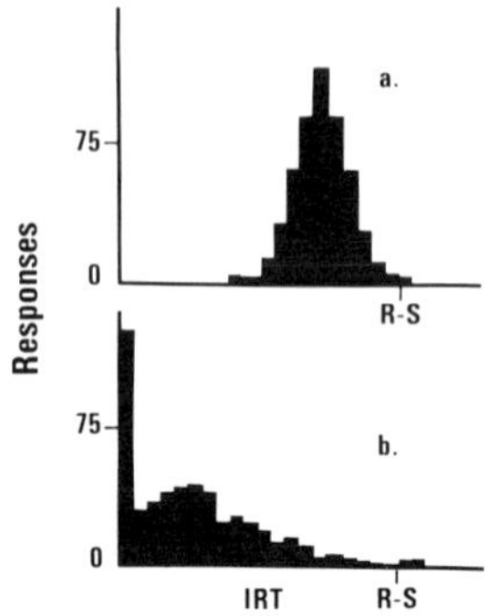

Fig. 4. Sidman schedule IRT distribution simulation: (a) accurate temporal perception, (b) inaccurate temporal perception.

An appropriate test of the model requires that it be applied to other behavioral situations with only the environmental transform being modified to fit the different contingencies. Such an application was done, using other temporally based operant–schedule contingencies for the environmental transforms. In the process, some minor organismic variable changes had to be made in the simulation programs, but none of the changes affected the basic application of the same model. For example, in fixed- and variable-interval schedule situations, the simulated organism had to be sensitive at the time since the receipt of the last reinforcement, whereas in the Sidman schedule, the sensitivity was to the time since the last response. These simulated organismic-variable changes were simply an expression of the organism's learning the different experimental contingencies.

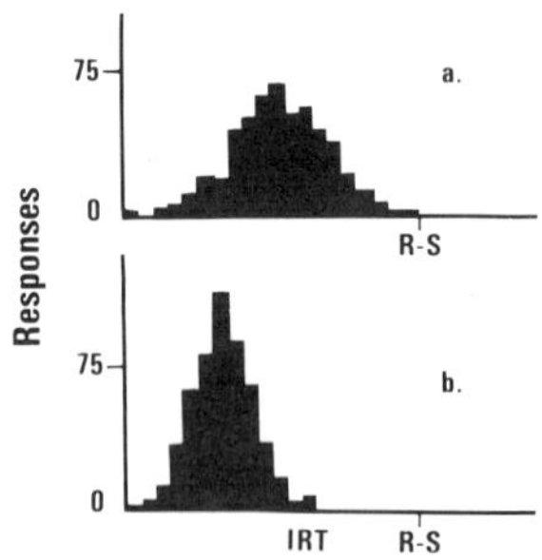

Fig. 5. Sidman schedule IRT distribution simulation: (a) high response threshold, (b) low response threshold.

Other Schedules

In a fixed-interval schedule, the first response that occurs at more than a given fixed interval after the receipt of the previous reinforcement is reinforced. The pattern of simulated responding shows a low response rate following reinforcement, and a higher rate later in the fixed interval. One of the more notable effects of varying parameter values is that an increase in the response cost depresses responding in the earlier portion of the fixed interval and reduces the average response rate.

In a variable-interval schedule, the first response that occurs at more than an interval, which varies randomly in length, after the receipt of the previous reinforcement is reinforced. The pattern of simulated responding shows a quite steady rate of responding throughout the interval. There is a tendency for increased response cost to decrease therate of responding. Temporal discrimination ability makes very little difference in the response pattern.

A simulation program was made for a nonstandard schedule, called a *mixed fixed-interval schedule.* Essentially, it is a random presentation of two fixed-interval schedules, one of length *1,* and the other of length *1/2.* This schedule was used because it can be conceived of as being transitional between fixed- and variable-interval (VI) schedules, and the behavior pattern should reveal the temporal discrimination abilities of organisms. Simulated behavior shows that with better temporal discrimination, the response distribution becomes more peaked, one peak occurring around the interval *1/2,* and the other around interval *1.*

Preliminary mathematical investigation of concurrent VI–VI performance according to the model has been done, but no computer simulation program has yet been made to simulate behavior in that situation. However, the work that has been done suggests that the behavior according to the model will exhibit the characteristics of Herrnstein's matching law (see Herrnstein, 1979), which states that in an alternative response-choice situation, the responding on each alternative is proportional to the reinforcement received from that alternative. Moreover, according to the model, the behavior of changing from one response alternative to another response alternative is consistent with experimental findings (Heyman, 1979), in that response alternative changeovers seem to be randomly distributed.

Conclusions

The potential advantages of a self-regulating control-system approach to behavior are strongly suggested by the application of a single model to the different experimental situations described above. The behavior of organisms in the several different experimental situations is quite disparate, and the situations have been considered quite separate from one another. Yet, a single control-system model incorporating the same variables and relationships appropriately arranged for the different experimental contingencies describes the different patterns of behavior typically observed in live organisms. Such a unification of the description of different behavior patterns in different situations under the umbrella of a single model indicates that the application of control system analysis to behavior has some promise of providing an improved conceptual framework for the field of psychology.

The mathematical application of control system analysis to the simple operant situations above was intended to be a test of the feasibility of such an application to well-defined behavioral situations in which behavior patterns are known to be stable in their characteristics for any given schedule, but patterns are different for different schedules. Operant schedules are well suited to mathematical description because of the limited number of variables involved and the precision with which those variables can be specified. However, those advantages, while helping mathematical description, separate operant schedule situations from situations encountered in the day-to-day affairs of human beings. Human affairs involve many variables, most of which cannot be specified with much precision. Consequently, the mathematical description of human affairs for computer simulations of behavior is not an appropriate beginning point for the investigation of the application of control system analysis to behavior. Yet, the application of control system analysis to human affairs would be quite desirable. Clearly, such an application must forego some precision, but it does mean that the application of control system analysis to human situations is appropriate, as is illustrated in the following section.

A Self-Environmental Regulation Model

The general systems-theory ideas were presented in the first section, and then the application of these ideas to a mechanical heating system and to operant temporal schedules was discussed. Building on these ideas about regulating systems, we now examine the application of systems theory to human research and applied practice. A number of behavioral researchers and professionals have been investigating and applying aspects of self-regulating systems to humans for some time. Bandura's research on self-reinforcement and self-control (Bandura, 1971; Bandura & Walters, 1963), Kanfer's development of a three-stage model of self-control (1971, 1977), Thoresen and Mahoney's (1974) writings on self-monitoring and self-management, and Schwartz's (1975) research on biofeedback and self-control are just a few examples of some of the behavioral work on self-control with humans.

In this section, we present a self-environmental regulation model (SERMOD) that attempts to incorporate the previously presented systems theory ideas with the human behavior modification literature. The heuristic value of this model is that (1) it helps translate some of the systems theory language into behavioral language; (2) it helps to relate operant, observational, and cognitive research at a conceptual systems theory level; and (3) it helps to emphasize the interactions of individuals with and the interdependence of individuals on their external environment.

The SERMOD

Figure 6 is a schematic diagram of the components necessary for any system to operate, whether it be a machine, an animal, or a human being engaged in simple or complex behavior. The general systems-theory notions are the same as presented in the first section; however, the schematic layout has been redrawn, and some of the terms have been relabeled so as to make these notions more compatible with the existing behavioral literature. The

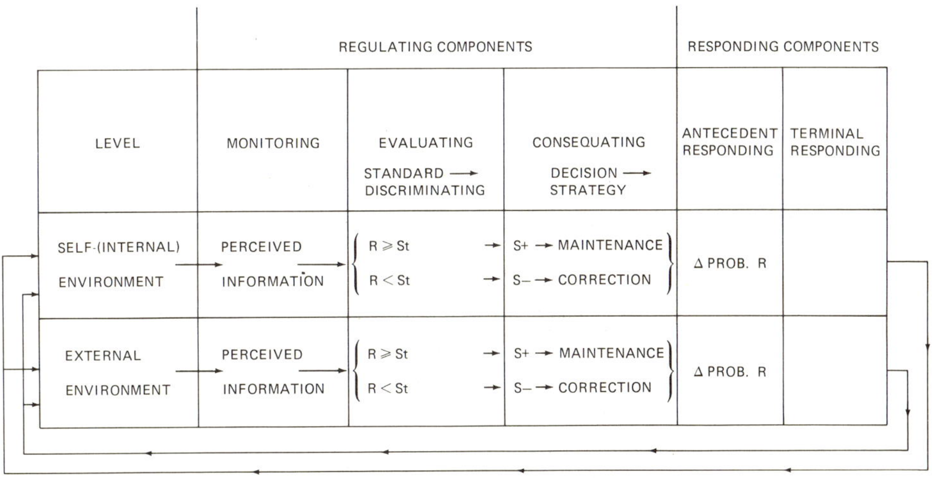

Fig. 6. Self-environmental regulation model (SERMOD).

regulating components consist of the following, and their translation to the control system terms presented in Figure 6 appear in parentheses:

1. *Monitoring* of information about the environment (input transform and perception).

2. *Evaluating* that information, which involves making a discrimination of that information against a standard of acceptable behavior. The response may be greater than or equal to the standard or less than the standard (reference state and perception).

3. *Consequating* or acting on the evaluation of that information. This consequation consists of a decision process of assessing whether the information is in a positive state (above the standard) or in a negative state (below the standard) and then adopting a behavioral strategy (error signal and behavioral strategy). The control process then leads to (in the right column of the diagram) the responding components. The control aspect of the system tells the organism or the machine how and when to respond. The response can be a simple response or a chain of responses, such as a number of antecedent responses that then lead to the final terminal response.

This system functions at several levels. The first is the self, or the internal environment, which is depicted at the top of the diagram. The self-environment refers to an individual,a human organism with its own internal biological and psychological control systems. The next level is the external environment, which consists of both the physical environment and the social environment that an individual interacts with. Since the former has already been discussed in the first section, and since we are examining human applications for the remainder of the chapter, we focus here on the social external environment.

The social environment consists of other human beings interacting with a particular individual or self-environment. The term *external environment* refers to a special case of an environmental transform in which the environmental transform is itself another control system. Thus, from a systems theory perspective, an individual is both a part of the self-environment—a human with internal controls—that is influenced by the external environment, and at the same time, a part of the collective external environment in terms of interacting with another particular individual. Furthermore, an individual's processing of the external environment's output and then his or her eventual behavioral response can be directed at modifying his or her internal environment or external environment, or both. This systems theory conceptualization rejects simple unidirectional, stimulus–response, nonfeedback causality models and, instead, emphasizes a model of continuous interaction and reciprocal influence of the external environment and the self-environment.

In addition, the regulating components of monitoring, evaluating, and consequating also apply to the external environment when the external environment is also composed of many and sometimes conflicting control systems. For the self and the external environments to regulate themselves successfully, all the regulating components must be working appropriately. If there is a breakdown in any one of the components, it can cause a breakdown in the behavior at either level. Also, if there is not a cooperative relationship between self and the external environment, there can be a breakdown in part or all of the self, the social environment, or both.

Illustrations of the SERMOD

Let us provide two examples with humans that illustrate the operation of this model. The first example is about toilet training, and the second is about academic and scholarly behavior.

With a 2-month-old infant, the regulating components are all internal. In terms of the monitoring stage, the baby responds to the propioceptive cues, that is, a full bladder. In the evaluating stage, the standard is "no pressure in the bladder," which leads to a positive state with a decision rule of no urination, which determines the response of no urination. The converse is "pressure in the bladder," which produces a negative state, which leads to the decision rule to urinate, the response that, in the case of a 2-month-old baby, is to urinate whenever and wherever it wants to.

From the perspective of a 2-month-old baby, it does have a self-regulating system for urination and bladder control. However, from the perspective of its parents and society, this infant would be considered a *non*-self-regulating human being. As is typically the case, the parents (see Figure 6) are the external regulating environment. The parents monitor when the baby is wet or dry, they set the standard that dry is good and wet is bad, and they compare the baby's state of affairs with their standard. Their decision rules are that "a positive state of dryness" means not changing the baby, and that "a negative state of wetness" means changing the baby. The parents' decision then leads to not responding or to changing their baby's diaper. In this example, the regulating components and the responding components are done by the parents—the external environment.

As part of the maturation and socialization of the child, he or she goes from being a non-toilet-trained, nonregulated baby to being an adult who can regulate himself or herself without difficulty.

Again, if there is a breakdown in any one of the components, it can cause a breakdown in the self-regulated behavior. As the reader is probably well aware, there are adults 30, 40, and 50 years old who have been institutionalized for much of their lives and have not been toilet-trained a day in their lives. The causes for the breakdown are many. For example, there can be organismic, physiological problems with the bladder and the muscles. These can be considered breakdowns in the mechanism or the responding components of the human being.

There can also be a breakdown in the regulating components because of inadequate or inappropriate learning. A common example is the 2-year-old child who had difficulty learning to be toilet-trained with a new baby in the house, or who was toilet-trained and then regresses when the parents bring a new baby brother or sister home from the hospital. Often, what happens in this type of case is that the wires, in a sense, get crossed in the consequating stage. When the child responds appropriately, the parents are often so involved with the new baby that they ignore the child. They do not provide positive reinforcement to the child for appropriate behavior. And then when the child has an accident, the parents inadvertently give a great deal of attention to the child, and we certainly know from the research on rewards and punishments that that is a very good way to shape and maintain wet pants.

Another common problem is the parents' setting unrealistic standards for the child. For example, they might set the standard that they believe their child should be toilet trained day and night at 18 months of age. This is such a high, unrealistic standard for the child that it can cause many problems between the parents and the child and may actually retard the child's later development of self-regulation.

In summary, this example of what we might initially consider simple human behavior is really a very complex set of behaviors in which there is a continuous interaction between the self and the external environment, with the environment influencing the individual and the individual influencing the environment. Furthermore, there can be a breakdown in this regulated behavior because of a malfunction in any one of the regulating or responding components of either the internal environment of the child or the external environment of the parents.

Let us now move on to even more complex human behavior of the type one often sees on a university campus: academic achievement and the lack of it. The case illustrations come from the clinical work of the first author (Jeffrey). We have a Student A, who is getting all As. Student D-1, Student D-2, and Student D-3 are getting all Ds and are on probation. Student A is aware of how well and for what amount of time he is studying—the monitoring stage. He sets high but realistic standards, always trying to do his best. He appropriately consequates his behavior when he achieves his standard, which leads to feeling good about himself, and goes out to reward himself overtly with some favorite activity. These positive feelings and activities, as well as the knowledge that his academic achievements will probably determine his acceptance into a professional graduate school, serve to maintain his high academic achievement. When he does not achieve his standard, this lack of achievement results in a clear negative state, which leads to a decision rule that is complex and adaptive. He asks himself what he did wrong and how he can do better next time. This behavioral strategy then leads to positive adaptive responses, such as analyzing the exam, talking to the teacher, and preparing differently for the next exam, all of which actions lead to a self-correcting system. In this case, Student A is also getting a great deal of support from his external environment. His parents and teachers set realistically high but achievable standards, and they reinforce his achievements richly.

Three students, D-1, D-2, and D-3, are all failing for different reasons that can be quickly analyzed with the SERMOD that has already been presented. Student D-1 is failing but is very relaxed and nonchalant. His standards are just to get Ds, and this outcome is satisfactory, not important. As long as he gets Ds or better, he keeps doing what he has been doing. In this particular case, the student has good study skills and abilities, so he has the responding capabilities but does not have the standards necessary to succeed in the school environment. Student D-2 has the incredibly high standard of having to be always Number 1 but seldom can reach this standard. Her lack of achievement leads to a negative self-statement, such as "I'm not good enough, and I need to work a little harder," which then leads to the actual responding of being very tense and anxious and of *freezing* on exams.

Student D-3 (we'll call him the poor-study-skills student) monitors his behavior fairly well and has appropriate standards; however, he has never developed really good responding capabilities. That is, he hasn't really developed good study skills, reading skills, and a game plan for making it in the school system. Thus, he has continuing difficulties in school.

Summary

The model that has been presented is not fully developed, nor perfect, but it does help to integrate a number of research findings and ideas. From this perspective, two things are clear:

1. All regulating or control systems involve the same regulating processes, whether it be a heating system, an animal, a child, or an adult. The more complex the behavior, typically the more complex the regulating system, including different behavioral strategies.

2. There is always an interaction of the self-regulating system with the environmental regulating system, with the self influencing the environment and the environment influencing the self. Therefore, we must take into account the self and the environment as a continuous, reciprocally interacting system.

The next section applies the general systems notions presented in the beginning of this chapter and the more clinically oriented systems notion of the SERMOD to specific treatment strategies that can be used in clinical settings.

Self-Environmental Regulation Treatment Strategies

The self-environmental regulation treatment strategies (SERTS) provide an organizing framework from a systems theory perspective for a variety of behavioral modification techniques that have been developed over the years by a number of people (see Bandura, 1969, and Goldfried & Davison, 1976, for general summaries of these techniques). The heuristic value of the SERTS is that (1) it emphasizes both self *and* external environmental change techniques within the encompassing content of regulating systems, and (2) it provides a convenient checklist of a set of principles and procedures that practitioners should attend to in assessing and treating a breakdown in some regulated behavior.

The SERTS model is summarized in Table 1. At the left-hand side of the column are the principles and procedures going down from top to bottom. Going across from left to right is the locus of control. The first column under the locus of control consists of externally initiated changes. These are changes made by therapists, teachers, parents, supervisors, and others who affect another individual. At the far right is self-initiated personal change, where the individual assesses his or her situation and decides to initiate some change in his or her covert behavior (that is, self-verbalizations) or overt behavior. The middle column consists of self-initiated assistance from others, as when the individual wants to change her or his behavior and asks for help from others.

Table 1. Self-Environmental Regulation Treatment Strategies (SERTS)

Principle/procedure	Locus of control		
	Externally initiated changes: Therapists, teachers, parents, supervisors	Self-initiated assistance from others	Self-initiated personal change
1. Monitor accurately			
2. Evaluate realistically			
3. Arrange antecedents			
4. Practice the behavior			
5. Provide consequences appropriately			
6. Go back to 1–5 and modify as needed			

The principle and procedures (that is, the left-hand column) consist of six stages: (1) monitoring accurately; (2) evaluating realistically; (3) arranging the antecedents; (4) practicing the behavior; and (5) providing consequences appropriately. The last one (6) really is a reiterative loop of going back to 1 through 5 as needed.

We will look at each of the principles and procedures as interventions that one could take in changing one's own behavior or, as a social change agent, that one could use in modifying the behavior of others.

1. *Monitoring accurately.* Under monitoring accurately, we know from the control systems and the SERMOD previously presented that accurate information is absolutely essential if the individual or the external agent, such as the parents, is to regulate her or his behavior, or the behavior of others, sensitively and appropriately. Accurate information is needed to adjust to the changing internal and external environment. This information can be of an informal or a formal nature. It can also be from an intermittent or a continuous source. We will go through examples from externally initiated change, from self-initiated assistance from others, and from self-initiated personal change. In the first case, examples are parents monitoring their child's behavior or a teacher monitoring a student's performance in class. An example of self-initiated assistance from others would be when a person who is trying to be more assertive asks others to provide information to him when he is not assertive. Another example would be of a person asking friends or neighbors to record in a diary the number of times she stutters, or the number of times she snacks on some food at their house. In the last column, self-initiated personal change, there are numerous examples of people monitoring their weight, the food they eat, the cigarettes they smoke, and their self-statements, such as bad thoughts about themselves.

In clinical practice, it is important to assess how accurately a client monitors his or her internal and external environment. If the assessment indicates that the person is not monitoring or is distorting the information, it is then essential to train the person. As a treatment technique, it is important to train people to accurately monitor and perceive their external and internal environment. Such training is often much more difficult than it would appear, since some people develop elaborate defenses against accurately seeing their environments. Although research shows that monitoring accurately is essential to effective functioning, it is not sufficient unless the problem of the maladaptive behavior exists only in the monitoring stage (Jeffrey, 1974b; Kazdin, 1974; Nelson, 1977.)

2. *Evaluating realistically.* Realistic evaluation consists of setting attainable standards, processing information as it comes in, and comparing it with the established standard. There are numerous examples of parents, acting as external change agents, setting unrealistic standards for their children. The

role of the therapist or teacher is to assess the actual potential of the child and then to set realistic standards that will help the individual to strive for excellence but not for goals beyond his or her capability. In clinical settings, realistic evaluation often involves changes in parents' behavior. In terms of self-initiated assistance from others, we often instruct our clients to check with others on what they think are realistic standards. This procedure allows the clients to become more aware of what constitute appropriate goals and, in the process, to begin to set more realistic standards for themselves. In terms of self-initiated personal change, we ask individuals who have problems with unrealistically high or low standards to monitor what effect those standards have on their behavior, and whether these standards facilitate or impede the types of things they want out of life. Becoming aware of their standards and seeing the connections between their standards, their feelings, and their behaviors often result in our patients' modifying their standards.

3. *Arranging antecedents.* This is often called *antecendent stimulus control,* which involves stimuli or events that precede and set the occasion for the target behavior to occur. This approach can consist of (a) rearranging the physical environment or (b) rearranging the social environment. As an example of self-initiated personal change, Skinner (1953) used an individual's setting an alarm clock for himself or herself the night before in order to get up the following morning. An example of self-initiated assistance from others is an individual's asking a parent or a roommate to set the alarm clock for him or her. An example of externally initiated change is the parents' setting the clock the night before to wake the child up.

In terms of rearranging the social environment, there are numerous examples. A mother and father who want their child to lose weight might buy, prepare, and serve low-calorie foods to the child. People who know that they will not exercise on their own often enroll in an exercise class at a university gym, a YMCA, or a health club as a way to get assistance from others. Jogging on one's own without any classes or anybody else would certainly be an example of self-initiated personal change.

4. *Practicing behavior.* In this category are a number of techniques, such as verbal instruction, modeling, behavior rehearsals, and role playing, that are used in a systematic way to teach new behaviors. All of the things previously discussed–monitoring, setting standards, and arranging antecedents–consist of behaviors that a person may be proficient or deficient in. If the assessment indicates deficiencies in any one or a combination of the designated behaviors, verbal instruction, modeling, and rehearsal techniques can be used to teach those behaviors.

We will provide a few examples here to illustrate these techniques. However, the reader who would like to know more about the clinical aspects of using these techniques should see the books by Goldfried and Davison (1976) and O'Leary and Wilson (1975).

In the case of externally initiated modeling, a therapist or a parent would demonstrate clearly and slowly the behavior that she or he wants in another individual. This technique is extraordinarily important because, as Bandura (1969) and others have shown, a great deal of behavior is learned by observing others, so the old maxim of practicing what one preaches is important when the change agent wants the designated behavior to occur in others.

An example of a self-initiated assistance from others would be an individual's asking somebody else to demonstrate how to do something.

In the technique of rehearsal, the individual practices the behavior, either overtly (out loud and going through the acts) or covertly (talking to herself or himself or imagining going through the desired behavior). For this technique to work, the person must obviously be conscientious about practicing the desired behavior.

5. *Providing consequences appropriately.* This involves applying the voluminous research of Skinner (1953), Bandura (1969), Ferster and Skinner (1957), and others on the controlling effects of consequences. This stage involves using the established principles of positive reinforcement, negative reinforcement, extinction, time-out, and punishment to increase or decrease specific behaviors.

Let us use positive reinforcement or rewards as an illustration. In terms of externally initiated change, there are numerous examples of parents praising their children and giving them privileges when they do something that the parents deem appropriate. An example of self-initiated assistance from others is individuals' asking friends or family members to reinforce them when they have achieved their goal, as in a jogging, weight-loss, or self-improvement program. In terms of self-initiated personal change, a person rewards himself or herself for having achieved a set goal. Self-rewards can be either covert actions (such as self-statements of approval and praise) or overt actions (such as going out and celebrating, buying oneself a gift, or going to a show). The research indicates that self-reward has properties similar to external reward in modifying and maintaining behavior (Bandura, 1971, 1976; Kanfer, 1971).

Much information and many techniques are needed to use consequences effectively. For example, the work on schedules of reinforcement–fixed ratio, variable ratio, fixed interval, and variable interval–all have demonstrated replicated effects on responding (Ferster & Skinner, 1957). Also, the work on successive approximations and shaping to increase the likelihood of a response's occurring or to eliminate a response gives many examples of the effective use of consequences (Honig, 1966).

An additional component of effective rewards and punishment is that they are based on accurate information about what the response was, which brings us back full circle to the role of monitoring behavior accurately in order to know when a behavior should be reinforced, or extinguished, or sometimes even punished. So, accurate monitoring of responding and knowledge of that information are essential to the application of effective rewards and punishments.

In summary, these five principles of monitoring accurately, evaluating realistically, arranging antecedents, practicing behavior, and providing consequences appropriately can be used in combination to allow an individual to regulate his or her own life effectively and to allow societal change agents to regulate others effectively. As can be seen in the discussion, these principles are not independent of each other but interact with each other in influencing behavior. And they are all behaviors that can be learned and modified. Thus, when an individual is trying to change her or his behavior, or a parent is trying to modify the behavior of the child, the SERTS outline provides a convenient checklist for diagnosing the cause of the maladaptive behavior and for determining how to go about correcting the problem.

In the clinical work at the University of Montana Psychology Clinic, the first author provides his graduate clinical students with this outline so that they can quickly diagnose deficits in any one or combination of the components that may be causing difficulties in their clients. Using the same SERTS outline, the therapists can then plan a comprehensive treatment program that helps the individual remediate his or her situation and develop to his or her fullest potential.

Application of the SERMOD and SERTS to the Individual Management of Obesity[1]

The application of systems theory and self-control techniques to a specific clinical problem can be richly illustrated with an examination of the behavioral treatments of obesity. Additional factors such as the client's medical and personal characteristics, the therapist's characteristics, and the situational constraints would obviously also need to be considered in treating an individual. Furthermore, the etiology, assessment, and treatment of obesity are complex (Jeffrey & Knauss, 1981). However, for the purposes of this chapter, we focus only on a discussion of the application of SERMOD and SERTS ideas to the individual treatment of obesity. In particular, we (1) summarize the major findings about the relative efficacy of self-control approaches to obesity; (2) examine the component analyses of self-control techniques; and (3) present an overview of acomprehensive self-control approach to the treatment of obesity. For an extensive summary of the literature, see the fine re-

[1]Appreciation is extended to Maxwell R. Knauss for his contribution to this section.

views by Abramson (1973, 1977), Bellack (1977), Jeffrey (1976, 1977), Leon (1976), and Stunkard and Mahoney (1976).

The cumulative results of a number of comparative outcome studies covering short-term treatment and follow-ups demonstrate the superiority of behavioral control treatments over no-treatment controls, attention-placebo controls, traditional insight and group psychotherapy, TOPS dieting clubs, and "willpower." Penick, Filion, Fox, and Stunkard (1971) concluded that "behavior modification may represent a significant advance in the treatment of obesity" (p. 49). The promising results of behavioral studies and the increasing interest in SERMOD notions (e.g., Thoreson & Mahoney, 1974) have led some investigators to examine the efficacy of self-control treatment packages relative to more external-control (therapist) treatment packages. Overall, the self-control packages appear to be as effective as or more effective than other behavioral programs in promoting weight loss (e.g., Abrahms & Allen, 1974; Hall, Hall, DeBoer, & O'Kulitch, 1977; Jeffrey, 1974a). The promise of the self-control approaches has led some investigators to conduct studies analyzing the components typically included in self-control packages to determine which are the most responsible for the treatment effects. Since these components can be related to SERMOD notions, and as they illustrate the analyses of SERTS procedures, they will be covered in greater detail.

Component Analyses of Self-Control Techniques

Self-monitoring is an integral part of self-regulating systems and has thus far received a thorough evaluation. Romanczyk, Tracey, Wilson, and Thorpe (1973) compared two types of self-monitoring (caloric intake and caloric intake plus daily weight) with complex self-control packages that included self-monitoring, stimulus control, covert sensitization, and contracting. Although the self-monitoring groups received no additional treatment components, in both studies the groups following the program of caloric intake plus daily weight self-monitoring lost as much weight as the more complex self-control groups. These results are difficult to evaluate because the brevity of the studies (4 weeks) may not have allowed true differences between the treatment groups to emerge. In a second study, Romanczyk (1974) found that the complex package produced more significant treatment effects and resulted in better maintenance at 12-week follow-ups than did the self-monitoring.

Two other studies also suggest that more complex treatment procedures are more effective than self-monitoring alone. Mahoney (1974) compared self-monitoring with two self-reward conditions (self-reward for weight loss and self-reward for habit change). Posttreatment and two-month follow-up results indicated that the self-reward conditions were more effective than self-monitoring alone. In addition, self-reward for habit change had greater efficacy than self-reward for weight loss. Bellack (1976) also demonstrated that self-reward was more effective than self-monitoring.

Bellack, Rozensky, and Schwartz (1974) evaluated two types of self-monitoring within stimulus-control treatment groups. Self-monitoring of intake before eating (premonitoring) was compared with self-monitoring of food after intake (postmonitoring) and a no-treatment control. The premonitoring treatment was most effective, while the postmonitoring treatment group did not differ from the control group at posttreatment.

Mahoney, Moura, and Wade (1973) compared three types of self-initiated consequences (self-reward, self-punishment, and self-reward plus self-punishment) for weight loss and habit change with self-monitoring only and with a no-treatment control. At a four-month follow-up, the groups containing self-reward instructions had lost more weight than either the self-punishment or the control groups.

The role of setting one's own standards as a component of self-reinforcement has not been sufficiently examined. In a study employing an additive design, Chapman and Jeffrey (1978) compared a situational management group with a group that set its own standards and with a self-reinforcement group. The situational management group employed self-monitoring, stimulus-control techniques, and exercise and nutritional counseling. The standard-setting group received the same instructions as the situational management group and, in addition, were instructed in setting realistic goals for weekly habit change and weight loss. The self-reinforcement group received both situational management and standard-setting instructions and were also instructed to reward themselves verbally and materially for successful weight loss and habit change. The results revealed, as predicted, that the standard-setting subjects lost significantly more weight than the situational management subjects. However, the standard-setting group was also superior to the self-reinforcement group, which did not differ significantly from the situational management group. These results demonstrated that the addition of self-reinforcement failed to enhance weight loss, as predicted, and in fact produced results inferior to those achieved by the situational management and the standard-setting techniques. At posttreatment, group members rated the helpfulness of the various techniques employed during the treatment. Both the standard-setting subjects and the self-reinforcement subjects rated standard setting as one of the most useful techniques, while subjects in the self-reinforcement group rated self-reinforcement as the least helpful technique they had learned during treatment.

In summary, the existing component analysis studies have examined the importance of self-monitoring, setting standards for oneself, self-reinforcement and self-attribution in treatment efficacy in complex self-control packages. On the basis of currently available evidence, it can be concluded that self-monitoring of food intake before eating is effective (Bellack, Rozensky, & Schwartz, 1974). Several studies have compared simple self-monitoring treatments with treatment packages combining self-monitoring and other behavioral techniques. While McReynolds, Lutz, Paulsen, and Kohrs (1976) found self-monitoring superior to the more complex treatment package, other studies (Romanczyk, 1974; Mahoney, 1974; Bellack, 1976; Mahoney, Moura, & Wade, 1973) have found the complex packages to be the most effective. Taken together, these findings suggest that self-monitoring facilitates weight loss but, by itself, is not as effective as when it is combined with self-reinforcement and other components.

Several studies have found that self-reward enhances weight loss when added to self-monitoring procedures (Mahoney, 1974; Bellack, 1976). At present, self-reward for habit change appears more effective than self-reward for weight loss (Mahoney, 1974). It has also been demonstrated that self-reward is superior to self-punishment in promoting weight loss (Mahoney, Moura, & Wade, 1973). While some aspect of the self-reward procedure enhances weight loss, Chapman and Jeffrey's (1978) results suggest that the standard setting inherent in the self-reward may be the effective component, rather than the self-administered reward per se. These results underscore the importance of standard setting in self-management programs and demonstrate that this component deserves further research attention. Finally, investigators have evaluated the impact of patients' self-attributions on treatment outcomes. The failure of "willpower" treatments (Jeffrey & Christensen, 1975; Tobias & McDonald, 1977) suggests that manipulating patients' attribution of responsibility for treatment outcome is not sufficient by itself to promote weight loss. However, when patients are given the attribution that they must be responsible for making habit changes through the use of self-control techniques, better results are achieved than when patients are given the attribution that the therapist is responsible for their weight loss (Jeffrey, 1974a).

At the present time, there are not enough data to allow any final judgments regarding the relative efficacy of these treatment components. However, from a SERMOD perspective, it can be argued that all the regulating and responding components are necessary for the individual to manage his or her weight effectively. The precise way that these components interact and the best way to teach these self-management skills are still not known. Thus, further research is clearly warranted. However, sufficiently promising basic and treatment-outcome research exists to suggest that therapists should employ comprehensive self-management treatment programs for obesity and should include all the previously discussed SERMOD notions and SERTS techniques.

Comprehensive Self-Control Treatment Programs

Currently, self-management approaches offer promising methods for the treatment of obesity in outpatient settings. Until a decade ago, there was no single source designed for use by the layperson that contained all the techniques encompassed by this approach. Instead, brief descriptions of self-management programs were scattered throughout the experimental literature. As research has accumulated, several good books have been written for the public on self-control approaches to weight loss (e.g., Ferguson, 1975; Jeffrey & Katz, 1977; Mahoney & Mahoney, 1976; Stuart & Davis, 1972).

For example, Jeffrey and Katz (1977) presented in their book, *Take It Off and Keep It Off: A Behavioral Program for Weight Loss and Healthy Living,* a comprehensive, multifaceted self-management program. The program is based on the SERMOD ideas and the SERTS techniques previously discussed here and on the most promising research currently available. This self-help book is written in a style that the average layperson can easily understand and use. It is also self-contained, in that it includes all the information and materials necessary to implement a self-management weight-reduction program. Therefore, it can be used alone in bibliotherapy as well as within the context of either individual or group behavior therapy. The components of this self-management package are:

1. Overview of the causes of obesity
2. Presentation of the rationale of behavioral self-management
3. Thorough assessment of readiness to lose weight
4. Training in self-monitoring, standard setting for oneself, and self-reward
5. Description of a "commonsense" diet and a "food-exchange" diet plan
6. Discussion of caloric expenditure and a physical activity plan
7. Training in techniques of effective food management
8. Techniques for gaining support from significant others
9. Ways to handle feelings without eating
10. Methods of contracting with a spouse or a friend for weight loss
11. Plans for long-range planning and maintenance of weight loss
12. Suggestions for preventing obesity in children

Jeffrey and Katz (1977) stressed the importance of gradual weight reduction achieved through self-modification and environmental modification. The book focuses on habit change rather than weight loss and on the importance of a lifelong commitment to a healthy, thin lifestyle.

In conclusion, the promise of the behavioral self-control approach to obesity does not imply that it offers a panacea to the treatment of obesity. It only opens the door to a more sophisticated understanding and treatment of obesity. Future research and practice will need to focus more on individual differences and long-term maintenance (Jeffrey & Knauss, 1981; Wilson, 1978). However, the brief examination of obesity literature illustrates the increasing use of systems theory ideas and specific SERTS techniques in the individual management of obesity.

From a systems theory analysis, one would expect to account for part of the variance by examining an individual's efforts to modify his or her own internal and immediate social environment. However, from a systems analysis, one would also expect to account for part of the variance by examining the influence of the external social environment in shaping and rewarding both overeating and normal eating. This latter focus is referred to as a macroanalysis of obesity (Jeffrey & Lemnitzer, 1981), and one aspect of this macroanalysis is the focus of the next section.

Application of the SERMOD and SERTS to the Analysis of Television Commercials and Eating Habits

In our earlier sections on SERMOD and SERTS, we presented the ideas of regulating and responding components and of the interactions of the individual (self-environment) and the external environment. Based on these models, if there is a major conflict between the external change agents over which external standards apply to an individual (say, a child), this conflict would probably cause some unhealthy functioning in that individual. Furthermore, if the external change agents wanted to influence or condition the behavior of an individual, the SERTS provides an outline of a variety of social learning procedures that could be used to control the child.

The increasing incidence of children's dental caries and obesity, all would agree, is unhealthy and, from a systems theory perspective, represents some breakdown in the self–environmental interaction. The etiologies of obesity and dental caries are complex, but the research does indicate one major contributing factor: children's eating habits. Since young children learn eating habits from their culture, it seems that the well-established field of social learning theory combined with systems theory would provide excellent conceptual models for understanding many of the factors that influence children's eating habits.

To clarify our discussion, the child will be considered the self-environment, and the external environment will be regarded as being composed of the major change agents, such as parents, health professionals, and advertisers. Since television advertisers purposefully intend to change children's specific eating habits by means of particular commercials, it appears that the macrosystems theory and the social learning theory offer appropriate conceptual models for analyzing this controversial area. Therefore, this section examines television advertising in greater detail. In particular, we briefly discuss (1) the health risks of the current American diet; (2) the food products advertised on television; (3) the research problem of analyzing the role of television in influencing children to eat foods that are considered unhealthful; (4) the results of one research program that is investigating this problem; and (5) the reasons that a systems theory and a social learning theory are useful models for understanding this area.

Health Risks of the Typical American Diet

In America and other affluent societies, it is becoming apparent that there is a connection between the consumption of foods rich in cholesterol, saturated fat, calories, sugar, and salt, and the occurrence of health problems such as arteriosclerosis, coronary heart disease, stroke, hypertension, obesity, diabetes, gallstones, and cancer of the colon and the breast (U.S. Senate Select Committee on Nutrition and Human Needs, 1971).

The cost of treating obesity is also enormous. A recent marketing survey indicated that $10 billion is spent annually on various diet foods, medication, devices, and programs. The psychological cost of obesity, while perhaps not so easily quantified, is nonetheless equally enormous. Overweight children are frequently teased by other children and may be the victims of damaging social pressure or the recipients of embarrassing nicknames. Obese girls have been shown to exhibit personality characteristics such as passivity, obsessive concern with self-image, expectation of rejection, and progressive withdrawal (Bruch, 1954; Monello & Mayer, 1963). Furthermore, whether because of psychological and/or physiological factors, it has been established that 80% of all obese children grow up to be obese adults (Eden, 1975). Thus, childhood obesity not only leads to a variety of difficulties for the child but also leads to adult obesity with its more serious health risks.

The health risks of the typical children's diet in America are being increasingly documented. The question that needs to be asked is: What role, if any, does advertising play in influencing children to eat large quantities of unhealthful foods?

Television Viewing and Programming Analysis

Critics of current nutritional practices have argued that television contributes substantially to children's health problems (Action for Children's Television, 1977; Choate, 1975). Television has become a universal experience for American children; that is self-evident. For example, by high school graduation, the average child will have logged approximately 15,000 hours in front of a TV set, more time than he or she will have spent in the classroom. In fact, the only single activity that will have consumed more of the adolescent's time is sleep (Mauro & Feins, 1977; Schramm, Lyle, & Parker, 1961). Of even greater importance, however, is that in any given year, the typical child will be exposed to roughly 22,000 commercials, a staggering total of 350,000 attempts to influence her or his buying behavior during childhood and adolescence (Choate, 1975). Over 50% of television commercials are for foods and beverages, most of which are high-calorie, high-sugar, low-nutrition items. A survey in the 1970s monitored four Saturday mornings of children's television advertising and found that 67% of the ads were for cereals, snacks, candies, sweets, chewing gum, and soda pop. In another survey it was found that only 7% of all food ads during weekdays were for foods such as dairy products, fruits, and breads (Barcus & Wolkin, 1977; Mauro & Feins, 1977).

From a systems theory perspective, this advertising represents a major conflict between the standards of what the advertisers are promoting and what dentists, physicians, and dieticians are recommending that children eat. Research has shown that the food children eat influences their health, and that a high percentage of the food advertised on television is considered unhealthful. However, the question remains whether television advertising actually influences children to eat the advertised foods, or whether other change agents–parents and health professionals–determine what children consume.

The Research Problem

When one becomes aware of these findings and questions, it is not difficult to see why researchers have devoted increased effort to the investigation of how television influences food choices and consumption patterns.

There is experimental evidence that a wide range of human behaviors, including eating, can be acquired through observational learning and reinforcement (Bandura, 1971). While the acquisition of eating habits and food preferences can be attributed to a variety of factors, a particularly potent source of modeled eating behavior may be children's television food commercials. It seems logical that food manufacturers and distributors would not invest heavily in advertising unless it increased the sales of their products. However, empirical verification of this "logical" conclusion is quite a different matter.

Some social science researchers have explored this area. In survey-based research, correlational investigators have found that television commercials do influence children's nutrition knowledge and purchase attempts (Atkin, Reeves, & Hocking, 1979; Ward, Wackman, & Wartella, 1977). Reviewers have discussed the problems of relying only on self-report and nonexperimental data and have recommended that more emphasis now be given to behavioral, experimental studies (National Science Foundation, 1977; Rychtarik, Kniivila, & Jeffrey, 1978).

The Television Research Program at the University of Montana[2]

Based on a system-theory and social-learning-theory approach, the first author (Jeffrey) and his research associates have undertaken a programmatic series of behavioral-experimental studies investigating the effects of television commercials on children's eating habits. Summarized briefly are two recently completed studies.

The first line of investigation was to create a procedure for measuring actual food consumption (Jeffrey, Lemnitzer, Hickey, Hess, McLellarn, & Stroud, 1980). The behavioral eating test involved allowing 25 preschool and kindergarten children to sample as they wished for eight minutes from a tray of 12 foods and beverages, 6 of which were considered high-nutrition (cheese, grapes, carrots, apples, orange juice, and milk) and 6 of which were considered low-nutrition (Hershey Chocolate, Chips Ahoy, Fritos, Honeycombs, Koolaid, and Pepsi). One week later, these children were again given the opportunity to sample as they wished for eight minutes from the same foods and liquids. Measurements of the amounts consumed at each testing were taken initially in grams and milliliters and were later converted to calories. Immediately following presentation of the behavioral eating test, the subjects were given the food attitude scale, which asked the subjects to rate each of the 12 foods and beverages, indicating how much each was liked. It was necessary to determine the consistency or stability of consumption and preference over the

[2]The TV research and preparation of this manuscript were supported in part by United States National Science Foundation Grant No. ISP-8011449, and the National Institute of Child Health and Human Development HD-12073. Appreciation is extended to Robert W. McLellarn and J. Scott Hickey for assistance with this research.

two test occasions in the absence of any experimental intervention, that is, without the introduction of any television commercials. Assuming adequate consistency was found, any change in consumption or preference in subsequent experiments could more clearly be attributed to the effect of a commercial and not simply to random fluctuations in the measurement procedure. The results of the study indicated that both measurement procedures possessed sufficient stability to warrant their use in future research studies.

We then applied these measurement procedures in an experiment designed to assess the effect of television food commercials on children's eating behavior (Lemnitzer, Jeffrey, Hess, Hickey, & Stroud, 1979). Forty-seven 4- and 5-year-olds were first given one administration of the behavioral eating test and food preference scale, as previously described. One week later, and just prior to the second presentation of the measurement procedures, the children were shown 12 minutes of children's programming that included a half-dozen commercials for low-nutrition foods, high-nutrition foods, or toys (a control group). In each group, three different 30-second ads were shown twice in the context of a 9-minute cartoon segment. In the low-nutrition group, the children saw ads for Pepsi, Fritos, and Hershey Chocolate. Children from the high-nutrition group saw ads for grapes, milk, and cheese. The control group saw ads for three popular children's toys. The results suggested that children exposed to the low-nutrition ads significantly increased the caloric consumption of low-nutrition foods. The high-nutrition commercials brought about only small increases,and the toy commercials had no effect at all. Additionally, children in the low-nutrition group, as compared with the high-nutrition group, had better recall of the commercials.

The failure of high-nutrition advertising to effect significant changes in the nutritional food consumed or to create a substantial impact on the memory of the products advertised raises several issues. Since the high-nutrition advertising in this study was representative of typical high-nutrition ads shown on children's television (all ads used in this study were recorded directly from children's network programming), it is highly unlikely that the lack of results was due to unrepresentative ads. Observations by the experimenters suggested that some of this differential effectiveness may have been due to differences in the overall quality and appeal of the various types of commercials. To determine if this was the case, independent ratings were obtained for all experimental conditions on visual interest, auditory interest, product appeal, and the technical quality. In all categories, the low-nutrition ads were rated as significantly better than the high-nutrition ads. Low-nutrition advertising is typically produced by large advertising agencies and appears to utilize many of the techniques that the modeling literature has proved to be successful (i.e., multiple models, peer groups, attractive models having fun, etc.). In addition, this advertising uses other attention-getting techniques, such as catchy songs and enhanced screen action. On the other hand, high-nutrition advertising is often produced by nonprofit organizations or by small local farm groups and typically uses few, if any, of these techniques. Thus, it is possible that the low-nutrition ads employed in this investigation were more successful because of their greater technical sophistication.

Concluding Comments

Additional studies are under way in which other variables of social learning theory, such as repeated exposures, will be examined. Still other studies will examine the interaction of television advertising with parenting and individual factors in influencing the child's food consumption. The findings from this laboratory and other research programs will establish more precisely the influencing role of television advertising. However, the main point of this chapter is how a combined systems theory–social learning theory provides conceptual models for analyzing and understanding this important area. Traditionally, advertising has been examined by marketing people from the motivation and communication perspectives. However, if one is interested in (1) how children learn new attitudes and behaviors by observational processes, (2) how the external environment (in this case, the advertiser) influences the self-environment (the child), and (3) how this advertising interacts with other external change agents to influence the child, it seems that SERMOD, SERTS, and observational learning theory provide a broader conceptual model for understanding the important social determinants of children's health.

Summary

In this chapter, we have introduced systems theory and discussed its application to machines, animals, and humans. We have pushed ourselves, and hopefully the reader, toward new horizons of conceptualizing and understanding behavior. Certainly, control systems analysis, computer-simulated programs of operant schedules, SERMOD, and SERTS will have their problems and will need to be revised and expanded. However, we are convinced that general systems theory offers an exciting, more sophisticated conceptual model for understanding a wide range of basic and applied areas of psychology.

References

Abrahms, J. L., & Allen, G. J. Comparative effectiveness of situational programming, financial pay-offs and group pressure in weight reduction. *Behavior Therapy,* 1974, *5,* 391–400.

Abramson, E. E. A review of behavioral approaches to weight control. *Behaviour Research and Therapy,* 1973, *11,* 547–556.

Abramson, E. E. Behavioral approaches to weight control: An updated review. *Behaviour Research and Therapy,* 1977, *15,* 355–363.

Action for Children's Television. *Petition to promulgate a rule prohibiting the advertising of candy to children on television* before the *Federal Trade Commission.* Newtonville, Mass.: Author, 1977.

Atkin, C., Reeves, B., & Hocking, J. *Children's responses to television food advertising: Survey evidence.* Paper presented at the annual meeting of the American Psychological Association, New York, 1979.

Bandura, A. *Principles of behavior modification.* New York: Holt, Rinehart, & Winston, 1969.

Bandura, A. Vicarious and self-reinforcement processes. In R. Glaser (Ed.), *The nature of reinforcement.* Columbus, Ohio: Merrill, 1971, 228–278.

Bandura, A. Self-reinforcement: Theoretical and methodological considerations. *Behaviorism,* 1976, *4,* 135–155.

Bandura, A., & Walters, R. H. *Social learning and personality development.* New York: Holt, Rinehart, & Winston, 1963.

Barcus, F. E., & Wolkin, R. *Children's television: An analysis of programming and advertising.* New York: Praeger, 1977.

Bellack, A. S. A comparison of self-reinforcement and self-monitoring in a weight reduction program. *Behavior Therapy,* 1976, *7,* 68–75.

Bellack, A. S. Behavioral treatment for obesity: Appraisal and recommendations. In M. Hersen, R. M. Eisler, & P. M.Miller (Eds.), *Progress in behavior modification,* Vol. 4. New York: Academic Press, 1977.

Bellack, A. S., Rozensky, R., & Schwartz, J. A comparison of two forms of self-monitoring in a behavioral weight reduction program. *Behavior Therapy,* 1974, *5,* 523–530.

Bruch, H. The psychosomatic aspects of obesity. *American Practitioner and Digest of Treatment,* 1954, *5,* 48–49.

Buckley, W. (Ed.). *Modern systems research for the behavioral scientist.* Chicago: Aldine, 1968.

Chapman, S. L., & Jeffrey, D. B. Situational management, standard setting, and self-reward in a behavior modification weight loss program. *Journal of Consulting and Clinical Psychology,* 1978, *46,* 1588–1589.

Choate, R. *Testimony before the House Subcommittee on Communications.* United States House of Representatives, Washington, D.C.: Council on Children, Media and Merchandising, 1975.

Eden, A. *Growing up thin.* New York: David McKay, 1975.

Ferguson, J. M. *Learning to eat: Behavior modification for weight control.* Palo Alto, Calif.: Bull, 1975.

Ferster, C. B., & Davison, B. F. *Schedules of reinforcement.* New York: Appleton-Century-Crofts, 1957.

Goldfried, M. R., & Davison, G. C. *Clinical behavior therapy.* New York: Holt, Rinehart & Winston, 1976.

Green, D. M., & Swets, J. A. *Signal detection theory and psychophysics.* Huntington, N.Y.: Krieger, 1974.

Hall, S. M., Hall, R. G., DeBoer, G., & O'Kulitch, P. Self and external management compared with psychotherapy in the control of obesity. *Behaviour Research and Therapy,* 1977, *15,* 89–95.

Herrnstein, R. J. Derivatives of matching. *Psychological Review,* 1979, *86,* 486–495.

Heyman, G. M. A Markov model description of changeover probabilities on concurrent variable-interval schedules. *Journal of the Experimental Analysis of Behavior,* 1979, *31,* 41–51.

Honig, W. K. (Ed.). *Operant behavior: Areas of research and application.* New York: Appleton-Century-Crofts, 1966.

Jeffrey, D. B. A comparison of the effects of external control and self-control on the modification and maintenance of weight. *Journal of Abnormal Psychology,* 1974, *83,* 404–410. (a)

Jeffrey, D. B. Self-control: Methodological issues and research trends. In M. J. Mahoney & C. E. Thorensen (Eds.), *Self-control: Power to the person.* Belmont, Calif.: Brooks/Cole, 1974, 166–199. (b)

Jeffrey, D. B. Behavioral management of obesity. In W. E. Craighead, A. E. Kazdin, & M. J. Mahoney (Eds.), *Behavior modification: Principles, issues, and applications.* New York: Houghton Mifflin, 1976.

Jeffrey, D. B. Self-control approaches to the management of obesity. In J. P. Foreyt (Ed.), *Behavioral treatments of obesity.* New York: Pergamon, 1977.

Jeffrey, D. B., & Christensen, E. R. Effect of behavior therapy vs. "will power" in the management of obesity. *Journal of Psychology,* 1975, *90,* 303–311.

Jeffrey, D. B., & Katz, R. C. *Take it off and keep it off: A behavioral program for weight loss and healthy living.* Englewood Cliffs, N. J.: Prentice-Hall, 1977.

Jeffrey, D. B., & Knauss, M. The etiologies, assessments, and treatments of obesity. In S. N. Haynes & L. Gannon (Eds.), *Psychosomatic disorders: A psychophysiological approach to etiology and treatment.* New York: Praeger, 1981.

Jeffrey, D. B., & Lemnitzer, N. Diet, exercise, obesity, and related health problems: A macro-environmental analysis. In J. Ferguson & B. Taylor (Eds.), *Advances in behavioral medicine.* Holliswood, N.Y.: Spectrum, 1982.

Jeffrey, D. B., Lemnitzer, N. B., Hickey, J. S., Hess, M. J., McLellarn, R. W., & Stroud, J. M. The development of a behavioral eating test and its relationship to a self-report food preference scale with children. *Behavioral Assessment,* 1980, *2,* 87–98.

Kanfer, F. H. The maintenance of behavior by self-generated stimuli and reinforcement. In A. Jacobs & L. B. Sachs (Eds.), *Psychology of private events.* New York: Academic Press, 1971, 39–57.

Kanfer, F. H. The many faces of self-control, or behavior modification changes its focus. In R. B. Stuart (Ed.), *Behavioral self-management: Strategies, techniques, and outcomes.* New York: Brunner/Mazel, 1977.

Kazdin, A. E. Self-monitoring and behavior change. In M. J. Mahoney & C. E. Thoresen (Eds.), *Self-control: Power to the person.* Monterey, Calif.: Brooks-Cole, 1974.

Lemnitzer, N. B., Jeffrey, D. B., Hess, M. J., Hickey, J. S., & Strand, J. M. *The effects of low-nutrition, pro-nutrition, and non-food commercials on the eating behavior of children.* Paper presented at the meeting of the Society for Research on Child Development, San Francisco, Ca., March 1979.

Leon, G. R. Current directions in the treatment of obesity. *Psychological Bulletin,* 1976, *83,* 557–578.

Mahoney, M. J. Self-reward and self-monitoring techniques for weight control. *Behavior Therapy,* 1974, *5,* 48–57.

Mahoney, M. J., & Mahoney, K. *Permanent weight control.* New York: Norton, 1976.

Mahoney, M. J., Moura, N., & Wade, T. The relative efficacy of self-reward, self-punishment, and self-monitoring techniques for weight loss. *Journal of Consulting and Clinical Psychology,* 1973, *40,* 404–407.

Mauro, F. J., & Feins, R. P. *Kids, food and television: The compelling case for state action.* Albany: New York State Assembly, 1977.

McReynolds, W. T., Lutz, R. N., Paulsen, B., & Kohrs, M. B. Weight loss resulting from two behavior modification procedures with nutritionists as therapists. *Behavior Therapy,* 1976, *7,* 283–291.

Monello, L. F., & Mayer, J. Obese adolescent girls: An unrecognized "minority" group? *American Journal of Clinical Nutrition,* 1963, *13,* 35.

National Science Foundation. *Research on the effects of television advertising on children: Review and recommendations.* Washington, D.C.: Author, 1977 (Grant NO. APR 75-10126, executive summary).

Nelson, R. O. Assessment and therapeutic functions of self-monitoring. In M. Hersen, R. M. Eisler, & P. M. Miller (Eds.), *Progress in behavior modification,* Vol. 5. New York: Academic Press, 1977.

O'Leary, K. D., & Wilson, G. T. *Behavior therapy: Applications and outcome.* New York: Prentice-Hall, 1975.

Penick, S. B., Filion, R., Fox, S., & Stunkard, A. J. Behavior modification in the treatment of obesity. *Psychosomatic Medicine,* 1971, *33,* 49–55.

Powers, W. T. *Behavior: The control of perception.* Chicago: Aldine Press, 1973.

Romanczyk, R. G. Self-monitoring in the treatment of obesity: Parameters of reactivity. *Behavior Therapy,* 1974, *5,* 531–540.

Romanczyk, R.G., Tracey, D. A., Wilson, G. T., & Thorpe, G. L. Behavioral techniques in the treatment of obesity: A comparative analysis. *Behavior Research and Therapy,* 1973, *11,* 629–640.

Rychtarik, R. G., Kniivila, C. M., & Jeffrey, D. B. *Effects of television advertising on children's behavior: A methodological review.* Paper presented at the American Psychological Association, Toronto, Canada, August 1978.

Schramm, W., Lyle, J., & Parker, B. *Television in the lives of our children.* Stanford, Calif.: Stanford University Press, 1961.

Schwartz, G. E. Biofeedback, self-regulation, and patterning of physiological processes. *American Scientist,* 1975, *63,* 314–324.

Sidman, M. Avoidance behavior. In W. K. Honig (Ed.), *Operant behavior: Areas of research and application.* New York: Appleton-Century-Crofts, 1966.

Skinner, B. F. *Science and human behavior.* New York: Macmillan, 1953.

Stuart, R. B., & Davis, B. *Slim chance in a fat world: Behavioral control of obesity.* Champaign, Ill.: Research Press, 1972.

Stunkard, A. J., & Mahoney, M. J. Behavioral treatment of the eating disorders. In H. Leitenberg (Ed.), *Handbook of behavior modification.* New York: Appleton-Century-Crofts, 1976.

Thoresen, C. E., & Mahoney, M. J. *Behavioral self-control.* New York: Holt, Rinehart & Winston, 1974.

Tobias, L. L., & MacDonald, M. L. Internal locus of control and weight loss: An insufficient condition. *Journal of Consulting and Clinical Psychology,* 1977, *45,* 647–653.

U.S. Senate Select Committee on Nutrition and Human Needs. *Dietary goals for the United States.* Washington, D.C.: Government Printing Office, 1971.

Ward, S., Wackman, D.B., & Wartella, E. *How children learn to buy.* Beverly Hills, Calif.: Sage Publications, 1977.

Wiener, N. *Cybernetics, or control and communication in the animal and machine.* New York: Wiley, 1948.

Wilson, G. T. Methodological considerations in treatment outcome research on obesity. *Journal of Consulting and Clinical Psychology,* 1978, *46,* 687–702.

CHAPTER 4

Emotionality and Aging

Richard Schulz

Institute on Aging
Portland State University
Portland, Oregon

Much has been written about mood, emotionality, and emotional behavior in humans, but rarely has this topic been addressed from an adult developmental perspective. Indeed, the major theorists on the determinants of human emotions (James, 1890; Cannon, 1927; Schachter & Singer, 1962; Pribram & Melges, 1967; Tomkins, 1962, 1963; Izard, 1972) have had little to say about emotionality through middle and old age. Likewise, major textbooks on adult development and aging, including the *Handbook of the Psychology of Aging* (Birren & Schaie, 1977), devote little space to the discussion of this topic. It is unclear whether this neglect is due to oversight, to the unavailability of relevant data, or to the assumption that age, beyond adulthood, is an irrelevant dimension with respect to emotionality. In any case, it is the aim of this discussion to focus on issues of emotionality and aging. It may be that the neglect of this topic is justified and that a synthesis of the literature on adult development and emotionality does little to enrich either, but it is more likely that there are important questions and answers to be found in such a synthesis.

It is difficult to discuss emotionality without first establishing some ground rules. Terms such as *mood, emotion,* and *motivation* are used interchangeably by both professionals and laypersons, thus creating considerable confusion in this area. The first part of this chapter focuses on some of the

Preparation of this chapter was in part supported by the Deutsche Forschungsgemeinschaft, Sonderforschungsbereich 24, Teilprojekt 6, and the University of Mannheim, Mannheim, West Germany.

semantic issues concerning the use of these terms. Theories of emotionality are briefly discussed in the second part. While none of these theories specifically addresses the issue of developmental change in emotionality, it may be possible to derive predictions regarding changes in emotionality by examining the social-psychological and biological changes associated with growing old in the context of these theories. This topic is the main focus of the third and fourth parts of the chapter. The available relevant data on emotionality and aging are examined in the fifth part. Data on both episodic and long-term emotional responses of the elderly are presented, with special emphasis on the situational factors that elicit such responses. Additionally, experimental attempts directed toward manipulating the emotional status of the aged are examined. An integrative summary and suggestions for future research complete this chapter.

Defining Emotions

There are literally hundreds of descriptive terms regularly used to discuss moods and emotions, as well as dozens of instruments designed to measure a wide variety of affective states ranging from one extreme (e.g., elation) to another (e.g., depression). From a Whorfian perspective, this richness in our language reflects both the strong interest in and the importance of this domain to our culture. From a researcher's perspective, the large lexicon of emotion-related terms can be either an asset or a liability: on the one hand, it presents opportunities for precision and nuance; on the other hand, it invites confusion and obfuscation.

Since the terms *emotion, mood,* and *affect* are frequently used interchangeably, the first question to ask is: Can one distinguish among them? According to one researcher (Buss, 1973), these terms can be differentiated on the basis of the level of arousal underlying each state. Thus, emotions such as rage and fear occupy the extreme end of the arousal continuum, while states such as grief, disgust, love, and shame are characterized by more moderate degrees of arousal and should properly be called moods or affective states. One critical factor distinguishing between emotions and moods, then, is level of arousal. In particular, arousal well beyond the range of normal wakefulness is believed to be crucial for emotions.

A second useful distinction between emotions and moods can be made on the basis of the localizability of their principal effects or consequences:

> Emotional behavior seems most usefully considered as part of a broad class of affective interactions, the primary consequences of which appear to change the

> organism's relationship to its external environment. Feelings or affective behavior, on the other hand, can be distinguished as a generic class of interactions, the principal effects of which are localizable withinthe reacting organism rather than in the exteroceptive environment. Many different subclasses of feelings may be identified within this broad affective category, but emotional behavior seems uniquely definable in terms of change or perturbation characteristically abrupt and episodic, in the ongoing interaction between organism and environment. (Brady, 1970, p. 70)

Implicit in Brady's and Buss's discussion is the idea that emotions are relatively rare and short-lived, while moods and affective states are more common and longer in duration. By adding this third dimension–time–we can differentiate not only emotions and moods but also personality types. As shown in Table 1, emotions are defined as involving extreme levels of arousal. They are likely to alter the organism's relationship to the environment, and they are brief in duration; moods or affective states are characterized by moderate levels of arousal, their effects are localizable primarily within the individual, and they are of moderate time duration; finally, certain personality types (e.g., depressives) have all the characteristics of mood states except that they are longer-lasting. Thus, we talk about an individual's being in a bad mood, with the expectation that it is likely to change at some time, or that she or he is perhaps a depressive type, suggesting that change is unlikely.

Keeping in mind the distinctions presented above, we can now consider some issues of emotionality and mood from an adult development perspective. The following list of questions, while couched in terms of emotion, can be applied to moods or affective states as well:

1. *Intensity:* Is the intensity of emotional experiences stronger or weaker among the aged than among the young? One of the popular stereotypes of the aged suggests that while the aged do experience emotions, their intensity is subdued relative to younger cohorts. Thus, the aged are often thought of as being happy but rarely as elated.

2. *Duration:* Once an emotional experience is instigated, do older persons experience a longer or a shorter duration of that emotion? Is it more difficult for an aged individual to return to a neutral baseline?

Table 1. Dimensions Used to Differentiate Emotions, Moods, and Personality Types

	Dimensions		
Affective category	Intensity of arousal	Primary locus of effects	Duration
Strong emotions	High	Environment	Short (minutes)
Moderate emotions, moods	Moderate	Individual	Moderate (hours or days)
Personality type	Moderate	Individual	Long (years)

3. *Variability:* Do the aged show less day-to-day or within-day variability in emotional states? Implicit in the popular view of the aged as more rigid than the young is the idea that they have reduced lability, that they are more set in their ways and therefore are less likely to experience mood swings.

4. *Frequency:* Are particular types of emotional experiences more or less frequent among the aged? Another stereotype of the aged suggests that negative affective states are more common among the aged than among the young. Are there data to support this view?

5. *Quality:* Are there qualitative differences in the experience of specific emotional states among the aged? For example, is an emotion such as love a qualitatively different experience for the aged and for the young?

6. *Elicitors, instigators:* Do the types of events that elicit emotional experiences change with age? What are the attributes or characteristics of instigators of emotional experiences for the aged?

Information concerning each of these questions will be presented. A prerequisite to any attempt at answering these questions, however, is an understanding of (1) theories regarding the determinants of emotions and (2) the biological and social-psychological changes that occur with age and their likely impact on the organism's ability to experience affect. If we believe, for example, that emotions are largely physiologically based and we know that there are relevant physical changes associated with age, then age differences in the intensity of emotions may be largely attributable to biological changes. In contrast, we might ask, are the aged exposed to particular environmental events that precipitate a characteristic set of emotional or affective reactions?

Theories of Emotion

The goal of a theory of emotion is to integrate three identifiable components of emotion: the motor behavior associated with emotions (what is expressed); the experiential aspect (what is felt); and the central and peripheral physiological mechanisms that underlie emotions (what happens inside the body). Each of these components receives some attention in all existing theories of emotion, although the emphasis varies.

Two types of theories have been advanced. The first, conceived primarily by psychologists, is perhaps best described as the psychophysiological approach to emotions. The emphasis is on understanding the physiological mechanisms underlying emotions and the relationship between them and the subjective experience of emotion. The major proponents of this perspective include James and Lange (James, 1890), Cannon and Bard (Cannon, 1927), Schachter and Singer (1962), Solomon and Corbit (1974), Pribram and

Melges (1967), and Tomkins (1962, 1963). The focus of the second class of theories, advanced primarily by sociologists, is more on the sociocultural conditions that affect both the experience and the expression of emotions rather than on physiological mechanisms. Proponents of this perspective include, among others, Kemper (1978a, 1978b) and Shott (1978).

Psychophysiological Theories

The ultimate goal of psychophysiological theories is to explain the mechanisms that lead to the experience of specific emotions. In all cases, physiological processes are identified, in greater or lesser detail, as necessary conditions for the experience of emotions, although the specific anatomical structures involved and their importance vary greatly among the different theories.

One of the earliest and most influential psychophysiological theories of emotion was proposed by James and Lange (James, 1890). Given their emphasis on visceral factors as the primary determinants of emotional experiences, their approach has been traditionally identified with the peripheralist perspective. According to James (1890), "the bodily changes follow directly the perception of the exciting fact, and that our feeling of the same changes as they occur is the emotion" (p. 449). This theory equates bodily changes and visceral feelings with emotions and implies that different emotions are accompanied by recognizably different bodily states and that the manipulation of bodily states directly affects emotional states. This peripheralist position survived intact for several decades until contraditory data collected by Bard and Rioch and others enabled Cannon (1927) to present his frequently cited critique of the James–Lange position:

1. The total separation of the visceral from the central nervous system does not alter emotional behavior.
2. The same visceral changes occur in very different emotional states.
3. The viscera are relatively insensitive structures.
4. Visceral changes are too slow to be a source of emotional feeling.
5. The artificial induction of visceral changes that are typical of strong emotions does not produce the emotions. (from Schachter, 1971, p. 1)

Cannon moved the locus of emotional experience from the viscera to the central nervous system. He proposed a thalamic theory of emotions: emotional expression results from the operation of the hypothalamic structures; emotional feeling results from stimulation of the dorsal thalamus (Pribram & Melges, 1967). With the development of modern techniques for electrical brain stimulation and the increasing sophistication in our understanding of the central nervous system, the Cannon–Bard view was superseded by an alternative proposed by Papez and elaborated by Maclean (1950). Instead of the thalamus, the limbic portion of the forebrain was identified as the seat of emotions. While this view is still popular today, increasing quantities of contradictory evidence suggest that major modifications of this view are imminent.

A less controversial but equally important theme among psychophysiological theories of emotion has been the concept of activation. It is generally accepted that the nonspecific reticular activating system is the central locus of arousal and that a correlation exists between the amount of hormone, the amount of neural excitation, and the amount of emotional arousal. According to this perspective, all emotional behavior can be described in terms of its intensity and whether or not it shows approach or avoidance. What activation theory alone does not explain is the qualitative difference among different emotional states (Pribram & Melges, 1967).

This problem was in part solved by Schachter and Singer (1962) with the theory emphasizing the cognitive determinants of emotional experiences. According to Schachter, a particular emotional experience is the result of perceived sympathetic arousal and the characteristics of the social environment in which the individual finds himself or herself. The sequence of events involved in defining an emotion, therefore, includes, first, the perception of sympathetic arousal, followed by a search for an appropriate explanation. When the social environment has supplied the information necessary for explaining the arousal, the emotion has been defined. These notions were tested and substantially supported in a series of experiments carried out by Schachter and Singer (1962), although there is some argument at present about the internal validity of these experiments (see Maslach, 1979; Marshall & Zimbardo, 1979; Schachter & Singer, 1979).

What happens after an emotion is identified? The answer to this question is provided by the opponent-process theory of emotions proposed by Solomon and Corbit (1974). This theory suggests that emotional states are automatically opposed by central nervous system mechanisms that reduce the intensity of both pleasant and unpleasant emotional feelings. The opponent process is manifested in the temporal pattern of emotional reactions. First, following the introduction of either a pleasurable or an aversive stimulus, an affective reaction begins and quickly rises to a peak. This peak is followed by a slow decline to a steady level, where the reaction remains if the quality and the intensity of the stimulus are maintained. Once the stimulus is terminated, the emotion quickly disappears and gives way to a qualitatively different type (i.e., opposite to the one originally experienced) of affective reaction, which reaches its own peak of intensity and then slowly disappears with time.

Two features of this model are important. First, the opponent process operates at the level of the central nervous system, suggesting that deterioration of that system may affect the operation of the process. Second, the model proposes that there are costs, both psychological and physical (e.g., metabolic, hormonal, and neural),involved in any departure from hedonic neutrality. Departures from emotional neutrality have correlates in increased autonomic and central nervous system activity aimed at reducing those departures. One important implication of this theory is that both pleasurable and aversive stimulation is stressful and that diseases of adaptation (e.g., psychosomatic diseases and behavior disorders) may result from either. The latter proposition is an interesting contrapuntal theme to the work of Holmes and Rahe (1967) on life stress and disease.

Any theory based on activity or arousal mechanisms necessarily requires the stipulation of a baseline of arousal or a background level of activity against which arousal occurs. This is a basic assumption of all the theories described above and is explicitly discussed by Solomon and Corbit in their description of opponent process theory. Although it is typically assumed that the impact of a given stimulus depends largely on the background activity existing at the time the stimulus is introduced, few theorists have specifically described how a baseline is established. One exception is a psychophysiological theory of emotions developed by Pribram and Melges (1967).

According to Pribram and Melges, this baseline is provided by the process of habituation of the orienting response. Habituation is not, however, as was thought earlier, the result of the progressive raising of threshold to input but of the "formation of a 'neuronal model'—a neuronal configuration against which subsequent inputs to the organism are matched. In essence, such neuronal configurations form the sum of an organism's expectancies" (Pribram and Melges, 1967, p. 322).

This model differs from earlier habituation models in that it emphasizes that not only increases but also decreases in level of stimulation may disturb the baseline of activity, bringing about dishabituation of visceral and autonomic activities. Subjectively, dishabituation can be felt as a mismatch between expected and actual heart rate, sweating, trembling, etc. Objectively, perturbations and stability can be assessed by measuring changes in the electrical activity of the brain. Additionally, while perturbations of baseline activity are usually the result of changes in external input, they can also be the result of internal changes in the organism. Thus, input that may ordinarily be processed smoothly may perturb a system that is already unstable, or internal changes in the organism may result in incongruity where match had previously existed (Pribram & Melges, 1967).

Given these basic processes, we can now proceed with a more detailed examination of how the organism is regulated at the neurological level. Specifically, the operation of two central processes of the system—(1) habituation and its perturbation and (2) orienting—need to be explained. Both processes are controlled by inhibitory processes in the afferent channels of the nervous system: the model states that habituation is a function of self-inhibition (the activity of a cell inhibits its own activity through negative feedback) and that orienting is a function of collateral inhibition (the activity of a cell inhibits the activity of its neighbors). Stated another way, self-inhibition stabilizes and brings the system back to baseline, while collateral inhibition enhances contrast and as a result maximizes perturbation. The adjectives *preparatory* and *participatory* are used to describe these processes. Thus, preparatory processes tend to lead the organism toward internal control. They function to reestablish continuity at the cost of simplification. Participatory processes tend to lead the organism toward external control. They tolerate the temporary instability of incongruity for the gain of flexibility through more complex organization.

The two types of processes can be further differentiated on the basis of the specific emotional states associated with each. Since preparatory processes operate to eliminate input—to return the organism to the previously equilibrated state—they are associated with negative emotions such as fear, anger, disgust, guilt, shame, and depression. By contrast, participatory processes deal with incongruity by searching and sampling the input and accommodating the system to it. Positive emotions, such as affection, compassion, admiration, interest, and awe, are associated with this process.

What determines which process will be invoked in a given situation? This is an important question, and its answer, as we will see later, serves to differentiate this from other theories of emotion. Basically, the choice between the preparatory and the participatory processes depends on the remembered outcome of previous appraisals in similar situations. Inputs that are a result of past experiences and existing dispositional states judged as relevant (that is, inputs over which external control can probably be achieved) elicit participatory processes. Inputs that are appraised as irrelevant, that is, those that, based on past experience, are not expected to lead to external control, lead to the activation of preparatory processes. It should be clear that memory and learning play important roles in this model. Probably, outcomes are appraised based on the memory of past reinforcements, and incongruities are sensed by comparing stimulus inputs with information stored in memory. Like Schachter and Singer's two-factor theory, this theory relies heavily on cognitive processes. The difference lies in the fact that Pribram and Melges have a much broader view of what constitutes a context. For them, it includes the immediate situation as well as the history of experiences that the individual brings to the situation.

A discussion of psychophysiological theories of emotion would not be complete without including a discussion of Silvan Tomkin's (1970) work on affects, although the complexity of his theory makes it difficult to present in a brief summary. We focus here on those aspects of his theory that may be useful in understanding emotionality and aging. Tomkins has identified nine innate primary affects that are expressed primarily through the face. Each affect has its own innate affect program, which effects changes in breathing and blood flow to the face and results in a patterned set of muscular responses on the face. The awareness of this set of responses is the awareness of affect. The three positive affective states identified are surprise or startle, interest or excitement, and enjoyment or joy. The negative affects include distress or anguish, fear or terror, shame or humiliation, and contempt or disgust.

According to Tomkins, the particular affect activated depends on the density of neural firing elicited within the central nervous system. Density is defined simply as the number of neural firings per unit of time. Sudden increases in neural firing are associated with the startle or fear response. If there is a gradual increase in the density of neural firings, the individual exhibits interest. High constant rates of neural firings are associated with the negative affects of anger and distress, and decreases in the level of neural activity are associated with joy.

Like Pribram and Melges, Tomkins strongly emphasizes learning and memory. Although some stimuli that activate specific emotional states such as distress, startle, disgust, and fear are unlearned and innate, the affect system is also capable of being instigated by learned stimuli. Thus, the human being is born with some approach and avoidance programs that are activated by a limited set of circumstances, but she or he is also capable of learning to acquire new objects of interest and disinterest. Indeed, the affect system, according to Tomkins (1970), provides the

> primary blueprints for cognition, decision and action. Man is responsive to whatever circumstances activate positive and negative affects. Some of these circumstances innately activate the affects. At the same time, the affect system is also capable of being instigated by learned stimuli. The human being is thus urged by nature and nurture to explore and to attempt to control the circumstances which evoke his positive and negative affective responses. It is the freedom of the affect system which makes it possible for human beings to begin to implement and to progress toward what he regards as an ideal state–one which, however he may describe it, implicitly or explicitly entails the maximizing of positive affect and minimizing of negative affect. (p.110)

For Tomkins, understanding emotionality in humans is the central question of psychology. The same can perhaps be said of many social gerontologists. To the extent that they are interested in explaining how old people feel, their primary mission is to understand emotionality in the aged human being.

The Sociological Viewpoint

This perspective acknowledges the importance of the physiological components of emotion but focuses more on the cognitive or interpretive determinants of both the experience and the expression of emotions. A good example of this perspective is Kemper's (1978a) relational theory of emotions.

Kemper's point of embarkation is a physiological theory of emotion that relates two different physiological conditions to two different emotional states: anger is related to the activation of the sympathetic system and the release of norepinephrine, whereas fear is associated with sympathetic arousal and the release of epinephrine. Positive emotions are associated with the activation of the parasympathetic system and the release of the neurochemical acetylcholine.

The activation of a particular system depends, however, on the interpretation or cognitions regarding real, imagined, or anticipated outcomes of social encounters. Kemper postulated that relationships between individuals and between individuals and organizations can be characterized in terms of two relational dimensions: power and status. In any interaction episode, any of five possible outcomes can occur. An individual can experience a gain or loss of power and/or status, or power and status relations may not change. It is hypothesized that loss of power is the social relational condition for anxiety and fear, while loss of customary, expected, or deserved status is the basic relational condition for anger. Thus, the theory comes full circle by relating cognitively defined social encounters to specific physiological mechanisms.

The importance of interpretive processes in defining emotions is again emphasized by Susan Shott (1978) in her symbolic interactionist analysis of emotions. How one defines an emotion (what one feels) is guided by one's culture and its feeling rules. Thus, individuals frequently do "emotions work" on their feelings in an attempt to arouse emotions that they think they should feel. Perhaps the distinguishing characteristic of this perspective is that the interpretive or cognitive processes associated with emotional experience are raised to the level of formative or creative processes in their own right. Thus, this perspective recognizes the importance of cultural contexts in shaping both the experience and the expression of emotions.

Theories of Emotionality: Some Integrating Comments

It was suggested earlier that one prerequisite to understanding emotionality and aging is examining the existing theories of emotionality. Having done this, we can now begin to speculate about those theoretical constructs that are likely to be important from an adult developmental perspective. The discussion below highlights and summarizes some of the important issues raised in the earlier discussion.

Physiology. Every theory reviewed above accepts the idea that the activation of physiological systems is correlated with emotional experiences. There is general consensus that both the parasympathetic and the sympathetic systems are involved, that the limbic system and the reticular formation play an important role in the experience of emotions, and that to the extent that cognitive processes are thought to mediate emotional experiences, those structures of the brain serving processing, learning, and memory functions must also be included. In short, there is little of the central nervous system that does not play a part. Therefore, from the perspective of an aging organism, the important question to be answered is: Are there structural and functional age changes in the central nervous system that might systematically affect the individual's experience of emotions?

Adaptation. A second common characteristic of all theories of emotion is the concept of an adaptation level or a relatively neutral background against which deviations occur. Adaptation can be specified as a physiological and/or cognitive state, with the emphasis on one or the other varying, depending on the particular theorist. Since the adaptation level of an organism is largely a function of prior input, and the aged have by definition a longer history of prior experiences, this factor is likely to play an important part in our efforts to understand emotionality in the aged.

Instigators. How is an emotional experience instigated, and how does it come to be defined as a particular emotional state? The answer to these questions constitutes the heart of most theories of emotionality. In many cases, the instigating event is also the defining event. For example, Kemper (1978a,b) suggested that a social relational event such as loss of power not only instigates an emotional experience but also defines the particular emotion (e.g., fear) elicited. A two-stage process is suggested by other theorists. Thus, Schachter and Singer (1962) suggested that an organism first becomes aroused and then cognitively defines that arousal as one emotional state or another.

Instigating events can also be described in varying degrees of abstractness. At one extreme, we have concrete interpersonal events that can perturb the system (e.g., Kemper), while at the other extreme, the density of neural firing elicited by external events is identified as the instigator for particular emotional experiences. Somewhere in between lie the appraisal mechanisms suggested by Pribram and Melges (1967), which activate processes that either bring the system back to baseline (preparatory processes) or accommodate the system to the perturbing input (participatory processes). Perhaps these different perspectives can be integrated if we take the point of view that different theorists are focusing on different slices of the input continuum. It is noteworthy that despite the variety of instigating mechanisms postulated by researchers of radically different backgrounds, there is little inherent contradiction in the different models of emotionality proposed. One could conceivably construct a single theory of emotionality that incorporated most of the contemporary viewpoints reviewed above.

Emotion and Motivation. This topic is discussed in detail by several theorists (e.g., Solomon & Corbit, 1974; Pribram & Melges, 1967; Tomkins, 1962, 1963). For the purposes of this discussion, it should suffice to point out that in none of the theories of emotionality are human organisms viewed as a passive receptacle of emotional experiences. Emotional experiences are actively constructed via interpretive and appraisal processes, and specific emotional experiences are actively sought out, while others are avoided. It is perhaps a truism, but most persons like to feel good and to avoid feeling bad, and much human behavior can be explained as serving those ends.

Emotion and Control. A persistent theme in several of the theories discussed is the idea that control plays an important role in determining emotional experiences. A critical component of the Pribram and Melges model of emotion is the appraisal process that enables the organism to make a judgment about the external controllability of the input. This, in turn, determines whether preparatory or participatory processes are invoked. Inputs over which external control can be achieved lead to participatory processes. A similar point of view is found in Tomkins's (1962, 1963) theory of emotion: control over the density of neural firing determines the emotion experienced. Finally, Kemper (1978a,b) emphasized the control over social interactions as the means for determining how one feels.

If we accept the basic premise that most persons desire to maximize positive feelings and minimize negative feelings, then each of these theories suggests means for achieving this goal. In each case, this goal is accomplished by exercising control, whether it be over social events or over the rate of stimulation. It follows, therefore, that the degree to which individuals feel capable of controlling the density of stimulation (Tomkins, 1970), assimilability (Pribram & Melges, 1967) of stimulus input, and/or the outcomes of social interactions governs the degree to which they are likely to experience positive rather than negative emotions.

Emotions and Biological Aging

Having reviewed some of the essential information on emotionality, we can now ask: What happens to the organism with age that might affect the experience of emotion? We limit the discussion for a moment to high-arousal emotional states, since they clearly involve physiological components of the organism.

No one would deny that important, clearly perceivable physical changes occur as humans age. But more important for the purposes of this discussion are those changes that occur beneath the skin, particularly in the central nervous system, and that are not readily detected by the naked eye.

There are several characteristic and commonly observable changes in both the structure and the function of the nervous system as it ages. First, there is a marked decrease in brain mass beyond the age of 30 in males and 20 in females (Rockstein & Sussman, 1979), particularly between the ages of 50 and 90. For example, by 80 years of age, most males have experienced a 10% loss in total brain weight; females show similar losses, but a decade earlier.

In addition to loss in the number of cells, the remaining cells exhibit drastic structural changes with age. Depending on which part of the brain we examine, we find that there are substantial structural changes in the Golgi complex, the mitochondria, and the endoplasmic reticulum. The amount of Nissl substance generally increases, and the nucleus of cells accumulates chromatin and exhibits infolding of the nuclear membrane. Another consistent correlate of aging is the accumulation of lipofuscin, a substance variously referred to as *aging* or *wear-and-tear pigment.* It is a brown pigment distributed intracellularly throughout the nervous system. To this growing list, we can also add neurological changes involving gliofibrillary degeneration, alteration in acetylocholinesterase activity, and neuroaxonal dystrophy. (see Brody & Vijayashankar, 1977, for a review).

These are all changes that occur in the central nervous system. It should be noted, though, that there are, in addition, significant changes in the entire peripheral sensory system of the organism that have both a direct physical and a profound psychological impact on the functioning of the organism.

But of what import are these changes? Do they have any functional significance, especially with respect to the experience of emotions? There is, of course, no easy answer to that question. Researchers in this area are still attempting to differentiate ontogenetic changes from cohort effects or accidents (e.g., since brain mass is correlated with body size and bodies have been getting larger over time, the differences in brain mass between young and old may reflect in part changes in body size as well as deterioration). Furthermore, when functional deficits related to central nervous system changes are identified, the cause is often not clear. For example, there are indications that the reserve capacity of the brain is reduced with age. However, it is not resolved whether this reduction is the result of a decrease in functional cells or a decreased function per cell, brought about by lipofuscin accumulation (Brody & Vijayashankar, 1977).

While there is some confusion concerning the ultimate causes of particular outcomes, there is little doubt that one of the major consequences of both CNS and end organ change is that the organism is less able with age to respond to stress. This phenomenon has been repeatedly demonstrated by subjecting animals and humans of varying ages to physical stressors such as heat, cold, and intense physical exercise and to psychological stressors such as high performance demands.

With respect to physical stressors, the aged individual's response to demands for intense physical activity is prototypical. Under conditions of heavy exercise, the tissue of the body requires increased amounts of oxygen. This increase is accomplished by accelerating heart rates, increasing the number of beats per unit of time. One of the major factors limiting oxygen uptake is the progressive decrement, with age, of the maximum heart rates that can be obtained (Brody & Vijayashankar, 1977). In middle age, for example, the heart rate may increase from a resting level of 60 beats per minute to as many as 200 beats per minute. In contrast, the maximum heart rate achieved by normal males 70–90 years of age during strenuous exercise is 125 beats per minute (Brody & Vijayashankar, 1977).

A similar response pattern is found when older subjects are exposed to heat or cold stress; compared with the young, they adapt less quickly and take longer to return to baseline. Using specific organs, such as the kidneys, as the level of analysis, we again find less effective response in older than in younger subjects. For example, the renal response to antidiuretic hormones is lower among the aged than among young and middle-aged subjects.

In general, it seems reasonable to conclude that aging is associated with a reduction in the sensitivity and the responsiveness of tissues to hormones and other substances. Furthermore, it appears that once a system is activated, the aged exhibit a decreased ability to return to baseline.

With respect to the impact on the aged of psychological stressors, some insight is gained from the research on laboratory performance on learning tasks. Several investigators have found that arousal increases and performance declines more for older than for younger subjects under fast-paced conditions (Eisdorfer, Axelrod, & Wilkie, 1963; Troyer, Eisdorfer, Bogdonoff, & Wilkie, 1967). It has been suggested that high levels of arousal may in general account for the learning deficits exhibited by the aged in laboratory settings. This phenomenon is relevant to this discussion since it may be prototypical of situations where age-related situational variables (e.g., novelty) interact with age-related biological changes (e.g., deterioration of the central nervous system).

In general, arousal results in a heightened level of activity of the autonomic nervous system. The constant stream of nervous impulses from the autonomic system impinges on the higher cortical processes. A certain amount of excitatory input to the cortex facilitates the firing of cortical cells. Thus, the cortex is better prepared to process information and organize a response. If, however, arousal becomes extreme, the excitatory input to the cortex is detrimental in two ways. First, too much activity causes cells to fire spontaneously, making the central nervous system noisy and processing difficult. Second, once a neuron has fired, it goes through a relative refractory period, during which it is more difficult, if not impossible, to get the neurons to fire again. High levels of activity would cause a larger proportion of cells to be in this refractory period at any point in time (Welford, 1965).

Arousal appears to increase in all subjects during a laboratory task (Powell, Eisdorfer, & Bogdonoff, 1964). However, there are two changes in the nervous system across the life span that increase the possibility that older persons will reach an unproductive level of arousal. First of all, the central nervous system appears to become more prone to overactivity with age (Welford, 1980). And second, the normal homeostatic feedback mechanism of the nervous system is not as efficient as in younger years (Kaack, Ordy, & Trapp, 1975).

The tendency toward overactivity in the central nervous system with age results in unwarranted high levels of arousal and anxiety. As indicated by the physiological tests employed by Powell, Eisdorfer, and Bogdonoff (1964), older subjects are more aroused from the start, and the stress of the experiment itself pushes their arousal levels well above those of younger subjects. Even a small rise in anxiety during the task will cause an increase in arousal and neural activity in the elderly beyond the optimal level.

Gregory (1957) termed this increase in spontaneous neuronal discharge "neurological noise." Heightened background noise in the central nervous system not only creates tension and anxiety, it also distorts information arriving from the senses. The central effect of a stimulus lasts longer, neural recovery is slower, and therefore preparation for the next stimulus is blocked (Eisdorfer, 1966).

Adaptation to the environment is necessarily at least part of the function of all organs and systems of the body. Of particular importance in regard to arousal is the feedback mechanism of the nervous and neuroendocrine systems, which attempt to maintain homeostasis. Changes in these two systems with age increase the deleterious effects of stress and anxiety. As indicated by Kaack *et al.* (1975), decreasing homeostatic adaptation to environmental challenges is one of the most fundamental manifestations of aging.

Assuming that we can generalize from these findings to other novel stress-inducing circumstances, we can conclude that the aged, when compared with the young, are more easily aroused, reach higher levels of arousal, and require more time to return to baseline. Applied to emotionality, these physiological and performance data suggest, if anything, that the intensity and duration of emotional experiences may increase with age.

Cognitive Changes

One universal characteristic of aging is the accumulation of a large number of experiences, many of which are stored in long-term memory. Since emotional experiences are frequently some of the most salient, it is likely that they also become some of the most memorable. These experiences, then, provide a context against which any new emotion-arousing events are evaluated.

The accumulated store of emotion-related experiences is likely to affect future emotional experiences in two ways. First, holding other things constant, the greater the number and variety of stored emotional experiences, the higher the adaptation level for similar emotion-arousing events (Tomkins, 1962). This reasoning would suggest, for example, that the threshold for falling in love the second time is a little higher than it is the first time.

A second and related consequence is that emotions become first more differentiated and then more mixed with age. From a developmental perspective, it is probably true that a few general affective states become differentiated into several specific identifiable emotions. For example, research carried out by Bridges (1932) suggests that infants evolve from a state of being able to experience unpleasant and pleasant states to a state where, later in childhood and early adulthood, they are able to differentiate approximately nine different emotional experiences. In addition, there is a growing body of recent research indicating that among adults, emotions are rarely experienced as discrete, pure states (Polivy, 1982; Schwartz & Weinberger, 1980; Izard, 1972). Any given experience is likely to elicit not just one emotional response but several related emotions as well. For example, inductions aimed at making an individual feel depressed also frequently elicit high levels of anxiety and hostility (Polivy & Doyle, 1980).

These cognitive changes have particular relevance for the aged. First, if the types of experiences encountered during old age are essentially similar to those stored in long-term memory, then their impact is likely to be relatively low because of changing adaptation levels. Second, it is likely that events that in the past elicited predominantly positive emotions acquire negative loadings over time and that events that in the past elicited predominantly negative emotions acquire positive loadings over time. This idea is reflected in the notion that with increasing age, persons increasingly see the bad side of good things and the good side of bad things. In sum, this reasoning suggests that there may be a decrease in the frequency of emotional experiences associated with age but that the proportion of positive and negative feelings remains roughly equivalent over time.

Alternatively, it can be argued that the aged are exposed to a class of new emotion-arousing events that can be broadly identified as losses (e.g., loss of spouse, reduction in income, and decreased physical mobility). Such events, in part because of their novelty, are likely to elicit immediate, intense, and long-lasting emotional responses that are generally negative in character. Given this greater predominance of objectively negative events experienced by older persons, one would expect a higher incidence of negative affective states among the old than among the young. Put another way, as one grows older, the number of new positive events decreases while the number of new negative events either stays the same or increases. And since the adaptation level for familiar events is likely to be higher than the adaptation for unfamiliar events, the net impact of positive and negative events for the aged is likely to be weighted on the negative side.

Another line of reasoning, based on theories of emotionality, leads to a similar conclusion. It was pointed out earlier that the degree to which individuals feel capable of controlling the density and/or the assimilability of stimulus input, and/or the outcomes of social interactions governs the degree to which they are likely to experience positive rather than negative affects. However, older persons' ability to control these factors is reduced for a variety of reasons, including decreased physical and cognitive capacity as well as the reduction in available resources. This reduction in control again suggests an increase in negative emotional experiences with age.

These converging lines of thought overwhelmingly lead one to the conclusion that human aging should be associated with a steady increase in negative affect. Some support for this notion is found in the increased rate of depression among the aged. Despite this evidence, the majority of data indicate that most old persons are not particularly depressed, angry, or afraid most of the time. In fact, it would be difficult to argue that the aged as a group evidence any more negative affect than their younger cohorts. This is the conclusion reached by Cameron (1975), who assessed the mood states of 6,452 persons aged 4–99 years and in four different situations: leisure, home, school, and work. Social class, sex, and situational differences in mood were found, but no significant age-related differences were discovered. The frequency of happy, sad, and neutral moods was identical among the young and the old, contradicting the stereotype of the aged as the least happy generation. How are we to reconcile these data with the conclusions derived earlier?

A partial solution to this puzzle is perhaps found when we ask the question: How do persons determine how they feel? What is the process that individuals go through to arrive at a negative, a positive, or a neutral affective state? We have already rejected the idea that emotions are determined exclusively by internal physiological responses, and we have stressed the importance of context, viewed as the immediate situation and the individual's cognitions about that situation, as a vital contributor to the person's affective state. An elaboration and some slight alteration of these ideas may provide an answer to the dilemma posed above.

With the possible exception of extreme cases, how we respond to a wide range of stimulus input (particularly social stimuli) is not a function of absolute levels of input but is instead a function of the discrepancy between expected and actual levels of input. Expectations may be based on a composite or an average of similar past encounters, as adaptation-level theory would suggest, or they may be based on current standards existing within a society or a subgroup of society.

Put another way, an individual can make *historical* or *temporal* comparisons (see Albert, 1977) based on similar events in his or her past, and/or the individual can make *contemporary* comparisons by noting how relevant others react to similar situations. When making contemporary comparisons, other persons in the individual's environment provide the standard for evaluating outcomes and hence the appropriate emotional response. When making historical or temporal comparisons, outcomes are compared with similar specific events or a composite of similar events from the individual's past. Regardless of the source of these expectancies or standards, anytime the outcomes fall short of what is expected, negative affective experiences should result, whereas outcomes that exceed expectations should result in positive affect.

With respect to the aged, then, the important question is: What types of comparisons (temporal or contemporary) do they make in evaluating their outcomes? Or, put another way, what is the source of their expectancies? The answer to this question, as we shall see, has important implications for the general emotional status of the aged.

Given the many real declines associated with reaching old age (e.g., declines in physical and cognitive ability and in economic resources), comparisons based on the past are likely to yield negative discrepancies and hence negative affective states. Thus, the individual who compares present events and circumstances with past abilities, accomplishments, and outcomes is likely to encounter many negative discrepancies. On the other hand, the person who uses a contemporary context to evaluate his or her outcomes is less likely to encounter negative discrepancies and hence negative affective states.

As an example, consider an institutionalized older person and the types of events that he or she is likely to encounter. Clearly, if such an individual compares past housing conditions, leisure activities, physical mobility, and daily events in general with present conditions, he or she is likely to experience negative affect. However, if the same individual uses as a basis for comparison the outcomes of similar individuals in the immediate environment (other institutionalized old persons), there is less likelihood of experiencing negative discrepancies.

The type of comparison processes that older persons engage in can be inferred from some recent data reported by Zemore and Eames (1979). In their study, residents of old-age homes reported no more symptoms of depression than either a group of waiting-list controls or a noninstitutionalized young group. This finding would be expected if individuals engage in contemporary rather than temporal comparison processes. A similar inference can be derived from the large number of studies of morale and well-being in the aged. Despite large differences in objective conditions of young, middle-aged, and aged individuals, few studies report any age-related differences in self-reports of well-being and morale. Apparently, individuals in different age groups adjust their expectancies to the prevailing conditions for that group. Such strategies are adaptive in that they minimize disappointment, but they also tend to promote the status quo.

In sum, two sets of opposing mechanisms can be identified as important determinants of the emotional status of the aged. Absolute changes in the adaptation level for positive events, the increased probability of novel negative events, and the decreased ability to control external events all contribute to the increased incidence of negative affect among the aged. Counteracting these mechanisms are changes in the individual's reference groups and expectation levels. Although there are few data bearing on this analysis, it is anticipated that the two mechanisms together will tend to promote stability over time in the emotional status of the individual as he or she ages.

The Data: Evidence on Affect and Emotion in the Aged

Much of the discussion has thus far focused on theories of emotion and speculation about their relevance to the aged. This information provides a point of departure for the remaining portion of this chapter, which concentrates on the available data regarding mood, emotionality, andaging.

Four types of data are discussed. First, we set the stage by examining data on the personality changes characteristically associated with growing old. Second, evidence on common emotional problems of the aged is discussed. Third, the determinants of mood and emotion in the aged are examined, with the focus primarily on their contextual correlates. And fourth, several field experiments are examined in which mood states were altered as by-products of interventions aimed at increasing the individuals' level of competence and their ability to control and predict their environment.

Personality Change and Aging

Are there characteristic personality changes associated with growing old? This question can be answered at several levels. From the theoretical perspective of psychoanalysts or ego psychologists (e.g., Jung, 1933; E. R. Erikson, 1959; E. H. Erikson, 1963; Buhler, 1935, 1959), the answer is certainly yes. There is some agreement among most of these theorists that there is an increase in introversion in middle and later life. A contrasting view is presented by a variety of social psychologists, symbolic interactionists, and role theorists, who emphasize the situational or environmental determinants of dispositional characteristics and play down the internal or intrapersonal changes associated with aging. But even representatives of the latter group would agree that there are important changes correlated with age. Their argument concerns the ultimate cause of those changes and not their presence or absence.

Most attempts to document personality changes with age have been based on standardized testing instruments administered to a cross section of the population. Catell (1957), for example, found that with older age, there is a shift from surgency toward desurgency. The surgent person is described as enthusiastic and happy-go-lucky, while the desurgent type is sober, serious, and often glum. Similar age-related trends have been documented by means of the Minnesota Multiphasic Personality Inventory (MMPI). Slater and Scarr (1964) interpreted age-related changes in Factor F of the MMPI as an indication or lower energy and impulsivity and a tendency to shy away from anger. Traits that show an increase with age include self-sufficiency and self-sentiment. The latter trait indicates the extent to which the individual "has crystallized for himself a clear, consistent and admitted pattern of socially-approved behavior to which he tries to conform" (Fozard & Thomas, 1975, p. 131).

These are only a few of the hundreds of cross-sectional studies that could be cited (see Neugarten, 1977, for a review) for or against the notion that personalities undergo changes with age. The findings from these studies are largely inconclusive, primarily because of the many different measurement instruments used and the large variety of populations sampled. There is, however, one generalization derivable from this work: introversion increases with age in the second half of life (Neugarten, 1977). The evidence for age-related changes in other traits is suggestive but not conclusive: the older individual is higher in rigidity and control and lower in impulsivity, activity, heterosexuality, and need for achievement (Fozard & Thomas, 1975). For our purposes, these changes would suggest that, at least for familiar events, the frequency and intensity of emotional experiences decline with age.

Long-Term Emotional Problems of the Aged

The most common affective disturbance of late life is depression. Although reported incidence and prevalence rates vary widely depending on the criteria used, it is estimated that between 21 and 54% of all geriatric admissions to hospitals are diagnosed as depressed. Among nonpatient populations, it is estimated that between 2 and 10% of the elderly warrant a clinical diagnosis of depression (Zarit, 1980). Indeed, some researchers have noted the many behavioral similarities between the depressed and elderly persons in general (e.g., Lewinsohn, 1974). On the positive side, the elderly depressed patient does appear to have a relatively good prognosis.

A second common response to traumatic events (such as the loss of a loved one) among the aged is frequently referred to as *adjustment reaction of late life.* It is characterized by a variety of emotional and physical disturbances, the most prominent of which is anxiety:

> Fear sometimes to the point of panic, perplexity, emotional lability, tearfulness, and feelings of helplessness dominate the psychological symptomatology. Tremulousness, muscular tension, a rapid heart rate, subjective feelings of shortness of breath, epigastric discomfort, and disturbed sleep characterize the physical side of this syndrome. (Pfeiffer, 1977, p. 658)

This pattern of response appears in many ways to be an extreme instance of the behavior exhibited by some aged people in laboratory testing situations.

Affect and Mood in the Aged

Data bearing on the affect and mood (emotional states associated with low levels of arousal) are less available than data on extreme emotional states, although items tapping mood are frequently found in life-satisfaction and morale scales. Of those studies assessing mood directly (Bradburn & Caplovitz, 1965; Gurin, Veroff, & Feld, 1960), Cameron's (1975) is probably the most extensive and the most carefully executed. The mood states of 6,452 persons aged 4–99 were assessed in four different situations: leisure, home, school, and work. While social class, sex, and situational differences in mood were found, no significant age differences were discovered.

The second major source of mood data is the numerous studies assessing life satisfaction and morale. Occasionally, life satisfaction of the aged is based on behavioral ratings, but more frequently, it is a score derived from true–false answers to approximately 15–20 standardized questions, the number varying with the specific test being used. The intent of these instruments is to measure the global subjective well-being of the aged individuals. Not surprisingly, all these instruments contain several mood questions: "My life could be happier than it is now," "I am just as happy now as when I was younger" (Life Satisfaction Index, Adams, 1969); "I get upset easily," "I have a lot to be sad about," "I sometimes feel that life isn't worth living" (Philadelphia Geriatric Center Morale Scale, Lawton, 1972).

Reviewing 30 years of research on the subjective well-being of older Americans, Larson (1978) concluded, "Folklore has it that health, wealth, and love are the basis of happiness. The studies reviewed in this paper suggest a similar formula is applicable to older Americans" (p. 116). Larson found that subjective well-being was most strongly related to health, followed by socioeconomic status, degree of social interaction, marital status, housing, and availability of transportation. As was the case with mood, no differences in subjective well-being were found as a function of age.

Both life satisfaction and morale scales have been frequently factor-analyzed, but mood rarely falls out as an independent factor. It is therefore difficult to determine to what extent psychological well-being is determined by mood per se. In addition, for many researchers, the factor analysis of life satisfaction or morale scales is an end in itself. Few have taken the next logical step and correlated the subscales with the personal and situational characteristics of the individual. One exception is a study by Campbell, Converse, and Rodgers (1976), in which global life satisfaction and happiness were independently assessed in a wide age cross-section of the population. Significant age differences were found. Younger persons scored high in happiness but low in life satisfaction. This pattern was reversed for older individuals, while middle-aged respondents scored low in both happiness and life satisfaction. George (1979) interpreted the lower levels of happiness among the aged as support for Neugarten's (1977) notion that affect in late life tends to flatten. This interpretation is consistent with the idea proposed earlier that for familiar events, the aged individual's adaptation level is probably higher than it is in the young, making the aged less affectively labile. Since this was a cross-sectional study, it is also possible, of course, that these differences merely reflect cohort effects. At the least, these data point to a pressing need for future research to separate such constructs as happiness and sadness from global life-satisfaction indicators.

Experimental Data

Experimental research has long been a tradition in adult development and aging, although its main focus has been on biological processes and sensory and cognitive abilities. Experimental research on the social-psychological aspects of aging is still relatively rare, and studies of affect and emotions are almost nonexistent. However, some data on the affective consequences of a variety of experimental interventions are now available. In particular, a growing body of research demonstrating the impact of social-psychological variables on the health and psychological status of the aged has coincidentally yielded some important findings regarding affect and emotions.

The underlying premise for much of the existing research (cf. Schulz, 1976, 1978; Schulz & Hanusa, 1978, 1979; Langer & Rodin, 1976) is that aging is characterized by many losses, the combined impact of which is to induce feelings of lack of control and helplessness. There is much correlational research to support this idea (e.g., see Schulz & Brenner, 1977; Schulz, 1978), although for obvious ethical reasons, this specific hypothesis has not been tested experimentally. However, the complementary idea, that increased control should have positive effects on the well-being of the aged, has been investigated in various guises. For example, Schulz (1976) demonstrated that increasing the predictability of or the control over a positive event (i.e., being visited) had a significant beneficial impact on the health and the psychological status of institutionalized aged individuals. Similar positive effects were reported by Langer and Rodin (1976), who enhanced aged subjects' feelings of control over important decisions affecting their lives. In both studies, affective states were also affected by these interventions. Schulz found that levels of happiness, hope, and "zest for life" were significantly higher among individuals in the control-enhanced and the predictability-enhanced groups. In addition, these persons were not as depressed as individuals in the comparison groups. Subjects in the control-enhanced treatment of the Langer and Rodin study similarly reported feeling happier than individuals in the control group. These results have been substantially replicated in several follow-up studies (Krantz & Schulz, 1980; Schulz & Hanusa, 1979), and in general, they support the theoretical derivation presented earlier that increased control over one's environment leads to positive affective states. Just as important, however, is what these data do not allow us to conclude. Since these interventions instigated changes in level of control among the subjects, we can only conclude that the impact on affective states was attributable to increases in *control* and not to *absolute levels* of control. This is an important distinction that deserves discussion.

The early experimental research on the effects of control on the institutionalized aged (e.g., Schulz, 1976; Langer & Rodin, 1976) implied that psychological well-being was related to absolute levels of control; the less control, the more unhappy or depressed the individual; hence the argument that the aged, since they experience absolute declines in their ability to control important outcomes, should be more depressed than younger cohorts. This may be true of individuals at the extreme ends of the control continuum. However, for the majority of individuals, occupying the middle range of this continuum, affective responses are the result of relative changes occurring over a short period of time and not absolute levels of control. Put another way, what we are arguing is that individuals have expectations of controlling outcomes largely determined by their reference group. It is likely that just as absolute levels of control decline with age, so do the expectations of control, and it is only when the level of available control is discrepant from the expected levels that positive or negative affect results; or alternatively, when the individual undergoes a sudden change in level of control, as he or she might as a result of an experimental intervention or a sudden change in environment caused by a relocation, positive or negative affective states are induced.

From a methodological perspective, it predicts that survey approaches investigating the relationship between environmental control and well-being are likely to yield little evidence of a relationship between these variables unless the survey is administered during or after some event that has altered the individual's level of control. For example, a survey of individuals residing in different institutional settings varying in the amount of environmental control allowed is unlikely to yield data showing that amount of control is related to level of subjective well-being. According to our point of view, this would be true because individuals adapt over time to their setting by adjusting their expectancies of control to reflect those of other individuals in their immediate environment. In short, temporal comparison processes that may dominate during transition periods are replaced by contemporary comparison processes. Since experimental studies on the effects of control require by definition some sort of control-related intervention and hence a change in level of control, the likelihood of finding a relationship between amount of control and affective states increases.

The policy implications of this analysis are more controversial. The last two decades in the United States are characterized by a substantial growth in programs for the aged as well as an increased sensitivity to the plight of the aged, on the one hand, and to the inaccuracy of many negative stereotypes regarding the aged, on the other. At the federal level alone, several new agencies have been created to provide services (e.g., the Administration on Aging) and to support research (the National Institute on Aging) dealing with the aged. The combined annual budgets of these agencies is well over half a billion dollars. The "real" capabilities of the aged in domains ranging from the sexual to the intellectual have been regular features in the popular media for the last decade. The consequences of these media programs are numerous and include an absolute change in the living conditions of older Americans as well as an improvement in stereotypes of the aged.

These changes seem long overdue and welcome. At the same time, it is important to be aware of some unforeseen and unintended consequences of these changes. Two can be readily identified.

First, given the gap between what social programs actually accomplish and what they are claimed or intended to achieve, the implementation of new programs is likely to lead to feelings of relative deprivation. Expectations of what a program will accomplish often outstrip real achievements, leaving the individual subjectively worse off than he or she might have been had those expectancies not been tampered with. Additionally, individuals who do not have access to programs for a variety of reasons may feel deprived of something that they are rightfully entitled to. In either case, aged persons may feel subjectively worse despite the fact that objectively, conditions have been improved.

Second, changing a negative stereotype may likewise have undesirable consequences. A stereotype may serve as one type of comparison other. Research on social comparison suggests that one motive for making comparisons is to validate that one is better than others (Suls & Miller, 1977). Obviously, a negative comparison other serves this end well. It is easier to come out on top comparing your car to a Corvair than to a Mercedes. One consequence of altering the negative stereotype of the aged is that it makes these positive comparisons more difficult. Indeed, there is a real danger of painting a picture of the aged that is much rosier than the facts warrant (see, for example, the debate on intellectual ability in the aged; Schaie, 1974; Baltes & Schaie, 1976; Horn & Donaldson, 1976, 1977). Consider, for example, the aged individual who is repeatedly exposed to information regarding the previously underestimated sexual prowess of the aged. Such an individual, who may have been perfectly content with his or her level of sexual activity or the absence of it, may now begin to question his or her adequacy because of widely publicized claims that the aged are just as sexually active as younger cohorts. The important point here is that stereotypes, if they do not accurately reflect reality, can be damaging even when they are weighted in what is generally thought to be a positive direction.

Summary and Discussion

This chapter began with a list of questions concerning aging and emotionality. Our attempt to find answers has led us through a diverse literature spanning almost half a dozen disciplines, including psychology, sociology, biology, and neurophysiology. It is appropriate now to return to those questions to summarize what we know and still need to know.

1. *Is the intensity of emotional experiences stronger or weaker among the aged than among the young?* The physiological data indicating a tendency toward overactivity of the central nervous system as well as higher levels of arousal would suggest that the aged experience emotions at least as intense as those of younger cohorts. The reduced coping capacity attributed to the aged also suggests that, at least with respect to negative emotions, intensity does not decrease with age.

2. *Does the duration of emotional experiences vary with age?* Here again, age-related physiological changes in the central nervous system suggest that once an emotion is instigated, it takes longer for the aged to return to baseline. This view is generally supported by the fact that the aged exhibit decreased homeostatic adaptation capacities.

3. *Do the aged show less variability in emotional states?* The decrease in homeostatic adaptation capacities of the aged also suggests that, at least in the short run (e.g., within-day), variability in emotional states is reduced. Little is known about the day-to-day variability of emotion among different age groups.

4. *Are particular types of emotional experiences more or less frequent among the aged?* Given the increased number of novel and negative events (e.g., loss of spouse, physical decline, and loss of income) associated with increased age and the higher adaptation level for positive events, one would expect a higher incidence of negative emotional states and a lower incidence of positive emotional states among the aged. It was also pointed out that the aged have a decreased capacity to control their environment in ways that lead to positive affective states. Together, these processes suggest that human aging may be associated with increased negative affect. This suggestion is in part supported by the increased rates of depression among the aged. However, counteracting these mechanisms tending toward negative affect are changes in the individual's expectations concerning the probability of negative events and the ability to control environmental events. The net impact of these opposing forces may be to promote stability over time in the emotional status of the individual as he or she ages.

5. *Are there qualitative differences in the experience of specific emotional states among the aged?* It is likely that emotional responses become less unidimensional with age. Events that in the past elicited predominantly positive emotions acquire negative loading over time. Emotions such as love, for example, may be less euphoric and may become a little more bittersweet the second, third, and fourth time around.

6. *Do the types of events that elicit emotional experiences change with age?* The answer to this question is yes. We have already indicated that identical

events may elicit different emotions over time. In addition, changes in adaptation levels as well as in expectancies indicate that types of eliciting events change with age. Thus, a seemingly trivial event such as a trip to town may elicit great happiness in an institutionalized old person but may elicit only indifference in a younger person. In general, to the extent that aging is correlated with changes in social context, the types of eliciting events are likely to change as well.

It will be obvious to any reader that the answers provided above are peppered with the tentative terminology of a speculator. This tentativeness is appropriate, since there is, in fact, little research available on emotionality and aging. It is, nevertheless, an important topic, and it is hoped that this chapter validates that point and provides some structure and direction for future research in this area.

ACKNOWLEDGMENT

Thanks are due to Leonard Cain for his valuable comments on earlier versions of this manuscript.

References

Adams, L. Analysis of a life satisfaction index. *Journal of Gerontology,* 1969, *24,* 470–474.

Albert, S. Temporal comparison theory. *Psychological Review,* 1977, *84,* 485–503.

Baltes, P. B., & Schaie, K. W. On the plasticity of intelligence in adulthood and old age. Where Horn and Donaldson fail. *American Psychologist,* 1976, *31,* 369–374.

Birren, J. E., & Schaie, K. W. (Eds.). *Handbook of the psychology of aging.* New York: Van Nostrand Reinhold, 1977.

Bradburn, N., & Caplovitz, D. *Reports on happiness.* Chicago: Aldine, 1965.

Brady, J. V. Emotion: Some conceptual problems and psychological experiments. In M. B. Arnold (Ed.), *Feelings and emotions.* New York: Academic Press, 1970.

Bridges, K. M. B. Emotional development in early infancy. *Child Development,* 1932, *3,* 324–341.

Brody, H., & Vijayashankar, N. Anatomical changes in the nervous system. In C. E. Finch & L. Hayflick (Eds.), *Handbook of the biology of aging.* New York: Van Nostrand Reinhold, 1977.

Buhler, C. The curve of life as studied in biographies. *Journal of Applied Psychology,* 1935, *19,* 405–409.

Buhler, C. *Der menschliche Lebenslauf als psychologisches Problem* (2nd ed.). Göttingen, West Germany: Hogrefe, 1959.

Buss, A. *Psychology—Man in perspective.* New York: Wiley, 1973.

Busse, E. W., & Pfeiffer, E. Functional psychiatric disorders in old age. In E. W. Busse & E. Pfeiffer (Eds.), *Behavior and adaptation in late life* (2nd ed.). Boston: Little, Brown, 1977.

Cameron, P.,Mood as an indicant of happiness: Age, sex, social class and situational differences. *Journal of Gerontology*, 1975, *30*, 216–224.

Campbell, A. Converse, P., & Rodgers, W. *The quality of American life.* New York: Russell Sage Foundation, 1976.

Cannon, W. B. The James-Lange theory of emotions: A critical examination and an alternative theory. *American Journal of Psychology*, 1927, *39*, 106–124.

Cattell, R. B. *Personality and motivation structure and measurement.* New York: World, 1957.

Eisdorfer, C. *New dimensions and a tentative theory.* Paper presented at the 19th Annual Meeting of the American Gerontological Society, New York 1966.

Eisdorfer, C., Axelrod, S., & Wilkie, F. L. Stimulus exposure time as a factor in serial learning in an aged sample. *Journal of Abnormal and Social Psychology*, 1963, *67*, 594–600.

Erikson, E. H. *Childhood and society* (2nd ed.).New York: W. W. Norton, 1963.

Erikson, E. R. Identity and the life cycle. *Psychological issues, Vol. 1.* New York: International Universities Press, 1959.

Fozard, J. L., & Thomas, J. C. Psychology of aging. In J. G. Howells (Ed.), *Modern perspectives in the psychiatry of old age.* New York: Brunner/Mazel, 1975.

George, L. K. The happiness syndrome: Methodological and substantive issues in the study of social-psychological well-being in adulthood. *Gerontologist*, 1979, *19*, 210–216.

Gregory, R. L. "Neurological noise" as a factor in aging. *Proceedings of the Fourth Congress of the International Association of Gerontology, Vol. I.* Merano, Italy: International Association of Gerontology, 1957.

Gurin, G., Veroff, J., & Feld, S. *Americans view their mental health.* New York: Basic Books, 1960.

Holmes, T. H., & Rahe, R. H. The social readjustment rating scale. *Journal of Psychosomatic Research*, 1967, *11*, 213–218.

Horn, J. L., & Donaldson, G. On the myth of intellectual decline in adulthood. *American Psychologist*, 1976, *31*, 701–719.

Horn, J. L., & Donaldson, G. Faith is not enough: A response to the Baltes-Schaie claim that intelligence does not wane. *American Psychologist*, 1977, *32*, 369–374.

Izard, C. E. *Patterns of emotions.* New York: Academic Press, 1972.

James, W. *The principles of psychology.* New York: Henry Holt, 1890.

Jung, C. G. *Modern man in search of a soul.* New York: Harcourt, Brace, & World, 1933.

Kaack, B., Ordy, J., & Trapp, B. Changes in limbic, neuroendocrine and autonomic systems, adaptation, homeostasis during aging. In J. Ordy & K. Brizee (Eds.), *Neurobiology of aging.* New York: Plenum Press, 1975.

Kemper, T. D. *A social interactional theory of emotions.* New York: Wiley, 1978. (a)

Kemper, T. D. Toward a sociology of emotions. *American Sociologist*, 1978, *13*, 30–41. (b)

Krantz, D., & Schulz, R. A model of lifecrisis, control and health outcomes: Cardiac rehabilitation and relocation of the elderly. In A. Baum & J. E. Singer (Eds.), *Advances in environmental psychology, Vol. II.* Hillsdale, N.J.: Erlbaum, 1980.

Langer, E., & Rodin, J. The effects of choice and enhanced personal responsibility for the aged: A field experiment in an institutional setting. *Journal of Personality and Social Psychology*, 1976, *34*, 191–198.

Larson, R. Thirty years of research on the subjective well-being of older Americans. *Journal of Gerontology*, 1978, *33*, 109–125.

Lawton, M. P. The dimensions of morale. In D. Kent, R. Kastenbaum, & S. Sherwood (Eds.), *Research, planning and action for the elderly.* New York: Behavioral Publications, 1972.

Lewinsohn, P. M. A behavioral approach to depression. In R. J. Friedman & M. M. Katz (Eds.), *The psychology of depression: Contemporary theory and research.* Washington, D.C.: Winston & Sons, 1974.

Maclean, P. D. Psychosomatic disease and the "visceral brain," recent developments bearing on the Papez theory of emotion. *Psychosomatic Medicine,* 1950, *11,* 338–353.

Marshall, G. D., & Zimbardo, P. G. Affective consequences of inadequately explained physiological arousal. *Journal of Personality and Social Psychology,* 1979, *37,* 970–988.

Maslach, C. Negative emotional biasing of unexplained arousal. *Journal of Personality and Social Psychology,* 1979, *37,* 953–969.

Neugarten, B. L. Personality and aging. In J. E. Birren & K. W. Schaie (Eds.), *Handbook of the psychology of aging.* New York: Van Nostrand Reinhold, 1977.

Pfeiffer, E. Psychopathology and social pathology. In J. E. Birren & K. W. Schaie (Eds.), *Handbook of the psychology of aging.* New York: Van Nostrand Reinhold, 1977.

Polivy, J. On the induction of emotion in the laboratory: Discrete moods or multiple affects. *Journal of Personality and Social Psychology,* 1981, *41,* 803–817.

Polivy, J., & Doyle, C. Laboratory induction of mood states through the reading of self-referent mood statements: Affective changes or demand characteristics. *Journal of Abnormal Psychology,* 1980, *89,* 286–290.

Powell, A. H., Eisdorfer, C., & Bogdonoff, M. D. Physiologic response patterns observed in a learning task. *Archives of General Psychiatry,* 1964, *10,* 192–195.

Pribram, K. H., & Melges, F. T. Psychophysiological basis of emotion. In D. C. Glass (Ed.), *Neurophysiology and emotion.* New York: Rockefeller University Press–Russell Sage Foundation, 1967.

Rockstein, M., & Sussman, M. *Biology of aging.* Belmont, Calif.: Wadsworth Publishing, 1979.

Schachter, S. *Emotion, obesity, and crime.* New York: Academic Press, 1971.

Schachter, S., & Singer, J. E. Cognitive, social and physiological determinants of emotional state. *Psychological Review,* 1962, *69,* 379–393.

Schachter, S., & Singer, J. E. Comments on the Maslach and Marshall-Zimbardo experiments. *Journal of Personality and Social Psychology,* 1979, *37,* 989–995.

Schaie, K. W. Translations in gerontology—From lab to life: Intellectual functioning. *American Psychologist,* 1974, *29,* 802–807.

Schulz, R. The effects of control and predictability on the psychological and physical well-being of the institutionalized aged. *Journal of Personality and Social Psychology,* 1976, *33,* 563–573.

Schulz, R. *The psychology of death, dying and bereavement.* Reading, Mass.: Addison Wesley, 1978.

Schulz, R., & Brenner, G. Relocation of the aged: A review and theoretical analysis. *Journal of Gerontology,* 1977, *32,* 323–333.

Schulz, R., & Hanusa, B. H. Long-term effects of predictability and control enhancing interventions: Findings and ethical issues. *Journal of Personality and Social Psychology,* 1978, *36,* 1194–1201.

Schulz, R., & Hanusa, B. H. Environmental influences on the effectiveness of control and competence enhancing interventions. In L. C. Perlmutter & R. A. Monty (Eds.), *Choice and perceived control.* New York: Lawrence Erlbaum, 1979.

Schwartz, G. E., & Weinberger, D. A. Patterns of emotional responses to affective situations: Relations among happiness, sadness, anger, fear, depression, and anxiety. *Motivation and Emotion,* 1980, *4,* 175–191.

Shott, S. Emotion and social life: A symbolic interactionist analysis. *American Journal of Sociology,* 1978, *85,* 1317–1334.

Slater, P. E., & Scarr, H. A. Personality in old age. *Genetic Psychology Monograph,* 1964, *70,* 229–269.

Solomon, R. L., & Corbit, J. D. An opponent-process theory of motivation, I: temporal dynamic of affect. *Psychological Review,* 1974, *81,* 119–145.

Suls, J. M., & Miller, R. L. (Eds.). *Social comparison processes: Theoretical and empirical perspectives.* New York: Hemisphere Publishing, 1977.

Tomkins, S. S. *Affect, imagery, consciousness, Vol. 1: The positive affects.* New York: Springer, 1962.

Tomkins, S. S. *Affect, imagery, consciousness, Vol. 2: The negative affects.* New York: Springer, 1963.

Tomkins, S. S. Affect as the primary motivational system. In M. B. Arnold (Ed.), *Feelings and emotions.* New York: Academic Press, 1970.

Troyer, W. G., Eisdorfer, C.,Bogdonoff, M. D., & Wilkie, F. L. Experimental stress and learning in the aged. *Journal of Abnormal Psychology,* 1967, *72,* 65–70.

Welford, A. T. Sensory, perceptual and motor processes in older adults. In J. E. Birren & R. B. Sloane (Eds.), *Handbook of mental health and aging.* Englewood Cliffs, N.J.: Prentice-Hall, 1980.

Zarit, S. H. *Aging and mental disorder.* New York: Free Press, 1980.

Zemore, R., & Eames, N. Psychic and somatic symptoms of depression among young adults, institutionalized aged and noninstitutionalized aged. *Journal of Gerontology,* 1979 *34,* 716–722.

CHAPTER 5

A Skill Deficit Approach to Loneliness

Richard R. Bootzin

Department of Psychology
Northwestern University
Evanston, Illinois

Issues regarding aloneness and loneliness have become increasingly prevalent in recent years as our society has become more urbanized and mobile and as families have become less stable. In this paper, I first discuss some consequences of aloneness, then briefly survey different approaches to loneliness, and finally describe a skill deficit approach and its implications for prevention and treatment.

Consequences of Aloneness

In recent years, a number of convergent trends have led to a dramatic increase in the number of people living alone. It is now more acceptable to delay marriage, the frequency of divorce has increased, and people are living longer. Women, in particular, often outlive their spouses. In 1950, the U.S. Census Bureau reported that there were 4 million single-person households. In 1960, the figure had increased to 7 million, in 1970 to 11 million, and in 1977 to 15.5 million (U.S. Department of Commerce, 1977). This increase far outstrips the increase in population in the United States over the same period. The largest percentage increase of people living alone has occurred among the young. For example, there has been a 141% increase from 1970 to 1977 in the 14- to 24-year-old age group. However, the largest proportion of people living alone are elderly women. Over 5 million of the 15.5 million single-person households are women over 65 years of age.

Not everyone who lives alone is lonely; nevertheless, the negative consequences of aloneness may be substantial. For example, figures for premature death (i.e., death before the age of 65) are consistently higher for those who are single, widowed, or divorced than for those who are married. This holds for males and females as well as for whites and nonwhites and is true for almost every cause of death including heart attacks, cancer, suicide, and even automobile accidents (Lynch, 1977).

One plausible explanation of the dramatic effect of aloneness is that the presence of others is anxiety- or stress-reducing. This general thesis has been supported by research in many diverse areas. Lynch (1977) reported that even comatose patients can respond to the physical contact of another person by immediate and dramatic changes in physiological indicators such as heart rate. In addition, the Office of the Surgeon General (1973) in an analysis of American casualties during World War II concluded that psychiatric breakdown in battle was caused primarily by the absence or inadequacy of sustaining interpersonal relationships within fighting units. And in a series of laboratory experiments, Schachter (1959) found that people seek out others when they are in stressful situations and that the presence of others is anxiety-reducing.

Even animals can be reassured by social support during stressful experiences. Lynch and McCarthy (1967) placed dogs in an experiment in which the dogs were shocked 10 seconds after a warning tone. The dog's heart rate usually accelerated about 50–100 beats per minute whenever the tone sounded. However, if the dog was petted throughout the entire period of tone and shock, there was no heart rate acceleration.

There are many possible explanations of why the presence of other people, particularly people we care about, is stress-reducing. One possibility is that this reaction is learned. The emotional relief associated with the care and security provided by parents may have been conditioned so that the presence of certain others during stress elicits a conditioned emotional relief. Another possibility is that it is no doubt easier to cope with a variety of environmental stresses if there is someone to share them with. This would be true if only because of the higher likelihood of being able to generate effective coping strategies.

Finally, it may not be that the presence of others is stress-reducing as much as that the absence of others is stress-inducing. Many people have observed that those who are lonely often report that they are restless (Weiss, 1973). They cannot concentrate on work, their attention wanders, and they feel driven to seek out other people. One rather speculative hypothesis about this restlessness is an evolutionary explanation, that is, that there was survival value to staying in groups. If one wandered too far from the group, survival was less likely. Thus, those who became uncomfortable when away from the group and who as a consequence would stay with the group or return quickly would be most likely to survive.

The data regarding the medical consequence of aloneness indicate that even today, there appears to be survival value to having other people with whom to share the stresses of modern life. An interesting question that cannot be answered from these data is whether those who are most distressed by being alone are most vulnerable to the consequences of aloneness. Or conversely, are those who have good coping skills and who enjoy living alone less vulnerable to the consequences of aloneness than those who are very distressed by aloneness? We will return to this issue later.

Approaches to Loneliness

In this section, I focus more directly on loneliness as opposed to aloneness.

Many writers describe two general types of loneliness. For example, Weiss (1973) distinguishes social isolation from emotional isolation. Loneliness produced by social isolation depends on the extent to which the person is isolated from some social network, as, for example, when a person moves his or her household from one location to another. At the old location, there was an extended social network in which the person was embedded. There were many friends and pleasurable activities. A move disrupts that network. Suddenly, the person may find that many of the pleasures of life were intertwined with friends and activities at the old location. If the move is job-related, the social isolation may be relatively brief because the social network at the job helps the person make the transition. However, a spouse who is not working is likely to have considerably more difficulty, since he or she is likely to have depended more on social networks that cannot be easily reconstituted in the new location.

A similar disruption of social networks occurs when a couple get divorced. The innumerable habits, routines, and social ties that were associated with the marriage, even an unhappy marriage, are suddenly disrupted. For example, in a household where the wife did not work and the husband did, the husband's coming home after work may have provided a stimulus for a complicated sequence of evening activities. When her husband is no longer there to provide that stimulus, the woman may feel restless and at a loss to know what to do. Even if the interactions were primarily aversive, the disruption of routine may make the person particularly vulnerable to feelings of loneliness.

Besides social isolation, loneliness is also produced by what Weiss (1973) called "emotional isolation." *Emotional isolation* means the nonfulfillment of the need for intimacy or the need to have an intimate relationship with one special person. The feelings produced by emotional isolation are probably very different from those produced by social isolation, and the skills necessary to effectively cope with emotional, as opposed to social, isolation may be quite different from one another.

The approach I am proposing for treating loneliness is a skill deficit approach. It asks what skills a person would need in order not to feel lonely. This approach does not imply that one should never feel lonely. There are skills, however, that a person might possess that would minimize the discomfort produced by temporary isolation and that would facilitate the development of social and emotional interconnectedness.

Of the skills that might be involved, an obvious candidate would be social skills. However, loneliness is often thought to be situational. Even people with effective social skills would be expected to feel lonely in some situations. Nevertheless, there are two points that reinforce the usefulness of social skills. First, people who report themselves to be lonely are also typically shy and possess a variety of other social deficits (Zimbardo, 1977). Thus, although there may be considerable situational variability, there is also variability due to individual differences in which some people are more vulnerable than others. Those who are most vulnerable may well be those who lack social skills. Second, social skills may be particularly important in limiting the impact of temporary dislocations. They enable people to begin developing contact with new social networks, thus limiting the degree of isolation experienced.

Besides social skills, there are other skills that might be important. For example, the expression of emotion and affection is likely to be necessary for the development of intimacy. A person who is lonely may focus on the fact that there is no one giving him or her affection. An important therapeutic question, however, may be whether the lonely person is expressing affection to others. Similarly, from a treatment perspective, it may be less important whether a person has friends than whether the person is capable of being a friend to others.

An additional set of skills has to do with how one copes with aloneness. Does the person have the resources available to enjoy life when alone, or is the person primarily dependent on other people? A construct that may be applicable to loneliness, as it is to depression, is rate of reinforcement (Lewinsohn & Graf, 1973). Those people who engage in few enjoyable activities when alone may be the ones who are most vulnerable to feelings of loneliness if circumstances force a period of extended social isolation.

A final set of skills necessary if one is to cope effectively with aloneness are cognitive skills. For example, self-statements may either facilitate or undermine the development of other coping skills (Meichenbaum, 1977). Cognitive constructs such as efficacy expectations (Bandura, 1977) or a sense of control (Schulz, this volume) would be relevant here, as well.

As the components of a skill deficit approach to loneliness are described, it can be seen that such a program is not specifically focused on loneliness but might be better described as a program to help people become more personally effective and autonomous (Johnson, 1977). Aloneness is just one of a number of stresses with which a person might have to cope. The skills that are likely to be useful for coping with aloneness are also likely to have a more general utility in coping with stress.

Before describing the skill deficit approach in detail, it may be useful to review recommendations for loneliness as found in the best of the traditional literature. The following recommendations are paraphrased from Weiss (1973).

First, lonely people should recognize that it is all right to be lonely. Being lonely does not mean that there is something wrong with the person. Loneliness should be recognized, accepted, and expressed.

Second, lonely people should stay in close proximity to social networks. If social networks are being disrupted, the person should do something to try and maintain them. For example, the person can keep in touch with friends by mail and telephone. Some effort may be required to keep in touch with social networks, but doing so will help the person through transition periods.

Third, lonely people should use supplementary or transitional relationships, if necessary. Included here would be therapy and groups such as Parents without Partners. An advantage of supplementary relationships is that there is then someone with whom to share the experience.

And fourth, lonely people should direct energy to some project or activity. The person should not sit home alone avoiding contact with others. Intead, the person should get involved in activities that are enjoyable and that are likely to bring him or her into new social networks.

The above recommendations are meant to help the person deal with social isolation. Weiss, and almost everyone else, has pointed out that there is little that one can do directly to go about finding that one special person. Instead, the best one can do is to be in situations where there are other people and let nature take its course.

The above suggestions are quite sensible and very compatible with a skill deficit approach. An alternate perspective that deserves some comment is the existential perspective. From the existential perspective (e.g., Moustakas, 1961), loneliness is not something to be treated. Since we are all ultimately alone, loneliness is the human condition. Thus, Moustakas proposed that one learns and grows from accepting and coming to terms with loneliness.

Existentialists distinguish between loneliness and fear of aloneness. Much of what has been discussed thus far would be considered a manifestation of fear of aloneness rather than loneliness. Whereas the acceptance of loneliness allows growth, fear of aloneness and its associated emotional arousal motivate a variety of avoidance activities. According to existentialists, people fear aloneness because they are unwilling to confront loneliness.

Fear of aloneness may be a useful concept from a more behavioral perspective, as well. Frequently, it is the negative emotional arousal accompanying aloneness that is labeled as loneliness. Thus, loneliness, or fear of aloneness, might be best treated as one would treat any fear. Performance-based treatments have been particularly effective in changing avoidance behavior (Bandura, 1977). Thus, to treat fear of aloneness, one might need to practice being alone for increasing periods of time (Johnson,1977). This approach would be compatible with the earlier suggestion regarding skills for coping with aloneness. As the repertoire of activities that a person enjoys doing alone increases, the fear of aloneness should decrease.

The discussion to this point has been very speculative. No data have been presented to support the viability of a skill deficit approach to loneliness. Before discussing our own results, there is one study of widows (Lopata, 1973) that reported some interesting findings. Not all widows were found to be lonely after the deaths of their husbands. Some experienced remarkably little prolonged distress. Interestingly, the amount of loneliness experienced was independent of how good the marriage was; rather, loneliness was related to how active or passive the widow was. The women who were most lonely were the ones who were most passive. Those who had learned to be most active were least lonely.

Loneliness, Coping Skills, and Pleasurable Activities

In order to begin the process of evaluating the skill deficit theory of loneliness, Allison Curley, Dara Vines, and I surveyed 78 Stanford University undergraduates (48 women and 30 men). The subjects completed the UCLA Loneliness Scale (Russell, Peplau, & Ferguson, 1978), the Pleasant Events Schedule (MacPhillamy & Lewinsohn, 1976), a set of questions about current social and academic adjustment, and some life-history items. The Pleasant

Events Schedule was modified and administered twice. Not all items of the schedule were included. Of the 320 items, 100 were used. However, all items that had been found to be related to mood (Lewinsohn & Graf, 1973) or that discriminated depressed from nondepressed subjects (MacPhillamy & Lewinsohn, 1974) were included. In addition, the usual instruction to rate the frequency and the pleasurableness of a list of activities was followed by another administration with instruction to rate the frequency and pleasurableness of 77 of the activities when engaged in alone.

In addition to completing the UCLA Loneliness Scale, the subjects were asked to rate their current loneliness on a 7-point rating scale. The correlation between the two measures was $r = .55$ ($df = 76$, $p < .001$). Although this correlation is substantially lower than the correlation ($r = .79$) reported by Russell, Peplau, and Ferguson (1978), there were few significant differences between the measures in the pattern of interrelationships with other variables. Nevertheless, correlations with both measures are reported here.

Loneliness among Stanford undergraduates was unrelated to gender, birth order, year in school, grade-point average, and whether the student lived on or off campus. Not unexpectedly, loneliness was related to aspects of the students' social life. As can be seen in Table 1, those students who were satisfied with their social life or who had an "important other" person in their life were less likely to be lonely.

One particularly interesting finding had to do with the students' upbringing. We hypothesized that children who were firstborns or who spent a consid-

Table 1. Correlates of Loneliness[a]

	Loneliness rating	UCLA scale
Satisfaction with social life	−.39[f]	−.44[f]
"Important other"	−.31[f]	−.19[d]
Encouraged to develop independence	−.22[e]	−.26[e]
Pleasant Events Schedule		
Mood items[b]	−.40[f]	−.36[f]
Depression items[c]	−.29[f]	−.28[e]

[a] $n = 78$.
[b] Items that discriminate between moods, scored so that the higher the score, the more pleasant the mood.
[c] Items that discriminate between depressed and nondepressed subjects. The higher the score, the less depressed the subject.
[d] $p < .10$.
[e] $p < .05$.
[f] $p < .01$.

erable amount of time alone would have developed the resources for dealing with aloneness and, thus, would report less current loneliness. However, loneliness was found to be unrelated to either birth order or the rating of how much time the student spent alone as a child, but it was related to whether the parents had encouraged the students to be independent as children. The more the parents had encouraged the student to develop independence as a child, the less current loneliness the student reported. Although there are methodological problems with these data since the students were reporting about both their current loneliness and their past upbringing, this result gives additional support to the proposition that an active, independent coping style provides protection from loneliness.

Lewinsohn and his colleagues (e.g., Lewinsohn & Graf, 1973; MacPhillamy & Lewinsohn, 1974) have found that a person's mood varies with the frequency with which she or he engages in pleasurable activities. In their research, one set of items from the Pleasant Events Schedule was found to be related to mood, and another overlapping set of items was found to discriminate between depressed and nondepressed subjects. As can be seen in Table 1, the mood and depression items are also related to loneliness. In other words, if the students reported that they were engaging in many activities that had previously been shown to be related to positive moods, they were less likely to be lonely. Similarly, if they engaged in many activities that nondepressed people engaged in, they were also less likely to be lonely. Here, then, is another indication that being active and engaging in reinforcing activities are incompatible with being lonely.

A more detailed analysis of loneliness and pleasant events is found in Table 2. The first thing to notice is that almost all of the activities were negatively correlated with loneliness; that is, people who were lonely engaged in these activities less frequently or found them less pleasurable than people who were not lonely. Not surprisingly, many of the activities reflected the quality of the individual's social life, but interestingly, there were also a number of activities associated with competence, particularly for women. Thus, doing a job well, planning or organizing something, learning to do something new, and doing a project in one's own way were all activities that were engaged in more frequently by students who were less lonely. This finding, too, supports the earlier observations regarding the utility of an active, coping approach to life.

The findings that have been discussed so far concern the frequency and the enjoyability of activities irrespective of whether they were engaged in with other people or alone. A major hypothesis, however, had been that those people who had the resources for coping with aloneness, and thus who engaged in more activities alone, would be the ones who were less lonely. However, our survey indicated that loneliness was, for the most part, unrelated to doing things alone. Only the frequency of three activities done alone was related to loneliness ($p < .05$). People who were lonely reported being at the beach

Table 2. Loneliness and Pleasant Events[a]

	Loneliness rating	UCLA scale
Loneliness related to the frequency of:		
Males and females		
Being with someone I love	−.48[d]	−.43[d]
Being with happy people	−.36[d]	−.39[d]
Watching wild animals	−.35[d]	−.34[d]
Being told I am loved	−.51[d]	−.50[d]
Doing a job well	−.29[d]	−.31[d]
Being with friends	−.24[c]	−.30[d]
Males only		
Being noticed as sexually attractive	−.61[d]	−.30[b]
Going to a sports event	−.32[b]	−.43[c]
Going to a health club, sauna bath	.28	.50[d]
Being praised by people I admire	−.35[b]	−.39[c]
Petting or necking	−.55[d]	−.25
Smiling at people	−.38[c]	−.48[d]
Females only		
Going to a bar, tavern, or club	−.38[d]	−.41[d]
Planning or organizing something	−.37[d]	−.25[b]
Learning to do something new	−.40[d]	−.10
Complimenting someone or praising them	−.41[d]	−.22
Doing a project in my own way	−.43[d]	−.20
Having people show interest in what I said	−.29[c]	−.45[d]
Having coffee, tea, Coke with friends	−.31[c]	−.30[c]
Being complimented or told I have done well	−.34[c]	−.34[c]
Loneliness related to enjoyability of:		
Males and females		
Going to school or government meetings	−.32[d]	−.25[c]
Males only		
Breathing clean air	−.40[c]	−.36[b]
Thinking about something good in the future	−.34[b]	−.54[d]
Going to health club, sauna bath	.33[b]	.63[d]
Females only		
Meeting someone new of the same sex	−.27[b]	−.34[c]
Kissing	−.38[d]	−.39[d]
Visiting friends	−.23	−.37[d]
Smiling at people	−.45[d]	−.22

[a] $n = 78$.
[b] $p < .10$.
[c] $p < .05$.
[d] $p < .01$.

alone more frequently but driving skillfully alone and breathing clean air alone less frequently than those who were not lonely. This pattern is not very informative. Thus, loneliness was not found to be related to the frequency of engaging in activities alone but was related to the frequency with which the person engaged in activities with or without other people. It must be remembered, however, that our sample of students included both people who might have been coping with aloneness as well as those in the midst of active social networks. It may be that the number of activities engaged in alone is relevant for those who are socially isolated.

Parenthetically, men and women gave remarkably similar reports regarding how frequently they engaged in activities alone. However, there were many activities that the males said that they would enjoy doing more than the women said they would ($p < .05$). These activities were being in the country, planning trips or vacations, rock climbing or mountaineering, going to races, going to a bar or tavern, boating, camping, exploring, playing pool or billiards, bowling, eating good meals, hiking, being noticed as sexually attractive, and water skiing or surfing. Neither the men nor the women engaged in these activities alone very frequently, but the men reported that if they did, they would enjoy the activity. This finding may have more to do with cultural stereotypes about what men ought to enjoy doing than with what they actually do.

In summary, there were a number of findings from the survey that indicated that a skill deficit approach to loneliness might be fruitful. Loneliness was negatively associated with engaging in a wide range of activities. These activities included activities associated with developing competence, as well as social activities. In addition, those students whose parents had encouraged the development of independence when they were children were less lonely than other students at the time of the survey. Learning to be an active, independent, coping individual seems to provide protection from loneliness.

The Prevention of Loneliness

In order to evaluate the treatment and prevention implications of a skill deficit approach to loneliness, a specific treatment or prevention program must be developed. I decided to focus on prevention rather than treatment in order to evaluate whether the development of particular skills to cope with aloneness would in fact be protective. There are many occasions when people move to new environments and must undergo a resulting period of adjustment during which they are particularly vulnerable to loneliness. One such population is graduating high-school seniors. Whether the student goes off to college or begins a new job, this is a time of many environmental changes and the disruption of social networks. From a skill deficit perspective, there are specific skills that could be developed that would ease the adjustments to be made.

One goal of such a program would be to expand the repertoire of activities that one could enjoy alone. This expansion would be particularly difficult to achieve in the midst of a crisis, while the person is lonely. On the other hand, this task might be accomplished more easily while the social networks are still intact and the person does not feel lonely. Thus, one advantage of a prevention approach is that skill development should be easier to accomplish. Those skills should then be available for use when social networks are disrupted.

Mijke McKee, Diana Dahlgren, John Buckner, and I designed a four-session workshop to develop skills that would make later adjustments easier. Each session was an hour and a halflong. All four leaders met with each group of six students. We conducted two four-session workshops. One group was recruited from a private girl's preparatory school in Palo Alto, while the other was recruited from a Palo Alto public high school and contained both males and females.

The workshops might be better described as being focused on autonomy training rather than as being focused on just the development of skills for dealing with loneliness. Since most of the students would be going to college, much of the workshop dealt with college adjustment. Among the topics covered were (1) meeting new people and making new friends; (2) learning to expand the repertoire of activities that one can enjoy alone; (3) learning to handle problems that might occur when one is out alone; (4) the role of self-statements in shaping one's reaction to new experiences; (5) practical considerations such as budgeting time and money; (6) learning a general problem-solving strategy for change; and (7) informal academic advice about college life.

For each topic, a written handout was distributed and discussed during one or more of the sessions. In addition, there were between-session assignments to engage in activities alone and to initiate social interaction. Tables 3 and 4 list a number of possible assignments for engaging in activities alone and for initiating social interaction. Each group member selected a number of items that varied in difficulty from each list. The group members were instructed to complete the less difficult items first, before attempting the more difficult ones. For all assignments, the group members kept a diary of their reactions and internal dialogues while carrying out the assignment. The reactions to assignments were then discussed at the next session.

Table 3. Possible Assignments of Activities in Which to Engage Alone

1. Going on a long walk
2. Going to a rock concert
3. Planning trips or vacations
4. Playing a round of golf
5. Going to a sports event
6. Going to the races (horse, car, or boat)
7. Reading stories, novels, poems, or plays
8. Going to lectures or hearing speakers
9. Eating lunch at school
10. Exploring
11. Going to a party
12. Going to church functions (socials, classes, or bazaars)
13. Going to a service, civic, or social club meeting
14. Snow skiing
15. Playing pool or billiards
16. Bowling
17. Sitting in the sun
18. Going to a fair, a carnival, a circus, a zoo, or an amusement park
19. Planning or organizing something
20. Going to school or government meetings
21. Gathering natural objects (wild foods or driftwood)
22. Seeing beautiful scenery
23. Eating at home
24. Hiking
25. Going to a museum or exhibit
26. Fishing
27. Going to a health club or a sauna bath
28. Sightseeing
29. Meeting someone new of the same sex
30. Shooting baskets
31. Learning to do something new
32. Going to a drive-in (McDonald's, Jack-in-the-Box)
33. Horseback riding
34. Going to the movies
35. Running, jogging
36. Going to the library
37. Shopping for clothes
38. Watching people
39. Going to banquets, luncheons, or potlucks
40. Bicycling
41. Having coffee, tea, or a coke
42. Going to auctions or garage sales
43. Listening to music
44. Meeting someone new of the opposite sex
45. Attending a concert, opera, or ballet
46. Going to a play
47. Doing errands
48. Grocery shopping
49. Practicing golf at a driving range or tennis against a backboard
50. Window shopping

Table 4. Possible Social Interaction Assignments

1. Asking someone for directions or the time of day
2. Asking someone for help
3. Asking a police officer for help or directions
4. Asking a clerk for help in buying something
5. Ordering something from a waiter or waitress
6. Buying something from a person
7. Talking to someone about a personal problem
8. Going up to someone of the opposite sex at school and eating with her or him
9. Calling a member of the opposite sex just to talk (someone you are not a boyfriend or girlfriend of)
10. Calling for estimates on repairs or for other information
11. Going to a meeting or club for the first time
12. Opening a checking account
13. Talking with landlords about apartments to rent
14. Talking with a teacher or a professor after class or during office hours
15. Asking someone out for a date
16. Starting a conversation with someone who sits down next to you at a sports event
17. Starting a conversation with someone at a movie
18. Starting a conversation with someone at a party
19. Starting a conversation with someone in a class or a meeting
20. Speaking to someone while waiting in line
21. Starting a conversation with someone when you are both doing some activity (jogging, hiking, or skiing)
22. Starting a conversation when you see someone you know of the same sex
23. Starting a conversation when you see someone you know of the opposite sex
24. Starting a conversation with a person you know who is much older than you
25. Ending a conversation
26. Meeting relatives you haven't seen in a long time
27. Asking a favor or something else of someone you don't know (donation)
28. Saying no to something you don't want to do or buy

The participants completed postworkshop evaluations and reported that they found the workshops to be valuable. A larger-scale implementation of the workshops would be necessary to adequately evaluate their value in preventing loneliness. However, there were some valuable informal observations.

First, the gains made were rather modest. There were many activities that competed with the workshops for the interest of the high school seniors. Thus, a disadvantage of a prevention strategy is that the participants are not likely to be as motivated as people who are already in distress. Nevertheless, some high school students were interested, and those who participated did carry out the assignments. We were left feeling, however, that more could have been accomplished.

Second, the high school girls were much more interested than the boys in the issues and problems of aloneness and autonomy. The boys wanted practical advice such as how to get an A in introductory psychology or how to budget. For the most part, they were uncomfortable with discussions about coping with emotional states such as loneliness or anxiety. They did talk about these issues and related their experience, but that was not the reason that the boys were participating. The girls, on the other hand, understood exactly what the workshops were attempting to do and how these skills might be helpful to them. The girls seemed to have been more protected than the boys and had been encouraged not to engage in activities alone. Thus, when they found themselves without social networks, the girls were much more at a loss to know what to do. Consequently, they felt that the workshops focused on issues that were of more concern to them.

Third, the people who gained the most from the workshops were the leaders. There was more change in our behavior than in that of any of the participants. In that sense, leading a workshop was truly a learning experience.

Although formal evaluations have not been done, the skill deficit approach appears to be a promising method for dealing with loneliness. It is applicable not only to high school students. The skills for becoming more active and autonomous are useful at all stages of life.

References

Bandura, A. Self-efficacy: Toward a unifying theory of behavioral change. *Psychological Review,* 1977, *84,* 191–215.

Johnson, S. M. *First person singular: Living the good life alone.* New York: Lippincott, 1977.

Lewinsohn, P. M., & Graf, M. Pleasant activities and depression. *Journal of Consulting and Clinical Psychology,* 1973, *41,* 261–268.

Lopata, H. Z. Loneliness: Forms and components. In R. S. Weiss (Ed.), *Loneliness: The experience of emotional and social isolation.* Cambridge, Mass.: MIT Press, 1973.

Lynch, J. J. *The broken heart: The medical consequences of loneliness.* New York: Basic Books, 1977.

Lynch, J. J., & McCarthy, J. F. The effect of petting on a classically conditioned emotional response. *Behavioural Research and Therapy,* 1967, *5,* 55–62.

MacPhillamy, D. J., & Lewinsohn, P. M. Depression as a function of desired and obtained pleasure. *Journal of Abnormal Psychology,* 1974, *83,* 651–657.

MacPhillamy, D. J., & Lewinsohn, P. M. *Manual for the pleasant events schedule.* Unpublished manuscript, University of Oregon, 1976.

Meichenbaum, D. H. *Cognitive behavior modification.* New York: Plenum Press, 1977.

Moustakas, C. *Loneliness.* Englewood Cliffs, N.J.: Prentice-Hall, 1961.

Office of the Surgeon General. *Neuropsychiatry in World War II, Vol. 2: Overseas theaters.* Washington, D.C.: Government Printing Office, 1973.
Russell, D., Peplau, A., & Ferguson, M. Developing a measure of loneliness. *Journal of Personality Assessment,* 1978, *42,* 290–294.
Schachter, S. *The psychology of affiliation.* Stanford, Calif.: Stanford University Press, 1959.
U.S. Department of Commerce, Bureau of the Census. *Population characteristics: Households and families by type.* Washington, D.C.: Government Printing Office, 1977.
Weiss, R. S. *Loneliness: The experience of emotional and social isolation.* Cambridge, Mass.: MIT Press, 1973.
Zimbardo, P. G. *Shyness.* Menlo Park, Calif.: Addison-Wesley, 1977.

CHAPTER 6

Alcohol and Anxiety

Recent Evidence on the Tension Reduction Theory of Alcohol Use and Abuse

G. Terence Wilson

Department of Psychology
Rutgers University
New Brunswick, New Jersey

The most remarkable feature of the tension reduction theory of alcohol use and abuse is how widely it is believed. The notion that alcohol reduces tension and that people drink in order to obtain this effect appears to make common sense and is deeply ingrained in folklore and clinical experience. Literary allusions to this effect abound, a particularly notable instance being Keats's expression in his *Ode to a Nightingale:*

> O, for a draught of vintage!. . . .
> Full of the true, the blushful Hippocrene,
> That I might drink, and leave the world unseen,
> Fade far away, dissolve, and quite forget
> The weariness, the fever, and the fret. . . .

Social and problem drinkers alike subscribe to the theory. For example, in a series of studies in my laboratory of male and female college students who were social drinkers, the vast majority expressed the view that alcohol reduces anxiety both in the population at large and in their own particular case (Abrams & Wilson, 1979; Wilson & Abrams, 1977; Wilson, Perold, & Abrams, 1979). Brown, Goldman, Inn, and Anderson (1979) conducted a factor analysis of the expectancies associated with moderate alcohol consump-

The preparation of this chapter and the research that it reports were made possible by Grant AA 00259=09 from the National Institute of Alcoholism and Alcohol Abuse.

tion in a diverse group of nonproblem drinkers and found that six factors emerged, one of which corresponded to tension reduction. Sample questionnaire items that loaded significantly on this factor included "Alcohol decreases muscular tension" and "Alcohol makes me worry less." Another factor corresponded to the expectation of enhanced sexual performance and experience. The perception of alcohol as an aphrodisiac by both men and women is commonly attributed to its anxiety-reducing or "disinhibiting" function (see Wilson, 1981, for a more detailed discussion of this relationship between alcohol consumption and sexual behavior). This assumed effect of intoxication is captured in the old definition of the superego as that part of the psyche that is soluble in alcohol!

Tension reduction was given as a reason for drinking by a representative sample of men living in a London suburb in a study by Edwards (1972). A factor analysis of this questionnaire showed that a number of items relating to tension reduction clustered together and constituted Factor 1. The items that loaded most highly on this factor were "I drink because it helps me to relax"; "I drink when things get me down"; "I drink because it helps me to forget my worries": and "I drink sometimes when I am restless or tense." Of particular interest is that the problem drinkers in this sample tended to show high scores on this tension reduction factor. In a related study, Deardorff, Melges, Hout, and Savage (1975) carried out a factor analysis of the responses of problem and nonproblem drinkers to a questionnaire that tapped situations that were related to drinking. Seven factors were derived from this analysis, one of which corresponded to tension reduction. A significant finding was that this factor was one of three factors that distinguished between the problem and nonproblem drinkers.

Social and problem drinkers are not alone in believing that alcohol reduces tension. Clinicians also share this view. Cappell (1975), for example, on the basis of a scholarly analysis of clinical interpretations of drinking, from 1941 through 1973, concluded that there "appears to be a relatively uncritical and widely shared view, based largely on clinical practice with alcoholic patients, that drinking and anxiety reduction are closely wed" (p. 178). While Cappell attributed this unchanging acceptance of the tension reduction theory to psychodynamic interpretations, some of the specific endorsements of the theory that he cited were learning-based analyses made by behavior therapists (e.g., Lazarus, 1965). Behavior therapy techniques that have been used in the treatment of alcoholics, such as relaxation training, systematic desensitization, and assertion training, have been predicated on the assumption that alcoholics drink excessively as a means of coping with anxiety and other sources of stress or tension.

A relatively recent development of considerable clinical importance has been the analysis of the specific variables that are related to relapse in abstinent alcoholics (Marlatt & Gordon, 1979). In their study of reasons for relapse among alcoholics, Litman, Eiser, Rawson, and Oppenheim (1977) concluded that there are four major categories of variables that govern relapse: unpleasant mood states such as anxiety and depression; external situations and euphoric feelings; social anxiety; and diminished cognitive vigilance and rationalizations. The results of studies by Marlatt and his colleagues on the situational and psychological factors associated with relapse can also be interpreted as providing support for the tension reduction theory of drinking. Alcoholics who relapsed were interviewed within a few weeks of their drinking episode with a view to pinpointing the specific circumstances surrounding their first drink. The relapse situations identified on the basis of these interviews were then assigned by trained raters to independent, operationally defined categories. In the first study (Marlatt & Gordon, 1979), most of the relapse situations were accounted for by two major categories: the experience of frustration or anger (29%) and social pressure to drink (21%). The category of negative emotional states, including feelings of anxiety, depression, and boredom, accounted for relatively few relapse episodes (10%). However, the term *tension* in the customary meaning of the tension reduction theory is a generic construct that encompasses negative emotional states such as fear, anxiety, and frustration (e.g., Cappell, 1975). In this sense, then, fully 40% of relapse situations could be linked directly to the reduction of tension or aversive emotional states that are assumed to motivate escape or avoidance behavior. In a second study (Chaney, O'Leary, & Marlatt, 1978), the same categories once again accounted for most of the relapse episodes in a sample of 25 male alcoholics, although the percentage of cases in each category differed from that of the first study. Significantly, 43% of relapse situations were attributed to the category of negative emotional states, 16% to frustration and anger, and 17% to social pressure from "drinking buddies."

In sum, it is clear that the public, alcoholic patients, and the professionals responsible for their treatment all agree that alcohol reduces tension and that this function motivates drinking. In a view of this impressive consensus among diverse groups, it behooves us to take seriously Hodgson, Stockwell, and Rankin's (1979) admonition that "drinking to relieve or avoid tension is so frequently mentioned that we must be very wary of 'objective' evidence to the contrary" (p. 459).

It is to a consideration of the objective evidence that I now turn.

Evidence from Animal Studies

Given the difficulty involved in developing an adequate animal model of alcoholism (Falk & Tang, 1977), and given the fact that this research inevitably overlooks the role of cognitive mediating processes in the regulation of drinking, I find it difficult to dispute too strongly Marlatt's (1979) conclusion that "the findings from the animal studies would seem to have little or no relevance to the understanding of drinking in humans" (p. 83). Consequently, this chapter focuses primarily on research with human subjects and patients. However, mention must be made of the major reviews of the animal literature on the tension reduction theory by Cappell and Herman (1972) and Cappell (1975). These reviews provide a comprehensive survey of studies on the effects of alcohol on conflict and experimental neurosis, avoidance and escape learning, conditioned suppression, and resistance to extinction following partial reinforcement. On the basis of these reviews, Cappel (1975) concluded that with

> the exception of the conflict literature (and even this was not totally exempt), equivocal, negative, and even contradictory evidence tended to predominate. (p. 190)
>
> When judged solely on its merits as a theory, the tension reduction theory is substantially undermined. In a sense this failure is perplexing since the rationale underlying the theory seems so plausible and so consistent with commonplace experience. But in the final analysis, the evidence can lead to no other conclusion. (p. 202)

Hodgson *et al.* (1979) have reexamined the animal literature and have arrived at a different conclusion from Cappell (1975). According to Hodgson *et al.*, the relevant animal experimentation provides the tension reduction theory with a solid, scientific basis. The key word here is *relevant*. Hodgson *et al.* offered an incisive analysis of the different animal conditioning procedures that were featured in Cappell's (1975) review, arguing that only those procedures that evaluate the effects of alcohol on fear or frustration (e.g., experimental neurosis, conflict, and passive avoidance) provide a fair test of the theory. Escape learning and well-learned active avoidance responses, they suggested, are not mediated by fear or frustration and therefore are ill-suited to testing the theory. Looked at in this more selective way, the data are more consistent with the tension reduction theory than previous reviews have indicated.

Evidence from Studies with Human Subjects

Excellent reviews of the experimental evidence on the tension reduction theory, based on studies with human subjects and patients, are available elsewhere (Cappell, 1975; Higgins, 1976; Marlatt, 1976), and it is not my purpose to try to cover the same ground. However, it is important to comment briefly on research with alcoholic subjects that has been widely interpreted as discrediting the tension reduction theory.

Laboratory studies of ad lib alcohol consumption by alcoholics in a research ward environment have repeatedly shown that continued drinking is associated with signs of *increased* anxiety and depression (McNamee, Mello, & Mendelson, 1968; Mendelson, La Dou, & Solomon, 1964; Tamerin & Mendelson, 1969). These findings have been limited to alcoholics' self-reported mood states and subjective psychiatric observations, but the consistency with which they have been replicated is striking. Nathan and O'Brien (1971) compared the effects of continued alcohol consumption in four chronic alcoholics and four matched nonalcoholic subjects and concluded that "most alcoholic subjects showed heightened depression, anxiety, and hostility and more symptoms of psychopathology during drinking. Nonalcoholics, by comparison, demonstrated essentially no change in affect with alcohol and only a mild increase in psychopathology" (p. 472). At first glance these results would seem to be especially damaging to the tension reduction theory, since alcoholics in particular would be expected to drink in order to reduce tension; yet they show the greatest increase in negative emotional states. However, there are plausible alternative explanations of these data that are consistent with the tension reduction theory.

An obvious explanation is that the initial effect of continued alcohol consumption is one of tension reduction, with subsequent increases in anxiety and depression. At least one of the studies referred to above (Tamerin & Mendelson, 1969) found this to be the case. In other words, the short-term consequences of drinking are negatively reinforcing, while the long-term effects are punishing. Since behavior is usually regulated to a greater degree by short-term rather than long-term consequences, this fact would account for the alcoholic's persistence in continuing to drink.

Hodgson *et al.* (1979) have advanced an alternative to these results in terms of the concept of the relativity of reinforcement. Specifically, they suggested that for the alcoholic the "increase in anxiety which follows prolonged drinking is actually reinforcing if it is less distressing than the frustration, anxiety or withdrawal symptoms that he expects to experience if he stops" (p. 461). Another way of characterizing the same idea is to state that the alcoholic's continued drinking is a partial avoidance response. One of the merits of this interpretation is that it is firmly grounded in recent conceptualizations of avoidance behavior (e.g., Herrnstein, 1969; Seligman & Johnston, 1973). Another is that this line of thinking has been extended to the explanation of obsessive-compulsive behavior in neurotic patients (e.g., Hodgson *et al.*, 1979; Levis & Hare, 1977). Obsessions, for example, are often associated with increased anxiety and emotional distress; yet, they not only persist but are often uncommonly resistant to extinction, as most clinicians will all too readily attest. Treatment strategies that are predicated on the notion that obsessions represent partial avoidance responses appear to be the most promising therapeutic techniques available (e.g., Rachman & Hodgson, 1980). Of course, the success of these treatment techniques does not directly establish the validity of the partial-avoidance-response explanation, but it is strongly suggestive.

Higgins (1976) has similarly challenged the automatic assumption in the alcohol literature that an increase in tension following drinking necessarily contradicts the tension reduction theory. Citing the theoretical analysis of conflict resolution by Brown and Crowell (1964), he suggested that increases in tension in response to alcohol consumption might more properly be interpreted as an *indirect* function of alcohol's tension-reducing effect as opposed to a direct effect of increasing tension. For example, by reducing anxiety, alcohol consumption might facilitate thoughts or actions that bring the person into contact with previously avoided conflict situations, thereby producing a *secondary* increase in anxiety.The advantage of this formulation and of the partial-avoidance-response hypothesis is that they explain otherwise contradictory findings and preserve the viability of the tension reduction theory. The danger, of course, is that these concepts could be used on a post hoc basis to "explain" all apparent discrepancies and thereby render the tension reduction theory critically untestable and hence useless as a scientific theory.

Methodological Problems in Evaluating the Tension Reduction Theory

Overall, research with human subjects on the tension reduction theory has yielded confusing and inconclusive results. Several methodological problems that may have contributed to this muddle and that make unequivocal interpretation of the data difficult can be identified. Among the major problems are the following:

1. The way in which the generic construct of "tension" has been operationalized in different studies complicates comparisons between studies. For example, the threat of receiving an electric shock is very different from the anxiety generated by interpersonal evaluation, as indicated below. Findings from studies using one definition of tension cannot be easily generalized to those of another.

2. Regardless of how the construct of tension is operationalized, a recurrent problem in the experimental literature has been the variable and subjective manner in which tension or anxiety is actually measured. The reliance on a single, subjective measure of anxiety in the majority of studies may help explain the discrepant findings, and it clearly limits the generalizability of the

results. It is now well established that the assessment of anxiety must include multiple measures of the behavioral, physiological, and subjective dimensions of this nonunitary construct (Lang, 1969; Rachman, 1978). In this triple-response-system analysis, changes in one response system may not always be correlated with changes in another; changes may also occur at different rates across the three systems, and each may be differentially affected by different variables.

3. Virtually all studies have failed to control adequately for the effects of expectations about alcohol consumption. The traditional drug-study control of including a placebo condition in which subjects are told that they are receiving alcohol but are actually given a nonalcoholic beverage equates the expectations that alcohol has been administered across groups and isolates the effect of alcohol *per se given this expectation*. However, it does not permit the study of alcohol's effects under different instructional conditions, such as the expectation that a nonalcoholic beverage has been consumed. In order to manipulate the independent factors of both the alcoholic content of a drink and the expectation that alcohol has been consumed, the balanced placebo design is necessary. This design was originally described by Lyerly, Ross, Krugman, and Clyde (1964), and its use in the study of alcohol's effects has been pioneered by Marlatt and his associates (see Marlatt and Rohsenow, 1981, for a comprehensive review of the methodological niceties of this design in alcohol research). The results of a series of studies employing this design have shown conclusively that expectations concerning alcohol consumption can be more important than ethanol's pharmacological impact in influencing such diverse behavior as aggression (Lang, Goeckner, Adesso, & Marlatt, 1975), sexual responsiveness (Briddell, Rimm, Caddy, Krawitz, Sholis, & Wunderlin, 1978; Wilson & Lawson, 1976), and alcohol consumption in both social and problem drinkers (Marlatt, Demming, & Reid, 1973). Research of this nature has clearly shown that cognitive mediating processes such as expectations about drinking must be taken into account in any analysis of the effects of alcohol on human behavior (Marlatt, 1979; Wilson, 1978).

Alcohol and Anxiety: A Social Learning Analysis

One of the reasons for the inattention to cognitive processes in experimental studies of alcohol's effects on tension and other aspects of human functioning has been the limited biomedical or behavioral models on which previous research has been based. A more comprehensive framework for conceptualizing the determinants and consequences of alcohol consumption is provided by social learning theory (Bandura, 1969; Marlatt, 1979; Wilson, 1978). This approach emphasizes the importance of cognitive mediating processes as well as antecedent and consequent situational variables and the pharmacological properties of ethanol in the cause and consequences of drinking. According to this social learning analysis, behavior commonly attributed to alcohol is related to it in a complex fashion (Wilson, 1981). Among the many variables that determine the effect of alcohol on tension and other emotional states are the amount of alcohol that is consumed; the person's prior experience with alcohol; individual differences based on physiological responsiveness to ethanol and specific social learning histories; learned expectations about alcohol and its effects; and the immediate physical and social setting in which drinking occurs. Moreover, alcohol consumption may have different effects on different measures of any particular emotional state such as tension. In view of the influence of all these psychosocial and pharmacological factors on the relationship between alcohol and anxiety, it is simply no longer useful to ask the question: Does alcohol reduce tension? In terms of social learning theory the more meaningful question to pose is: Under what conditions, at which doses, in whom, on what measures, and how does alcohol affect specific forms of tension?

The studies described in the following section are part of an ongoing research program directed toward elucidating the role of the different psychosocial and pharmacological influences listed above in alcohol's effects on social anxiety. Social anxiety was chosen as the target behavior because previous research had indicated that social anxiety or interpersonal evaluation is more likely to elicit drinking than other sources of tension induction that have often been used in studies of the tension reduction hypothesis, such as the threat of an electric shock (Higgins & Marlatt, 1975). In line with this finding, clinical experience strongly suggests that interpersonal anxiety and stressful social situations are among the most common and prominent determinants of alcohol abuse. If alcohol has clinically significant effects on tension, we should be able to demonstrate this relationship using social anxiety as the case in point.

Specifically, the experimental procedure for studying social anxiety in these studies was adapted from Borkovec, Stone, O'Brien, and Kaloupek's (1974) method of asking male subjects to talk to and make as favorable an impression as possible on a female confederate who remained silent and unresponsive during the interaction. Continuous measures of autonomic arousal were taken during this five-minute interaction. Subjects were also aware of the fact that the entire social interaction sequence was being recorded on video tape. This procedure reliably induces anxiety, and Borkovec *et al.* (1974) have shown that it provides a clinically relevant experimental situation. Thus, heart rate measures obtained during the interaction discriminated between socially anxious and nonanxious subjects, did not habituate over repeated measures, and were not influenced by demand characteristics. Moreover, this procedure allows multiple measures of social anxiety–including physiological, subjective, and behavioral indexes–to be made.

Expectations and Alcohol's Effects on Social Anxiety

The tension reduction theory comprises two assumptions: (1) that alcohol consumption reduces tension, and (2) that this tension-reducing effect motivates drinking. The studies in this section are addressed to the first of these assumptions. In the first study, we used the balanced placebo design to partial out the joint and separate effects on social anxiety in male social drinkers of both ethanol and the belief that alcohol had been consumed (Wilson & Abrams, 1977). College students between the ages of 18 and 23 were randomly assigned to the four cells of this 2 × 2 factorial design. The drink administration procedure, which was used in all the studies reported here, was as follows. First, the subject gargled with Chloraseptic mouthwash under the guise that this was important in obtaining accurate estimates from the breathalyzer that was used to measure blood alcohol level (BAL). The real purpose was to reduce the subjects' ability to discriminate the presence or absence of alcohol in their drinks. The operation of the breathalyzer was deliberately explained to each subject to enhance the deception at a later point in the study. The subject was given a breathalyzer test to ensure he had a zero BAL, was shown the reading, and was told how it was estimated.

Thereafter, one of the nurses at the Rutgers Alcohol Behavior Research Laboratory, where all these studies were carried out, delivered to the researcher a tray containing the ingredients for the subject's drink and a Styrofoam cup in which it was to be served. In the condition in which the subject was told that he was to receive an alcoholic beverage, the tray contained a chilled vodka bottle and a bottle of chilled tonic water. The research assistant announced that the subject was in the "experimental group," explaining that this meant that his drink consisted of vodka and tonic. The assistant then proceeded to mix the drink, according to a previously constructed dosage table, in full view of the subject. In the alcohol content condition, the vodka bottle contained 80-proof vodka; in the nonalcoholic content condition, it contained only decarbonated tonic water. In the latter case, the subject's cup had been smeared with alcohol to enhance the credibility of the placebo.

In the condition in which the subject was told that he was to drink a nonalcoholic beverage, the tray contained only a chilled tonic-water bottle. The research assistant announced that the subject was in the "control group," which meant that his drink consisted of tonic water. The rationale given for consuming the tonic was as follows: "In order to keep the experimental procedures constant for all subjects, it is necessary for the control subjects to consume the same volume of beverage as the subjects in the experimental group, who drink an alcoholic beverage. It is only in this way that we can determine that alcohol and not some other difference in the experimental procedure accounts for the results we obtain."

In the alcohol content condition, the tonic bottle contained vodka mixed with tonic; in the nonalcoholic condition, it contained only tonic water. Only the nurse knew the actual content of the bottles, ensuring a double-blind drink-administration procedure. The subject was told how many milliliters of beverage he received and its approximate equivalent in ounces. The mixture of vodka and tonic water consisted of 1 part vodka to 5 parts tonic. In addition, three squirts of lime juice were added to all drinks in all conditions so as to further reduce taste acuity. The alcohol content of the drinks was .5 g of ethanol per kilogram body weight.

Subjects were asked to consume their drinks within 20 min. Following an additional 20-min absorption period, a second breathalyzer test was administered, the results of which were read aloud. Unbeknown to the research assistant, a nurse had specially prepared the breathalyzer for use with the subjects who had been deceived as to the contents of the beverages they had consumed. For subjects who consumed only tonic but who were told that they had also been given vodka, the nurse had preset the BAL indicator to read 40 mg%, when the actual BAL was zero. For subjects who had consumed the vodka-and-tonic mixture but who were led to believe that they had drunk only tonic, the nurse had disconnected the breathalyzer photometer, causing the instrument to indicate a zero BAL. In the latter case, the nurse subsequently reconnected the photometer and obtained the subject's actual BAL reading. At this point the subjects participated in the social interaction described above.

The results were clear-cut. The subjects who believed that they had consumed alcohol showed significantly less increase in heart rate than those who believed that they had consumed tonic only, regardless of the actual content of their drinks. There was no effect of alcohol itself. A self-report measure of anxiety–the Spielberger, Gorsuch, and Lushene (1970) State Anxiety Inventory (STAI)–also showed that the subjects who believed that they had consumed alcohol felt less anxious than their counterparts who believed that they were sober, although this difference only approached statistical significance. As in all the studies reported here, the success of the expectancy manipulation was checked in two ways. First, the subjects' answers on a postexperimental evaluation form in which they were asked what beverage they had consumed showed 100% agreement with the experimental manipulation. Similarly, when asked whether the experimental procedures deviated in any way from what he had been told, no subject indicated any uncertainty about the nature of the beverage he received. Second, the subjects' postsession estimates of the number of ounces of 80-proof alcohol they had consumed were evaluated. Every subject in the two groups who expected only tonic water estimated zero consumption of alcohol. The mean estimates of the subjects in the two "expect-alcohol" conditions were 4.1 and 3.7 ounces. Roughly comparable success in sustaining the deception was achieved in the other studies reported here.

Ratings of the videotapes of the subjects' interactions with the confederate by observers who were unaware of the experimental conditions yielded results strikingly consistent with the heart rate and STAI findings (Woolfolk, Abrams, Abrams, & Wilson, 1979). Since the observers were shown the videotapes without the audio component, their ratings were based on nonverbal cues. The subjects who believed that they had been drinking were rated as more relaxed, less anxious, less inhibited, and more dominant than the subjects who believed that they had consumed only tonic water. The actual content of the drinks had no significant effect on the raters' judgments of the subjects' behavior. It should be noted that these significant observational data were limited to the three female raters. The three male raters were unable to discriminate among the experimental conditions.

To summarize, these results are consistent with the tension reduction theory of alcohol consumption. However, they suggest that this effect of alcohol consumption may be mediated by a different mechanism from one that has been commonly assumed. Rather than the depressant pharmacological action of alcohol on the central nervous system that has always contributed greatly to the plausibility of the tension reduction theory, the present findings indicate that the person's learned expectations about the role of alcohol determine its effects, at least at low to moderate BALs. To borrow once more from Keats, it might be said that escape from tension is mediated not by "Bacchus and his pards," but on the "viewless wings of Poesy"–*poesy* obviously being an archaic form of the more precise and contemporary term *cognition!*

In a similar study, Polivy, Schueneman, and Carlson (1976), using the balanced placebo design, found that alcohol decreased anxiety, whereas the belief that alcohol had been consumed appeared to increase anxiety. The generalizability of these results is limited, since they were based on a single, subjective measure of anxiety (the STAI). However, these data differ sharply from those reported by Wilson and Abrams (1977) and by Woolfolk *et al.* (1979). The major procedural difference between the two studies is that Polivy *et al.* used the threat of an electric shock as their source of anxiety. Although this procedure has its disadvantages (Higgins, 1976), it alone cannot plausibly explain the inconsistency in the findings. Differences in specific subject characteristics provide a more likely explanation, as the data from the following study suggest.

In a second study in my laboratory, we sought to replicate the Wilson and Abrams (1977) findings with female social drinkers (Abrams & Wilson, 1979). Using the same design and experimental procedure, we found that the subjects who believed that they had been drinking showed significantly increased physiological arousal and were rated as more anxious on the observational measures of social behavior than the subjects who believed that they were sober. Self-report measures failed to show any significant differences among the groups. These results confirm the importance of expectations in the effects of alcohol on social anxiety in particular and on human social behavior in general. An interesting aspect of these results is the fact that the direction of the expectation effect differed from our previous finding with male social drinkers. Whereas the belief of having consumed alcohol decreased social anxiety in the men, its effect in the women was to increase anxiety.

The sex difference in anxiety reactions that is shown in these results indicates that caution should be exercised in generalizing about the effects of alcohol on tension or any other aspect of human behavior. The overwhelming majority of studies on the tension reduction theory in particular and in the alcohol literature in general have included only men as subjects. Although it would be premature to draw any conclusion about the existence of a sex difference on the basis of the results discussed here, it might be noted that my research on alcohol and sexual behavior has also revealed a sex difference in sexual arousal in response to alcohol and the belief that alcohol has been consumed (Wilson, 1981).

Rather than there being an overall sex difference in anxiety reactions to alcohol, it may be that the results of the Abrams and Wilson (1979) and Wilson and Abrams (1977) studies reflect the influence of specific subject characteristics that could apply to either males or females. Consistent with this view is the fact that Polivy *et al.*'s (1976) results on the effect of the belief that alcohol had been consumed in male subjects were similar to those of Abrams and Wilson's results with female subjects. Both showed increased anxiety. The women in the Abrams and Wilson study had less drinking experience than their male counterparts, and this potentially critical factor needs to be carefully controlled in future studies before interpretations about sex differences can be made with any confidence. An attempt was made to assess the subjects' expectations about alcohol's effects on anxiety prior to the experiment proper, and men and women reported virtually identical beliefs that alcohol does indeed reduce tension. However, in terms of social learning theory, cognitions about drinking differ across individuals as a function of their unique social learning histories with alcohol and also across settings and at different times, even in the same person (Mischel, 1968).

Given this specificity of cognitive influences, Abrams and Wilson (1979) suggested that the inconsistency between the women's predictions of alcohol's likely effects and their subsequent behavior during the social interaction might be attributable to the particular circumstances of the experimental setting:

> In affirming their belief that alcohol reduces tension, subjects might have been responding to naturally occurring interactions with which they would be more familiar and comfortable. The laboratory setting, by contrast, represented an unfamiliar and possibly unpredictable environment that is anything but comfortable. According to this account, the effects of the expectations of having consumed alcohol are more powerfully moderated by specific psychosocial factors in women than in men. Regardless of its validity . . . both men and women in our society appear to believe that women's resistance to carnal temptation is soluble in alcohol. Since there is also a double standard concerning sexual behavior, women learn to be more wary when they are drinking (or when they believe that they have been drinking). Anecdotal comments from female subjects about their perceived need to monitor their sociosexual behavior when drinking have lent support to this notion. It may be that under less threatening circumstances, the belief that they have consumed alcohol would, in accordance with their self-ratings, reduce tension in women social drinkers. (p. 171)

Presumably it would be possible to select male subjects who would feel equally uneasy in the experimental setting and for whom the belief that they had been drinking would make them feel more vulnerable to social influence and would hence produce an increase in anxiety. In this connection, it is noteworthy that Polivy (personal communication, 1979) has reported that the male subjects in her investigations were a relatively inhibited and "uptight" sample.

The results from the Abrams and Wilson study also highlight the importance of obtaining both objective and subjective measures of anxiety. Had we relied on self-report measures, as has so often been the case in previous research, we would have found little of interest. Undoubtedly, inadequate or overly narrow measures have contributed to the conflicting findings in the literature on the tension reduction theory. The studies described here point out another reason for the mass of contradictory data that Cappell (1975) and others have commented on: the failure in past studies to take account of the critically important effects of psychological set and the experimental setting. The belief that alcohol had been consumed was a more potent determinant of anxiety than the pharmacological properties of a relatively low dose of alcohol in our studies with men and women. Moreover, the same expectancy set had different effects in the male and the female subjects, illustrating both the diversity and the specificity of the cognitive mediating processes of alcohol's effects. There can be little surprise then, at the conflicting findings from previous studies that have often disregarded the importance of such factors. We seem finally to have recognized Washburne's (1956) thoughtful warning about

> a tendency to ignore the important social and psychological variables which help determine behavior in situations where alcohol is being used. Individuals . . . show wide differences in behavior which can be explained only by incorporating psychological and social situational variables. These factors change the actual physiological effects of alcohol, because they can affect the physiological system in just as "real" a way as chemicals. (p. 122)

Increasing Levels of Intoxication and Social Anxiety

The emphasis in this chapter on the psychosocial determinants of drinking and alcohol's effects is not intended to minimize the powerful pharmacological consequences of consuming ethanol. Alcohol is a potent drug, and it follows that its effects are dose-related. With respect to the tension reduction theory, Bandura (1969) concluded that small doses have no consistent effect but that moderate to large quantities may produce substantial reductions in affective arousal. Russell and Mehrabian (1975) predicted that alcohol would reduce anxiety only in large quantities. The available data, however, are conflicting. On the one hand, Kalin, McClelland, and Kahn (1965) reported that social anxiety was reduced only after more than 10 oz of alcohol were consumed. On the other hand, Logue, Gentry, Linnoila, and Erwin (1978) obtained a significant positive relation between increasing doses of alcohol and increases in subjective anxiety. Williams (1966) found that anxiety decreased at low levels of alcohol consumption (4–6 oz) but increased at higher levels (8 oz or more). Methodological difficulties with these studies complicate their interpretation.

A person's prior experience with drinking creates specific expectations about its effects, affects his or her tolerance for alcohol, and can be predicted to influence alcohol's effects on social anxiety. For example, Smith, Parker, and Noble (1975) reported that subjects with greater experience with drinking showed less anxiety during social interaction than comparable subjects with less drinking experience. Accordingly, the third study of tension reduction in my laboratory investigated the effects of both dose and drinking experiences on social anxiety.

Forty-eight male social drinkers were randomly assigned to the six cells of a 2 (drinking experience) × 3 (dose) factorial design. The three dose levels were placebo, .5 g/kg, and 1 g/kg. "Light" and "heavy" social drinkers were selected on the basis of their scores on the Oates and McCoy (1973) drinking profile, which assesses the times, the amount, the context, and the physical consequences of customary alcohol consumption. Light drinkers were those with scores of 18 or less, and heavy drinkers were those with scores of 25 or more. A typical light drinker reported consuming a maximum of 2–3 oz of distilled spirits on any one occasion; drinking only with friends; drinking only in the evening on a weekly basis; and never becoming ill as a result of drinking. A representative heavy drinker reported that he drank 5–6 oz of spirits on an occasion; drank only with friends; drank at lunch, in the afternoon, and in the evening, the latter several times each week; and had become ill as a result of drinking.

Cognitive set regarding the nature of the beverage that the subjects consumed was not experimentally manipulated as in the first two studies, but an attempt was made to control for expectations. All three alcohol doses were administered under the same expectancy set. In a variation of the drink administration procedure described above, the nurse delivered to the researcher a tray containing a chilled bottle of tonic water, a vodka bottle filled with fluid, a beaker, and a Styrofoam cup. In the placebo dose condition, the vodka bottle contained only decarbonated tonic water, and the inside of the Styrofoam cup was smeared with vodka to enhance the credibility of the placebo. In the .5 g/kg dose condition, the vodka bottle was filled with a 160-proof vodka–ethanol mix. Both researcher and subject were blind as to the true contents of the vodka bottle. The researcher announced that the subject would be in the "experimental" group and therefore would receive alcohol. In full view of the subject, the drink was poured according to a previously constructed dose by body weight chart. This chart listed the number of milliliters of 80-proof vodka necessary for a .5 g/kg dose, and the amount of tonic necessary for a 1.5 dilution of the vodka. In all cases, the researcher poured between 2 and 7 oz of fluid from the vodka bottle, depending on subject's body weight. Dosage was determined by the alcohol concentration of the fluid, rather than by volume, since the 160-proof fluid resulted in twice as much ethanol (i.e., 1 g/kg) as the 80-proof vodka. Thus, in all three dose conditions, the subjects were led to believe that they were consuming the same amount of vodka and tonic based on body weight.

Consistent with the tension reduction theory of alcohol's effects, a significant negative relation between dose and an increase in heart rate during the social interaction was found. The more they drank, the less anxious the subjects appeared as measured by this index of autonomic arousal. The mitigating effect of alcohol on the anxiety induced by the social interaction is impressive, since one of the natural effects of alcohol on psychophysiological functioning is an increase in heart rate. The anxiety-reducing effect of alcohol at higher doses seems to supersede the specific physiological impact it has on heart rate under normal conditions. The amount of alcohol consumed also had a significant influence on the observational measures of social anxiety and differed according to the sex of the raters. In line with the heart rate data, the male raters observed the least social anxiety at the highest alcohol dose. However, the fact that they also viewed the subjects as more anxious at the .5 g/kg dose level than at zero BAL is inconsistent with the pattern of the physiological findings. The female raters showed a significantly different pattern. In their observations, the low (.5 g/kg) alcohol dose produced less social anxiety than the placebo dose. To this degree, the tension reduction hypothesis, is supported. Yet, in contrast to the tension reduction hypothesis, the heart rate data, and the male raters' observations, the female raters perceived the subjects to be most anxious at the high alcohol dose. Subjective measures of anxiety failed to discriminate among the experimental conditions, thereby replicating Abrams and Wilson's (1979) results.

An important methodological finding was that the attempt to hold constant the subjects' belief regarding the amount of alcohol they had received was unsuccessful. Subjects' estimates of the amount of alcohol they had consumed differed significantly across all three dose levels. As a result, it is impossible to disentangle the specific effects of ethanol and expectation in this study. This finding emphasizes the importance of checking the expectations that subjects develop rather than simply assuming that experimental instructions produce their intended effect. The subjects' drinking experience had no significant effect on any of the measures. The absence of an effect might be attributable to the way in which this variable was tested. It is likely that more extreme differences between groups of subjects with light and heavy drinking patterns than those tested in the present study might show an effect of drinking pattern. The mean quantity-frequency-variability score of the subjects in the light-drinking pattern group on the Cahalan, Cissin, and Crossley (1969) drinking profile is 1.8 indicating that they are more appropriately seen as moderate drinkers. Subjects whose drinking experience is lighter might respond differently. Similarly, caution must be observed in generalizing these results with heavy drinkers to the alcoholic population.

One of the measures obtained in this study was an index of tolerance-standing stability (static ataxia) under a standard dose of alcohol. Standing stability has been shown to be a sensitive measure of intoxication, and Lipscomp and Nathan (1980) have found that male social drinkers who show the greatest increase in sway under alcohol (subjects defined as low tolerant) respond differently to BAL discrimination training from those who show the least increase in sway (subjects defined as high tolerant). Accordingly, Lipscomb, Nathan, Wilson, and Abrams (1980) divided those subjects in the low (0.5 g/kg) and high (1.0 g/kg) alcohol dose groups in the original Wilson *et al.* (1980) study into high- and low-tolerant groups based on changes in standing stability following alcohol consumption. An analysis of the subjects' reactions along these lines during the anxiety-eliciting social interaction showed that the heart rate of the high-tolerant subjects increased significantly more than that of the low-tolerant subjects. In addition, measures of both skin conductance and heart rate indicated significant dose-by-tolerance interactions. High-tolerant subjects were more aroused than low-tolerant subjects at the low but not at the high dose, a result suggesting that high-tolerant subjects must consume more alcohol in order to experience an autonomic effect comparable to that experienced by low-tolerant subjects.

An intriguing finding from this study is that the low-tolerant groups did not differ in terms of their self-reported drinking patterns. One would assume that the latter would greatly influence the former. Lipscomb and Nathan (1980) have proposed that in young, relatively inexperienced drinkers, tolerance may be more a function of initial reactivity to alcohol than of drinking pattern. This explanation remains speculative until put to the empirical test. Nonetheless, the data from the Wilson *et al.* (1980) investigation seem to have implications for understanding both the role of tolerance in alcohol consumption and the tension-reducing effects of alcohol. The analysis by Lipscomb *et al.* (1980) shows that to the degree that alcohol serves to reduce anxiety, it functions less effectively for the drinker with greater tolerance. As a result, the highly tolerant drinker who has learned through past experience to drink during interpersonally stressful experiences must consume more alcohol to achieve the desired effect. Increasing consumption may lead, in turn, to even higher tolerance, further increasing the dose of alcohol required to reduce or control anxiety. In short, tolerance and the anxiety-reducing effect of alcohol interact to promote continued drinking. Future research must examine these hypothesized mechanisms in older and more experienced drinkers in order to clarify the relation between tolerance as measured by the standing stability test and drinking patterns.

Expectations of Self-Intoxication and Partner's Drinking Dyadic Social Interaction

Alcohol is typically consumed in a social setting, and the interpersonal context can exert a significant influence on consumption and its consequences. By its very presence, alcohol defines a set of social role conditions that can greatly affect behavior (Wilson, 1981). Drinking usually contributes to a more open, looser interpersonal setting in which otherwise socially inhibited actions are disinhibited. The fourth study to be described here investigated the effects on social anxiety of beliefs about which of the partners in a dyadic social interaction had been drinking (Wilson *et al.*, 1979). It was hypothesized that the belief that alcohol had been consumed in the dyadic situation would reduce anxiety in male social drinkers, irrespective of to whom the expectation about drinking was attributed (i.e., to self, other, or both).

Male social drinkers were randomly assigned to the four conditions of a 2 × 2 factorial design that controlled for differential expectations concerning alcohol consumption in a dyadic social interaction. Subjects were led to believe that they had consumed alcohol or tonic water (no alcohol was actually administered) prior to interacting with a female confederate in the manner described in the previous studies. Half of each of these groups were told that the confederate was another subject in the study who had just consumed a moderate amount of alcohol; the other half were simply informed that the confederate was another subject. The results showed that on both the observational and the self-report measures, the subjects who believed that the partner with whom they interacted had been drinking showed less anxiety than their counterparts who did not share this belief. The subjects who had been led to believe that their partner had consumed alcohol were not only rated as less anxious but were also seen as more personally attractive and likable. Despite the failure to find like physiological differences, it seems that at least in the eyes of objective observers, the male social drinker's belief that the female stranger with whom he was interacting had consumed alcohol conferred favorable psychological and interpersonal benefits on him.

In contrast to the earlier finding (Wilson & Abrams, 1977), the subjects' belief that they themselves had consumed alcohol did not significantly mitigate their anxiety during the social interaction. The subjects who held this belief did report less anxiety prior to the social interaction as a result of the drink administration procedure. However, the greater equanimity of these subjects disappeared rapidly during the social interaction iteself. A careful analysis of the heart rate data indicates that these subjects experienced a sudden surge of arousal when they were informed that the female confederate was about to enter the situation. We have speculated that this pattern of arousal indicates the negative rebound effect of a disconfirmed expectation. Subjects who believed that they had consumed alcohol were intially less anxious, presumably because they believed that the alcohol would mitigate their anxiety. However, the palliative effect of this expectation was eroded by the unnerving autonomic feedback that they experienced at the precise point of the female subject's entry. Confronted with their suddenly perceived vulnerability, these subjects displayed even higher levels of anxiety than their counterparts who had not had the initial buffer of believing that they had consumed alcohol. Expectations are a double-edged sword, which when disconfirmed, can produce a swing in the opposite direction of the intended effect (Wilson, 1979).

Do People Drink to Reduce Tension?

The discussion thus far has centered on the question of whether alcohol can reduce tension. The second assumption of the tension reduction theory is that this effect of alcohol motivates drinking. As noted in the introduction, both social and problem drinkers assert that this is one of the major reasons for drinking. The laboratory evidence on this part of the tension reduction theory is not free from conflicting findings, although some studies provide strong support for the notion. For example, Higgins and Marlatt (1975) showed that anticipation of interpersonal evaluation produced significantly increased consumption of alcohol. An earlier study by the same researchers, using threat of electric shock as the source of anxiety, failed to show significant results (Higgins & Marlatt, 1973). Miller, Hersen, Eisler, and Hillsman (1974) found that negative social evaluation in a role-playing situation resulted in significantly greater drinking by alcoholics but not nonalcoholic subjects, although there were no differences in physiological arousal between the two groups. This differential effect of anxiety on alcoholics and nonalcoholics can be accommodated by postulating that the social drinkers in this study were insufficiently experienced to have learned this strategy for coping with tension.

If people drink to reduce tension, it can be predicted that providing them with alternative means of coping with that tension would reduce, if not eliminate, the negative reinforcing function of alcohol consumption. Indeed, this is the central basis for commonly used behavior-therapy techniques such as social skills training (e.g., Chaney *et al.*, 1978) and relaxation training (e.g., Marlatt & Marques, 1977). Laboratory studies bear out this prediction. Marlatt, Kosturn, and Lang (1975) showed that subjects who had been angered and who were given the opportunity to retaliate against the aggressor subsequently drank less than subjects who were denied the opportunity to express their aggression. Similarly, relaxation training has been found to reduce drinking in subjects who anticipated an anxiety-provoking interpersonal evaluation (Strickler, Tomaszewski, Maxwell, & Suib, 1979).

In the fifth study in the series of investigations of the tension reduction theory reported here, Wilson and Lipscomb (1980) first exposed chronic alcoholics to the social interaction task used in the previous experiments. Thereafter, their consumption of alcohol was measured unobtrusively. Each subject served as his own control in a counterbalanced design in which the same opportunity to drink was provided the subjects under nonstressful conditions. Although the social interaction reliably induced high levels of social anxiety as indicated by the measures of autonomic arousal and confirmed by the subjects themselves, drinking was not significantly greater following the anxiety-eliciting interaction than following the nonstressful control procedure.

The likely reason for this latter failure to find support for the tension reduction theory is that tension is not tension is not tension. As Higgins and Marlatt (1975) pointed out in their analysis of why some situations seem to trigger drinking while others do not, alcohol consumption increases only in those particular situations that are defined as stressful by the individual subject and in which she or he expects alcohol to reduce tension. To predict otherwise would be to fly in the face of a cardinal tenet of social learning theory, namely, that assessments of the determinants of drinking must be tailored to the individual. This is undoubtedly one of the reasons that behavior therapists, who routinely conduct such individually based assessments of their clients' behavioral problems, have often reported that tension is a major antecedent of problem drinking. The attempt to develop a standardized procedure for generating anxiety in the laboratory setting may be inherently self-limiting, since it can never capture the idiographic nature of the specific psychosocial situations that provoke drinking in the natural environment. Simply ensuring that anxiety per se is generated, as in the Wilson and Lipscomb study reported here, does not suffice, since not all anxiety, even interpersonal anxiety, necessarily triggers increased drinking.

Conclusion

The results of the studies described here show that the effects of alcohol on social anxiety are governed by a complex set of psychosocial and pharmacological variables. Instead of inquiring about whether alcohol does reduce tension, the more useful question to investigate is under what conditions, at which doses, in whom, and on what measures alcohol reduces anxiety. Clearly, alcohol does reduce tension under some circumstances, and to this degree, the first assumption of the tension reduction theory has been validated. The fact that several studies have produced conflicting evidence need not be cause for discarding the tension reduction theory. Rather, this contradictory evidence means that the particular variables that determine alcohol's effects on anxiety have not been specified and that the theory must be refined to accommodate these different and often complex influences.

A major finding of the research presented here concerns the important role that cognitive mediating processes play in regulating alcohol's effects on social anxiety. The belief that alcohol has been consumed can exert a greater influence on behavior than the pharmacological impact of ethanol, at least at a low BAL. Moreover, these expectations can either decrease or increase social anxiety, depending on individual subject characteristics that remain to be fully identified. This expectancy effect applies not only to beliefs about self-intoxication but also extends to beliefs about one's partner in dyadic social interaction. The significanceof cognitive processes such as expectations has been largely overlooked in past research on the tension reduction theory, an oversight that may well have contributed to the often equivocal or contradictory evidence in this area.

The research described here emphasizes another reason for the conflicting evidence in the literature: the lack of adequate measures of anxiety. Multiple measures of the three main response systems–physiological, behavioral, and subjective–are essential if a comprehensive picture of the effects of alcohol on tension is to emerge. Failure to include all three measurement domains in the studies reported here would have led to very different conclusions. Neither tension nor anxiety is a unitary construct, and it is unreasonable to expect that different measures of these constructs will necessarily correlate well under different conditions. Future research that maps out the ways in which alcohol effects these three response systems and the interactions among them will go far toward clarifying the relationship between alcohol and anxiety.

The results reported here have theoretical, methodological, and clinical significance. From a theoretical viewpoint, the replicated finding of the critical importance of expectations in mediating alcohol's effects underscores the necessity of taking account of cognitive processes in any conceptual account of the determinants and consequences of alcohol consumption (Marlatt, 1979; Wilson, 1978). Methodologically speaking, the subjects' cognitive set about their drinking should be considered more seriously in subsequent research in this area. Subjects' expectations about their drinking and their potential effect on behavior must be assessed directly and must not merely be inferred from the subjects' performance. One of the significant lessons we have learned from the recent explosion of research on fear reduction processes in behavior therapy has been that simply labeling a procedure a placebo does not guarantee that this procedure equates for the specific variables (e.g., expectation of therapeutic outcome or credibility of the treatment rationale) it was designed to control. Finally, the balanced placebo design should be used more widely in order to partial out the effects of expectation of alcohol consumption and drinking *per se*. Particularly important would be methodological strategies for isolating these effects at higher BALs than those reported here.

In some ways, laboratory research on the tension reduction theory has lagged behind what therapists "knew" to be the case based on their treatment of individual problem drinkers. The results described will come as no surprise to most practitioners, and until single-case experimental designs are used in the analysis of drinking as a form of negative reinforcement, it is unlikely that the second assumption of the tension reduction theory will be tested adequately. However, there is one respect in which the findings here should influence clinical practice. These data emphasize the significance of cognitive processes in mediating alcohol's effects. The implications are that clinical assessment and treatment should increasingly reflect this emphasis on cognition in behavior change techniques. Treatment approaches rooted in outdated biomedical models and simplistic notions of "disease" as well as behavioristic models that concentrate exclusively on environmental determinants and consequences of drinking, are no longer tenable conceptual frameworks for understanding and treating alcohol-related problems. A broader view, such as the social learning account that incorporates an emphasis on cognitive mediating processes, provides a more compelling alternative.

ACKNOWLEDGMENTS

I wish to express my gratitude to David B. Abrams, Thomas R. Lipscomb, Peter E. Nathan, and Etienne Perold for their assistance in the research program that is described here.

References

Abrams, D. B., & Wilson, G. T. Effects of alcohol on social anxiety in women: Cognitive versus physiological processes. *Journal of Abnormal Psychology*, 1979, *88*, 161–173.

Bandura, A. *Principles of behavior modification.* New York: Holt, Rinehart & Winston, 1969.

Borkovec, T. D., Stone, N. M., O'Brien, G. T., & Kaloupek, D. G. Evaluation of a clinically relevant target behavior for analogue outcome research. *Behavior Therapy*, 1974, *5*, 504–514.

Briddell, D. W., Rimm, D. C., Caddy, G. R., Krawitz, G., Sholis, D., & Wunderlin, R. J. Effects of alcohol and cognitive set on sexual arousal to deviant stimuli. *Journal of Abnormal Psychology*, 1978, *87*, 418–430.

Brown, J. S., & Crowell, C. R. Alcohol and conflict resolution: A theoretical analysis. *Quarterly Journal of Studies on Alcohol*, 1964, *35*, 66–85.

Brown, S. A., Goldman, M. S., Inn, A., & Anderson, L. R. Expectations of reinforcement from alcohol: Their domain and relation to drinking patterns. *Journal of Consulting and Clinical Psychology*, 1980, *48*, 419–426.

Cahalan, D., Cissin, I. H., & Crossley, H. M. *American drinking practices.* New Brunswick, N.J.: Center of Alcohol Studies, 1969.

Cappell, H. An evaluation of tension models of alcohol consumption. In R. J. Gibbins, Y. Israel, H. Kalant, R. E. Popham, W. Schmidt, & R. G. Smart (Eds.), *Research advances in alcohol and drug problems*, Vol. 2. New York: Wiley, 1975.

Cappell, H., & Herman, C. P. Alcohol and tension reduction: A review. *Quarterly Journal of Studies on Alcohol*, 1972, *33*, 33–64.

Chaney, E., O'Leary, M., & Marlatt, G. A. Skill training with alcoholics. *Journal of Consulting and Clinical Psychology*, 1978, *46*, 1092–1104.

Deardorff, C. M., Melges, F. T., Hout, C. N., & Savage, D. J. Situations related to drinking alcohol. *Journal of Studies on Alcohol*, 1975, *36*, 1184–1195.

Edwards, G. J. Motivation for drinking among men: Survey of a London suburb. *Psychological Medicine*, 1972, *2*, 260–271.

Falk, J. L., & Tang, M. Animal model of alcoholism: Intrigue and progress. In M. M. Gross (Ed.), *Alcohol intoxication and withdrawal*, Vol. 3, New York: Plenum Press, 1977.

Herrnstein, R. J. Method and theory in the study of avoidance. *Psychological Review*, 1969, *76*, 46–69.

Higgins, R. Experimental investigations of tension reduction models of alcoholism. In G. Goldstein & C. Menninger (Eds.), *Empirical studies of alcoholism*. Cambridge, Mass.: Ballinger, 1976.

Higgins,R., & Marlatt,G. A. The effects of anxiety arousal on the consumption of alcohol by alcoholics and social drinkers. *Journal of Consulting and Clinical Psychology*, 1973, *41*, 426–433.

Higgins, R., & Marlatt, G. A. Fear of interpersonal evaluation as a determinant of alcohol consumption in male social drinkers. *Journal of Abnormal Psychology*, *84*, 644–651.

Hodgson, R. J., Stockwell, T. R., & Rankin, H. J. Can alcohol reduce tension? *Behaviour Research and Therapy*, 1979, *17*, 459–466.

Kalin, R., McClelland, D. C., & Kahn, M. The effects of male social drinking on fantasy. *Journal of Personality and Social Psychology*, 1965, *1*, 441–452.

Lang, A. R., Goeckner, D. J., Adesso, V. J., & Marlatt, G. A. Effects of alcohol on aggression in male social drinkers. *Journal of Abnormal Psychology*, 1975, *84*, 508–518.

Lang, P. J. The mechanics of desensitization and the laboratory study of fear. In C. M. Franks (Ed.),*Behavior therapy: Appraisal and status*. New York: McGraw-Hill, 1969.

Lazarus, A. A. Toward the understanding and effective treatment of alcoholism. *South African Medical Journal*, 1965, *39*, 736–741.

Levis, D. J., & Hare, N. A review of the theoretical rationale and empirical support for the extinction approach of implosive (flooding) therapy. In M. Hersen, R. M. Eisler, & P. M. Miller (Eds.), *Progress in behavior modification*, Vol. 4. New York: Academic Press, 1977.

Lipscomb, T. R., & Nathan, P. E. Effect of family history of alcoholism, drinking pattern and tolerance on blood ethanol level discrimination. *Archives of General Psychiatry*, 1980, *37*, 571–576.

Lipscomb, T. R., Nathan, P. E., Wilson, G. T., & Abrams, D. B. Effects of tolerance on the anxiety-reducing function of ethanol. *Archives of General Psychiatry*, 1980, *37*, 577–582.

Litman, G. K., Eiser, J. R., Rawson, N. S. B., & Oppenheim, A. M. Differences in relapse precipitants and coping behaviors between alcohol relapses and survivors. *Behaviour Research and Therapy*, 1979, *17*, 89–94.

Lyerly, S. B., Ross, S., Krugman, A. D., & Clyde,D. J. Drugs and placebo. *Journal of Abnormal and Social Psychology*, 1964, *68*, 321–327.

Marlatt, G. A. Alcohol, stress and cognitive control. In I. G. Sarason & C. D. Spielberger (Eds.), *Stress and anxiety*, Vol. 3. Washington, D.C.: Hemisphere Publishing, 1976.

Marlatt, G. A. Alcohol use and problem drinking: A cognitive-behavioral analysis. In P. Kendall & S. Hollon (Eds.), *Cognitive-behavioral interventions: Theory, research, and procedures*. New York: Academic Press, 1979.

Marlatt, G. A., & Gordon, J. R. Determinants of relapse: Implications for the maintenance of behavior change. In P. Davidson (Ed.), *Behavioral medicine: Changing health lifestyles*. New York: Brunner/Mazel, 1979.

Marlatt, G. A., & Marques, J. K. Meditation, self-control, and alcohol use. In R. B. Stuart (Ed.), *Self management: Strategies, techniques and results*. New York: Brunner/Mazel, 1977.

Marlatt, G. A., & Rohsenow, D. J. Cognitive processes in alcohol use: Expectancy and the balanced placebo design. In N. K. Mello (Ed.), *Advances in substance abuse: Behavioral and biological research*. Greenwich, Conn.: JAI Press, 1980.

Marlatt, G. A., Demming, B., & Reid, J. Loss of control drinking in alcoholics. *Journal of Abnormal Psychology*, 1973, *81*, 233–241.

Marlatt,G. A., Kosturn, C. F., & Lang, A. R. Provocation to anger and opportunity for retaliation as determinants of alcohol consumption in social drinkers. *Journal of Abnormal Psychology*, 1975, *84*, 652–659.

McNamee, H. B., Mello, N. K., & Mendelson, J. H. Experimental analysis of drinking patterns of alcoholics: Concurrent psychiatric observations. *American Journal of Psychiatry*, 1968, *124*, 1063–1069.

Mendelson, J. H., La Dou, J., & Solomon, P. Experimentally induced chronic intoxication and withdrawal in alcoholics, III: Psychiatric findings. *Quarterly Journal of Studies on Alcohol*, 1964, *2*, 40–52.

Miller, P., Hersen, M., Eisler, R., & Hillsman, G. Effects of social stress on operant drinking of alcoholics and social drinkers. *Behaviour Research and Therapy*, 1974, *12*, 67–72.

Mischel, W. *Personality and assessment*. New York: Wiley, 1968.

Nathan, P. E., & O'Brien, J. S. An experimental analysis of the behavior of alcoholics and nonalcoholics during prolonged experimental drinking. *Behavior Therapy*, 1971, *2*, 455–476.

Oates, J. F., & McCoy, R. T. *Laboratory evaluation of alcohol safety interlock systems, Volume 3: Instrument performance at high BALs*. Report to the Highway Research Institute, National Highway Traffic Safety Administration, Department of Transportation, Washington, D.C., 1973.

Polivy, J., Schueneman, A. L., & Carlson, K. Alcohol and tension reduction: Cognitive and physiological effects. *Journal of Abnormal Psychology*, 1976, *85*, 595–600.

Rachman, S. *Fear and courage*. San Francisco: Freeman, 1978.

Rachman, S., & Hodgson, R. *Obsessions and compulsions*. Englewood Cliffs, N.J.: Prentice-Hall, 1980.

Russell, J. A., & Mehrabian, A. The mediating role of emotions in alcohol use. *Journal of Studies on Alcohol*, 1975, *36*, 1508–1536.

Seligman, M. E. P., & Johnston, J. A cognitive theory of avoidance learning. In J. McGuigan & B. Lumsden (Eds.), *Contemporary approaches to conditioning and learning*. New York: Wiley, 1973.

Smith, R. C., Parker, E. S., & Noble, E. Alcohol and affect in dyadic social interaction. *Psychosomatic Medicine*, 1975, *37*, 25–40.

Spielberger, C. D., Gorsuch, R. L., & Lushene, R. E. *The state-trait anxiety inventory (test manual)*. Palo Alto, Calif.: Consulting Psychologists Press, 1970.

Strickler, D. P., Tomaszewski, P., Maxwell, W., & Suib, M. R. The effects of relaxation instructions on drinking behavior in the presence of stress. *Behaviour Research and Therapy*, 1979, *17*, 45–52.

Tamerin, J. S., & Mendelson, J. H. The psychodynamics of chronic inebriation: observations of alcoholics during the process of drinking in an experimental group setting. *American Journal of Psychiatry*, 1969, *125*, 886–889.

Washburne, C. Alcohol, self and the group. *Quarterly Journal of Studies on Alcohol*, 1956, *17*, 108–123.

Williams, A. F. Social drinking, anxiety, and depression. *Journal of Personality and Social Psychology*, 1966, *3*, 689–693.

Wilson, G. T. Booze, beliefs and behavior: Cognitive factors in alcohol use and abuse. In P. E. Nathan, G. A. Marlatt, & T. Loberg (Eds.), *Alcoholism: New directions in behavioral research and treatment*. New York: Plenum Press, 1978.

Wilson, G. T. Perceived control and the theory and practice of behavior therapy. In L. C. Perlmuter & R. A. Monty (Eds.), *Choice and perceived control*. Hillsdale, N.J.: Lawrence Erlbaum, 1979.

Wilson, G. T. The effects of alcohol on human sexual behavior. In N. K. Mello (Ed.), *Advances in substance abuse: Behavioral and biological research*. Greenwich, Conn.: JAI Press, 1981.

Wilson, G. T., & Abrams, D. B. Effects of alcohol on social anxiety and physiological arousal: Cognitive versus pharmacological processes. *Cognitive Therapy and Research*, 1977, *1*, 195–210.

Wilson, G. T., & Lawson, D. M. Expectancies, alcohol and sexual arousal in male social drinkers. *Journal of Abnormal Psychology*, 1976, *85*, 587–594.

Wilson, G. T., & Lipscomb, T. L. *Effects of inducing social anxiety on alcohol consumption*. Unpublished manuscript, Rutgers University, 1980.

Wilson, G. T., Perold, E. A., & Abrams, D. B. *The effects of expectations on self-intoxication and partners drinking on anxiety in dyadic social interaction*. Unpublished manuscript, Rutgers University, 1979.

Wilson, G. T., Abrams, D. B., & Lipscomb, T. L. Effects of increasing levels of intoxication and drinking pattern on social anxiety. *Journal of Studies on Alcohol*, 1980, *41*, 250–264.

Woolfolk, A., Abrams, L., Abrams, D. B., & Wilson, G. T. Effects of alcohol on nonverbal communication of anxiety: The impact of beliefs on nonverbal behavior. *Environmental Psychology and Nonverbal Behavior*, 1979, *2*, 205–218.

CHAPTER 7

Controlled Drinking

A Concept Coming of Age

Mark B. Sobell and Linda C. Sobell

Clinical Institute
Addiction Research Foundation
33 Russell Street
Toronto, Ontario, Canada

In terms of self-regulation of behavior, it can be argued that alcohol problems stand apart from other types of substance abuse. The differences derive not from scientific findings but from popular beliefs. Public attitudes generally view excessive eating, smoking, and use of drugs as largely under an individual's control. Thus, it has been popularly assumed that people engage in these excessive behaviors by choice. Popular conceptions of alcohol problems, however, are somewhat more clouded. While there appears to be considerable ambiguity about the nature and treatment of alcohol problems among the general public, a majority of paraprofessionals and professionals in the alcohol field have long supported an ideology that views alcohol problems as largely beyond an individual's control. This stance has greatly complicated research and treatment directed toward exploring the extent to which alcohol abusers can control their drinking.

This chapter considers issues of self-control over alcohol on two levels. The first is an overview of scientific investigations of control over drinking and the development of effective treatment interventions aimed at control. The second is the way in which such information can influence typical treatment practices and notions about the nature of alcohol problems.

A brief history of the alcohol field is presented so that those unfamiliar with the field will have an appropriate context for understanding the issues raised in this chapter. Following that history, empirical evidence derived from basic research, applied research, and follow-up studies is summarized as providing strong evidence that control over drinking is within an individual's capacity. Then, a more difficult question is considered: Since control is possible, in what instances and for what individuals might control enhancement strategies be suitable or desirable? A necessary consideration in this regard is how traditionalists in the alcohol field have reacted to the research evidence and the suggestion that control enhancement might have value. Attention is also devoted here to caveats regarding the advocacy of self-regulation approaches. Finally, the current state of alcohol treatment practice and ideology is addressed.

At present, the alcohol field can be described as being in serious ideological crisis. Although Thomas Kuhn (1970) developed his theory of paradigmatic change and scientific revolution to describe changes in the physical sciences, the alcohol field, in many ways, can currently be characterized as being in a state of scientific and ideological revolution. In this regard, the ways in which control enhancement strategies have had an impact on the alcohol field provide a good example of the differences that can exist between science and practice, and evidence and beliefs. Others might derive valuable lessons from the experiences of the alcohol field. When evidence contradicts strongly held beliefs, that evidence is likely to be resisted. The road to acceptance is at best difficult and slow.

The Origins of Traditional Ideology

Scientific clinical studies of alcohol problems were largely nonexistent prior to the 1960s. Nevertheless, despite its lack of a scientific basis, a popular and highly influential conceptualization of alcohol problems developed. These popular ideas derived from the only available resources: the experiences of persons who had alcohol problems and the clinical experiences of those who had to deal with the pervasive consequences of drinking problems. These popular ideas, which have been described by Pattison, Sobell, and Sobell (1977) as the traditional model of alcoholism, became the determining principles on which treatment procedures were formulated. In fact, it has been argued by some that these beliefs have become so reified by workers in the alcohol field, that the defense of and the proselytization for the traditional model have taken on evangelical religious fervor. Perhaps largely because of such actions, alcohol problems have come to be recognized as extremely serious and pervasive health problems, and they have become the focus of intensive scientific study. The widespread acceptance of traditional concepts, however, has also provided the foundation for contemporary controversy.

The sources of the traditional model are diverse, but there are two main sources that have to a great extent formed the basis of those ideas. These are the ideology of Alcoholics Anonymous (1939) and the disease concept of alcoholism formulated by the late E.M. Jellinek (1960).

Alcoholics Anonymous (AA) has been the most successful of several self-help movements that became quite active in the United States during the post-Depression era, when concerns for human welfare were championed. In part, its development can be traced to a pervasive noninvolvement by professionals with individuals suffering from alcohol problems. Alcoholics Anonymous filled a void characterized by a lack of interest and a verbalized antipathy on the part of health-care providers. The AA notion of alcohol problems, first published in the 1930s, was simplistic and was also congruent with the then existing medical science. The plight of the alcohol abuser was characterized as deriving from psychological and medical aberrations. The alcoholic was said to suffer from an allergy to alcohol. The allergy referred to was the development of a physical dependence on alcohol, and it was postulated that after some years of drinking experience, some individuals–alcoholics–developed such an allergy that even the consumption of a minute amount of alcohol would often initiate physical dependence. The physically dependent state, sometimes characterized by "cravings," was thought to be such that the person had to continue drinking in order to avoid the onset of alcohol withdrawal symptoms. Furthermore, it was explained that the reason individuals continue to initiate drinking despite being vulnerable to physical dependence and having suffered serious detrimental consequences from their previous drinking was that they were afflicted with an "obsession." This obsession was experienced as a powerful desire to drink in a normal and non-dependence-inducing fashion. Two quotations from the book *Alcoholics Anonymous* (1939) best illustrate how AA perceived the chronic alcohol abuser as lacking the ability to self-regulate his or her drinking:

> The idea that somehow, someday he will control and enjoy his liquor drinking is the great obsession of every abnormal drinker. (p. 41)

> We believe . . . that the action of the alcohol on these chronic alcoholics is a manifestation of an allergy; that the phenomenon of craving is limited to this class and never occurs in the average temperate drinker. These allergic types can never safely use alcohol in any form at all. (p. 4)

While Jellinek had a more comprehensive and scientific orientation to alcohol problems, he explicitly acknowledged that his views were not empirically grounded. His theory was developed primarily to meet humanitarian and sociopolitical needs rather than to synthesize scientific findings. More specifically, he hoped to encourage medical practitioners to assume the responsibility for dealing with the serious medical complications related to alcohol problems, and to change societal attitudes about alcohol abusers from a moral and legal posture to one of concern for human welfare. Only those parts of Jellinek's theory relevant to control issues are summarized here.

Jellinek essentially gave scientific statement to the basic ideas of AA, although he dispensed abruptly with the notion of a physical allergy to alcohol. He also postulated a psychological explanation why a previously addicted drinker should choose to drink again, after a period of not drinking. Jellinek, however, viewed this psychological impetus to drink as a "compulsion" whereby the individual had learned to drink to excess as a way of coping with emotional problems. The origin of the individual's alcohol problems was that as tolerance to alcohol developed with repeated drinking experiences, the individual had to drink more to achieve the desired effect. Some individuals, Jellinek postulated, after enough drinking experiences, developed a sensitivity to alcohol similar to that described in the allergy concepts of AA. That is, they experienced changes in their physiology so that the consumption of a small amount of alcohol was sufficient to initiate physical dependence. When such a person drank, he or she experienced what Jellinek chose to call a "loss of control" over drinking. Therefore, it was not that persons lacked volitional control over their behavior, but that they could not simultaneously stop drinking and avoid withdrawal symptoms. Thus, they were compelled to continue drinking in order to forestall an alcohol withdrawal reaction. It deserves mention that Jellinek purposely phrased his ideas in this regard as a "working hypothesis" that might, as a result of research, be found in need of modification.

While Jellinek did not explicitly address the question of reversibility, it is clear from his collective writings that he thought that the physiological changes causing physical dependence could not be remediated. Consequently, both Jellinek and AA strongly emphasized abstinence as a treatment goal, because in their view an individual who had been previously addicted to alcohol could never drink again without rapidly initiating a process of physical dependence. If this, in fact, were the case, questions of control or self-regulation of drinking would be moot. Amazingly, however, even as late as 1960, the development of physical dependence in alcoholics had not been experimentally investigated.

Basic Research on Control over Drinking

Behavioral research on drinking behavior and alcohol problems received its first major impetus from the pioneering work of Mendelson, LaDou, and

Solomon (see Mendelson, 1964) in the early 1960s. From a series of daring studies that examined the drinking behavior of chronic alcoholics within a controlled experimental setting came the first glimmer of evidence that a substantial conflict might exist between traditional ideology and empirical evidence. In one of the earliest studies, Mendelson *et al.* (1964) reported that 10 chronic alcoholics who received up to 24 oz of 86-proof alcohol daily for several days developed no cravings for alcohol. Similar evidence is now prodigious in amount, constituting well over 100 reports. This review, describes only a sampling of those studies.

In 1966, Merry reported a double-blind study using a within-subjects design. Nine alcoholics were at some times administered vitamin mixture solutions containing small amounts of alcohol and were at other times administered the same mixture but with the alcohol replaced by water. It was found that the subjects reported more cravings when a less concentrated or control solution was administered than when the most concentrated alcohol solution was ingested.

In a similar study, Engle and Williams (1972) investigated the effects of 1 oz of vodka on alcoholics' desire for alcohol. Forty chronic alcoholics who were in a residential treatment program served as subjects in a balanced placebo design. In this design, half of the subjects received 1 oz of vodka in a heavily flavored vitamin solution, while the other half received a placebo solution. Then, a random half of the subjects in each of the groups were told that they had received a solution containing alcohol. Since all the subjects had been receiving a nonalcohol vitamin solution daily prior to the test day, they were used to completing a daily questionnaire inquiring about cravings for alcohol. Therefore, after consuming their beverages on the test day, all subjects completed the cravings questionnaire as usual (the subjects were unaware of the test day). The results indicated that the different groups of subjects reported no differences in cravings for alcohol. Finally, as a behavioral indication of desires for alcohol, the subjects were told at the time they completed the questionnaire that, if they felt the need, they could request an additional drink. Interestingly, the one subject who did request an additional drink had been told that he had received alcohol when, in fact, he had received the placebo solution. Engle and Williams concluded that "no evidence was found for a physiological relation between one drink of alcohol and an increased desire for alcohol in the alcoholic" (p. 1103).

In 1973, Marlatt, Demming, and Reid introduced the taste test as an analogue and unobtrusive measure of drinking behavior. In the taste test, the subjects were informed that they were to compare and rate a variety of beverages for their taste characteristics. At the conclusion of the taste test, the total amount of beverage consumed by each subject was determined and constituted an unobtrusive measure of alcohol consumption. That is, for subjects who believed that the purpose of the test actually was a taste comparison (usually an effective manipulation as determined by postexperimental assessment), the alcohol consumption was measured without their awareness. Combining this task with a balanced placebo design, Marlatt and his colleagues investigated the effects of a priming dose of alcohol on the drinking of alcoholics and nonalcoholics. Half of the subjects were told that they would be comparing different vodka-and-tonic mixed drinks, and half were told that they would be comparing different types of tonic. Then, within each instructional group, half were actually given the beverage containing vodka (which by pretest was found to be indistinguishable from tonic water alone), and half were simply given tonic to rate in the taste test.

The important feature of the results of the Marlatt *et al.* (1973) study was that the amount of beverage consumed by both the alcoholic and the nonalcoholic subjects was primarily determined by the instructions rather than by the actual beverage content. In both beverage conditions, the alcoholic subjects consumed more total beverage than the nonalcoholics. However, both the alcoholic and the nonalcoholic subjects consumed more total beverage when they had been led to think that the beverage contained alcohol, whether or not it actually did.

As part of a controlled intoxication experiment, Paredes, Hood, Seymour, and Gollob (1973) investigated the loss-of-control phenomenon and the effects of chronic alcohol consumption on alcoholics. For 30 of the 131 total subjects, the experimental paradigm included a drinking schedule that required two consecutive days of drinking to a maintained blood alcohol concentration of 0.14%, a level reached by the consumption of approximately 7–8 oz of whiskey in an hour's time. It was found that no subject experienced alcohol withdrawal symptoms on cessation of drinking. Further, although all 131 subjects were free to discontinue their participation in the experiment at any time, it was found that the risk of not completing the five-week program tended to be greater for nondrinking subjects than for those assigned to the two scheduled drinking days. These investigators concluded that "The loss of control hypothesis as commonly understood is not supported by empirical evidence" (p. 1155).

In another study, Cohen, Liebson, Faillace, and Speers (1971) found that chronic hospitalized alcoholics who had access to 24 oz of 95-proof ethanol per day could either abstain or drink in a controlled fashion, if they were provided monetary incentives ranging from $7 to $20 per day. The financial reward could be earned by drinking exactly 5 oz of the beverage on a given day. As a result of these contingencies, all the subjects were able to demonstrate well-controlled drinking behavior. Similar kinds of control over drinking behavior were also elicited when the consequences involved gaining access to an enriched environment (Cohen, Liebson, Faillace, & Allen, 1971).

Another set of studies has examined the effects of the acute consumption of large amounts of alcohol and has similarly found that alcoholics do not experience a rapid onset of physical dependence on alcohol. For example, in early work done at Patton State Hospital in California, we conducted several studies in which chronic alcoholics consumed from 1 to 16 oz of 86-proof ethanol (reviewed in Sobell & Sobell, 1978). Of 214 chronic alcoholic subjects who were housed in an inpatient open ward, none experienced any alcohol withdrawal symptoms following their drinking sessions, and only 7 (3.3%), left the hospital to get more alcohol.

A questionnaire study conducted at Patton State Hospital with 30 chronic alcoholics sheds additional light on the relevance of environmental factors to drinking behavior (Sobell, Sobell, & Christelman, 1972). In that study, almost all of the subjects believed that they could ingest either 1 or 16 drinks and then stop if they were in a controlled hospital setting. However, less that one-quarter of those subjects thought they could stop after consuming 16 drinks if they were in their natural environment. These findings suggest that the subjects had a more realistic conceptualization of their own drinking than the traditional concepts that have attempted to describe their behavior.

Demonstrations that the chronic consumption of alcohol does not initiate a process of physical dependence have been produced using populations clearly within the domain of the traditional concepts of alcoholism. These studies have involved state hospital alcoholics, skid row alcoholics, and chronic alcoholics at Veterans Administration hospitals. Collectively, these studies indicate that even in chronic alcoholics, physical dependence on alcohol is not a consequence of the consumption of just a few alcoholic drinks or even initial alcohol intoxication. In fact, when physical dependence has not occurred, even chronic alcoholics can provide surprising demonstrations of control over their drinking. These studies, however, should not be taken as indicating that physical dependence on alcohol does not occur. Similar studies of chronic intoxication in alcoholics have produced evidence of physical dependence. However, such dependence typically ensues only when consumption occurs in large quantities. (e.g., 40 oz of whiskey per day) and over a substantial period of time, usually a few days (e.g., Gross, 1973). This is not to say that individuals who have had serious drinking problems can easily control their drinking in their natural environment, but the cumulative evidence distinctly implies that the critical variables involved in making drinking decisions—and also decisions not to drink—are motivational and environmental rather than physical.

Applied Research on Control over Drinking: Treatment and Follow-up Studies

There are three major sources of data concerning whether persons who have suffered alcohol problems can acquire a pattern of drinking without experiencing adverse consequences (nonproblem drinking). The three sources are epidemiological studies, follow-up studies of treated alcoholics, and experimental trials of treatments specifically aimed at achieving moderation. Although limited in number, a few studies have investigated the natural history of individuals who have had alcohol problems. These studies (reviewed by Pattison *et al.*, 1977, and others) have consistently shown a substantial incidence of spontaneous remission of drinking problems.

An impressive amount of data has resulted from studies that have investigated treatment outcomes for traditionally treated alcoholics and alcohol abusers, and from a small number of experimental treatment programs. In 1977, Pattison *et al.* cited 74 such studies, and a year later, Sobell added 7 additional studies to that review. Such evidence continues to proliferate. In fact, the number of such studies probably now exceeds 100. Why these studies have been relatively ignored and what the response of traditionalists is to these studies are considered later in this chapter. For now, it suffices to describe a few general characteristics of those studies.

First, it is useful to consider the types of individuals we are talking about. Over the years, definitions of *alcoholism* have varied, and to some extent, that term has become meaningless. When defining alcoholism, two crucial distinctions tend to recur. First, has the individual suffered any identifiable adverse life consequences as a result of using alcohol? Second, has the individual experienced physical dependence on alcohol as indicated by the presence of withdrawal symptoms on the cessation of drinking? With regard to the ability to drink in a nonproblem manner, the literature is clear: more than half of the studies have identified their subject populations as alcoholics who have experienced physical dependence on alcohol.

A second point of interest is that although successful nonabstinent outcomes have repeatedly been referred to as rare occurrences, a review of the literature presents a different picture. Successful nonproblem-drinking outcomes are no less rare than successful outcomes of total abstinence. This is an important point. In responding to findings on nonproblem drinking, it has often been mentioned that the numbers of individuals achieving such an outcome following traditional treatment are small, often less than 10% of the total sample. This statement loses much of its significance, however, when it is realized that well-designed studies of treated chronic alcoholics typically find that only 10%–15% of all subjects are able to maintain abstinence for as long as one year, and those figures further diminish as the follow-up interval lengthens. So, even using stringent criteria of success, it seems that the incidence of successful nonabstinent outcomes parallels that of successful abstinent outcomes.

Finally, successful nonabstinent outcomes are best considered as a *set* of outcomes. They include drinking behaviors ranging from extremely minimal and infrequent drinking, to daily drinking of limited quantities, to the occasional intake of excessive but not debilitating amounts of alcohol. In fact, it is becoming clear that one cannot define successful nonabstinent outcomes simply in terms of the amount of ethanol consumed. Rather, it is the adverse consequences that result from drinking or the risk of such consequences that defines drinking problems. In summary, successful nonabstinent outcomes do occur, and their frequency is astonishingly high, when one considers the lack of treatment services supporting goals alternative to abstinence.

Treatment programs that use the explicit goal of nonproblem drinking for their subjects have been very recent and were first reported from Japan, South Africa, and Australia, before proliferating in North America. The first reports to have significant impact on the field were experimental studies published in the behavior therapy literature in the early 1970s. In the first such report, Lovibond and Caddy (1970) investigated the use of blood-alcohol-concentration discrimination training, aversive conditioning, and a broad program of behavioral counseling in modifying the behavior of Australian alcoholic outpatients. The subjects were taught how to calculate their approximate blood alcohol levels, and how to determine what levels would eventuate from consuming a specified amount of ethanol over a specified period of time. They were also administered various doses of alcoholic drinks and taught to attend to their internal sensations (e.g., warmth, numbness, and tingling sensations) as cues to their blood levels. When the subjects exceeded a blood alcohol level of .065% during a training session, they received a painful electric shock. Although recent research has found that alcoholic and nonalcoholic subjects alike are not able to correctly identify their blood alcohol levels simply on the basis of internal cues (Nathan, 1978; Maisto & Adesso, 1977),this finding does not detract from the Lovibond and Caddy study since education in blood-alcohol-level estimation provided a reasonable basis on which subjects could monitor their level of intoxication. Also, it deserves mention that the behavioral counseling aspects of this study are often overlooked. Lovibond and Caddy reported that of 31 subjects who had received the experimental treatment, 24 had successful outcomes and were able to drink in a nonproblem manner.

The second study—henceforth referred to as individualized behavior therapy, or IBT, for alcoholics—was conducted at Patton State Hospital in California during 1970–1971. It is important to note that this study was influenced by a series of basic research studies that had been conducted earlier at the same facility (Sobell & Sobell, 1978). The IBT study was designed to examine specific treatment implications derived from an operant conceptualization of excessive drinking, and particularly from one viewing drinking as a discriminated operant response. Thus, it was suggested that the drinking of alcoholics occurred, and was initiated, only within the context of certain setting events, and that the behavior was maintained by its consequences. On the basis of previous research and a review of the literature, the study included a goal of controlled drinking for some subjects, while other subjects were assigned to a goal of nondrinking. From a treatment standpoint, since self-control of drinking was to be a goal of the therapy, the treatment procedures focused on (1) learning control enhancement strategies; (2) understanding the nature and functions of drinking and of setting events, and of the short- and long-term consequences of drinking; and (3) developing effective alternative responses to situations in which excessive drinking had previously occurred and was likely to occur in the future.

A group of 70 male gamma alcoholics who were voluntarily in treatment for alcoholism at Patton State Hospital served as subjects in the IBT study. The term *gamma alcoholic*, defined by Jellinek (1960), denotes that these men had histories of chronic alcohol abuse and had suffered physical dependence on alcohol. While the study had two treatment goals, controlled drinking and nondrinking, few discussions of the IBT study mention, other than in passing, the abstinent, or nondrinking, treatment goal. However, in designing the study, it was clearly recognized that for physical health and/or psychosocial reasons, either many alcohol abusers would probably not be able of attain a successful controlled drinking outcome or pursuit of that goal might involve unjustifiable risks.

Of the 70 subjects in the IBT study, 40 were assigned to a goal of controlled drinking, and 30 were assigned to a goal of nondrinking. It should be emphasized that the subjects were assigned to these goals on the basis of a research staff decision, rather than randomly. This procedure was used in order to minimize risk to the subjects. Within each treatment-goal condition, the subjects were then randomly assigned to either a control or an experimental group. All control-group subjects, regardless of their assigned treatment goal, received the conventional state-hospital treatment program and were strongly advised that complete abstinence would be in their best interest.

The IBT program has been extensively described elsewhere and will not be described again here. The results of that study, however, are germane to the present discussion. Evaluating the effectiveness of controlled drinking as a treatment goal required the development of more sophisticated outcome-evaluation procedures than had been used in the field prior to that time. All subjects and their collateral informants were contacted and interviewed monthly for a period of two years. At each contact, information was collected about multiple areas of the subjects' functioning, including a fairly precise delineation of the subjects' daily drinking behavior over the period covered by the interview. In addition to this very intensive follow-up, a separate follow-up evaluation was conducted three years after the subjects' discharge from the hospital. This third-year evaluation, which has now been published, was conducted independently of the first two-year follow-up and, importantly, confirmed the results of the earlier evaluation using a double-blind procedure (Caddy, Addington, & Perkins, 1978).

Based on drinking behavior and adjunctive measures of other areas of life health, it was found that the subjects who received the program of IBT with a treatment goal of controlled drinking ("Controlled-drinker experimental subjects") functioned significantly better throughout the follow-up period than did the respective control subjects, who received conventional abstinence-oriented treatment. The nondrinker groups, while differing significantly during the first year of follow-up, did not differ significantly either the second or the third year of follow-up. In each case, the conclusions based on differences in drinking behavior were supported by either differences or the lack of differences on adjunctive measures of outcome.

Two aspects of the outcome data for the controlled-drinker experimental subjects are of relevance here. First, many of those subjects engaged in limited, nonproblem drinking throughout the follow-up period. This fact of course, is hardly surprising since controlled drinking had been a goal of treatment for these subjects. Also, consistent with the literature on outcomes for traditionally treated alcoholics, a small proportion of subjects in each of the other three groups engaged in some amount of nonproblem drinking during the follow-up period. Second, and unanticipated, the controlled-drinker experimental subjects were also abstinent a substantially greater number of days during each of the three years of follow-up than were their respective control subjects or the subjects in the other two groups. Accordingly, these subjects also experienced the fewest number of drunk, or out-of-control, days during the total follow-up period. One possible interpretation of these results is that the treatment oriented toward the enhancement of self-control provided an unexpected benefit in helping the subjects gain control over their drinking behavior in terms of both abstinence and controlled drinking.

The nature and frequency of the controlled drinking outcomes in the IBT study are a topic that has generated considerable controversy. Several lines of evidence, however, have supported those outcomes as viable. First, although a somewhat arbitrary criterion of controlled drinking (defined as the consumption of less than or equal to 6 oz of 86-proof ethanol or the equivalent in alcohol content) had to be formulated for use in the statistical evaluation of the outcome results, the type of limited drinking in which the subjects actually engaged did not approach this criterion. Individual-subject drinking profiles suggested that most of the subjects' controlled drinking amounted to the consumption of from one to three drinks either a few days per week or a few days per month. When the subjects engaged in controlled drinking, they drank mostly mixed drinks or beer and only rarely consumed straight drinks. Also, when the experimental subjects drank in a controlled manner, that drinking did not tend to precipitate excessive drinking episodes. Lastly, the profiles indicated that situational determinants may have influenced whether subjects engaged in controlled drinking. Subjects who successfully attained a controlled drinking pattern typically drank in their own homes or in a social context conducive to moderate drinking. In many ways, these findings parallel the original criteria for the selection of the subjects for the controlled-drinking goal, one of which has that the subjects anticipated returning to an environment after hospitalization where limited drinking would be likely to be socially condoned. Another indication of the degree of control manifested by these subjects was attained by calculating a drinking-control index for each subject. This index was computed by dividing the number of the days during which the subject engaged in controlled drinking by the total number of days during which the subject drank at all. Thus, a subject could receive an index score ranging from 1.00, indicating totally controlled drinking, to 0.00, indicating totally uncontrolled drinking. In this analysis, the controlled-drinker experimental subjects again were statistically superior to their control subjects.

Several studies recently reported in the literature have provided similar findings, and it appears that one can find strong evidence of at least some successful nonabstinent outcomes wherever one looks. Before considering the reaction of the alcohol field to the empirical evidence, however, it will be useful to take a brief look at the nature of successful nonabstinent outcomes. First, as mentioned earlier, such outcomes are best defined as a set or class, rather than as a distinct entity. Perhaps Orford (1973) has suggested the best way to consider nonabstinent outcomes. He described individuals' drinking as lying along a continuum, with one end of the continuum representing totally controlled drinking and the other totally uncontrolled drinking. Orford has found that the majority of cases actually fall between these endpoints, and such a classification schema probably yields a much more realistic consideration of drinking practices and problems than the traditional dichotomy of either normal drinking or alcoholic drinking. It was also mentioned earlier that the amount of drinking probably bears only a partial relationship to whether an individual's drinking should be considered a problem. More important is the extent to which the person has experienced or risked adverse consequences by drinking. Thus, it seems that the recognition that successful nonabstinent outcomes do occur is forcing a more prudent consideration of the "meaning" of drinking when evaluating treatment outcome. Seemingly, these aspects of drinking can be operationalized in terms of measuring urges to drink, thoughts about drinking, the circumstances when drinking occurs, and the consequences that follow drinking. These facets of drinking and associated behaviors have seldom been assessed in studies reporting nonabstinent outcomes, including studies that have used behavioral methods. Also, it might be added that there is every reason to expect that abstinent outcomes are subject to the same variety of interpretations. That is, a person might be abstinent, yet experience repeated urges to drink and have a high likelihood of drinking in a pathological manner should conducive circumstances arise.

This critical distinction, between drinking per se and the *functions* of drinking, raises issues pertinent to abstinent as well as nonabstinent outcomes and suggests that self-control issues are relevant to both types of outcome. Surely, some nonabstinent outcomes incorporate factors of high risk and have a greater potential for relapse to problem drinking than do other nonabstinent outcomes. Similarly, one can expect that abstinent outcomes are subject to the same liabilities. Simply put, current abstinence does not guarantee future abstinence, nor does current nonproblem drinking guarantee a continuation of that status.

A considerable amount of more recent research could be cited to substantiate the point that successful nonabstinent outcomes do occur, and that the frequency of such outcomes is astonishingly high when one considers the lack of treatment services oriented toward or accepting of alternative goals. Rather than discussing the evidence at greater length, it will be more useful to consider the second level of debate about alcohol abusers' potential for control over their drinking: the conflict between ideologies. This conflict and the strength of the belief systems involved can best be considered by examining the responses of traditionalists to the accumulating evidence.

A Critical Evaluation of the Responses of Traditionalists

A popular way of criticizing the reports of non-problem-drinking outcomes has been to argue from personal experience as a clinician that such outcomes are not possible. Needless to say, such arguments are difficult to refute. The current evidence does suggest, however, that persons who achieve non-problem-drinking outcomes are not likely to maintain contact with abstinence-oriented clinicians or programs.

Another proffered explanation of reports of nonproblem drinking is the claim that anyone able to return to some type of limited nonproblem drinking must, by fiat, never have been a "true" alcoholic. In its extreme, this argument maintains that even individuals who have suffered distinct alcohol withdrawal symptoms must have been misdiagnosed as alcoholics. The position that such cases merely represent misdiagnosis, a conclusion that results from circular reasoning, lacks practical utility.

Non-problem-drinking outcomes have also been assailed as simply reflecting early states of a full relapse into noncontrolled drinking. While research data do not support this argument, this position possibly has some validity. On the other hand, it should also be noted that this same line of reasoning can be applied to abstinent outcomes. That is, abstinent individuals who are constantly preoccupied with thoughts of drinking and urges to drink, and who find it necessary to structure their daily activities so as to avoid access to alcohol, may be likely to resume pathological drinking, should particular circumstances arise. Obviously, relapse into problem drinking does not mean that the treatment has failed or indicate that the goal of abstinence should be discarded. Rather, in these cases, treatment is typically resumed, and the original objectives are maintained.

An important criticism of reports of nonproblem drinking is that such events have been newsworthy. It has been speculated that such news coverage might unintentionally lead abstinent alcoholics to unknowledgeably experiment with controlled drinking, leading to deleterious consequences. Since it is important to minimize any detrimental public impact of scientific findings, this criticism clearly has some validity. In this regard, however, two observations are relevant. First, although scientific publications and findings can be inaccurately reported and misrepresented by the news media, that surely is not an argument against reporting such findings in scientific journals. Second, reports of non-problem-drinking outcomes have had some impact on the public by virtue of the exaggerated reactions and the categorical denials of traditionalists. In these case, a more cautious reaction would have been possible, such as statements to the effect that such outcomes are of unknown frequency, should not be expected to result from home remedies, and may be unwise objectives in many cases.

These are just a few of the criticisms directed at scientific reports of enhanced control over drinking by alcohol abusers. The gist of the arguments is clear, and until recently, their influence has prevailed. In essence, the majority of criticisms either view non-problem-drinking outcomes as "freak" or exceptional occurrences or simply deny that they even occur. Nevertheless, the debate has also generated a series of arguments advocating the acceptance of the data and suggesting changes in the field.

The single most compelling reason for recognizing successful nonabstinent outcomes results from considering the sheer mass of evidence that demonstrates that such outcomes are both possible and numerous. In this regard, a number of arguments have been offered in support of nonabstinent approaches (Sobell, 1978). For instance, the reported rarity of successful outcomes based on a criterion of total abstinence could be the result of the extraordinary difficulty of treating alcohol problems. On the other hand, while undeniably a positive outcome in most cases, total abstinence may be an unreasonably strict and unrealistic treatment outcome criterion for general use and may obscure the recognition of actual improvement. One unfortunate consequence of insisting on evaluating treatment effectiveness in terms of total abstinence is that this insistence may actually have helped create the popular myth that treatment for alcohol problems seldom works.

Another problem with the criterion of total abstinence is that traditional treatment programs may have inadvertently prevented many persons from seeking or obtaining early treatment for developing drinking problems and may have hampered the development of appropriate clinical services for such individuals. For instance, recent statistics show that there continues to be little participation by persons under 30 years of age in Alcoholics Anonymous, even though survey data suggest that, at least among males, it is individuals in their 20s who report the highest incidence of drinking problems. At present, there are no separately identifiable services for persons who have less serious drinking problems. Consequently, these individuals often go without services or are referred to programs oriented toward treating the chronic, physically dependent alcoholic. A treatment program that is not solely abstinence-oriented might be appealing to this population. Moreover, research suggests that this population is the one most likely to achieve successful nonabstinent outcomes.

Traditional notions about alcoholism offer few reasons for problem drinkers to curtail their drinking and, in fact, may provide them with a basis for repeated attempts to prove that they are not "alcoholics." The term *alcoholic*, with its many connotations, has been applied rather indiscriminately to all varieties of drinking problems, including those of children. A preferred orientation would be to illustrate that recovery is possible, and that one can minimize future handicaps by early, and sometimes limited, actions.

Finally, although the social stigma of being an alcoholic is severe, an even worse stigma can result for individuals who have had serious drinking problems and think that they can drink without experiencing further problems. Such individuals can encounter unexpected hostility and ostracism. Thus, individuals who successfully engage in nonproblem drinking might not reveal this or their past drinking problems to others. It is ironic that traditional concepts of alcoholism may actually encourage many persons to be "hidden ex-alcoholics." *Only* if it becomes publicly acceptable for some persons, no matter how small a minority, to recover from serious drinking problems and successfully engage in nonproblem drinking will we be able to determine accurately what proportion of persons are capable of achieving such a goal.

Possible Predictors of Controlled-Drinking Outcomes

The evidence that has accrued to date allows for some speculation about who might be the better candidates for non-problem-drinking treatment goals. Nearly all of this evidence has been garnered either from studies that have reported non-problem-drinking outcomes for individuals treated in a traditional abstinence-oriented treatment program or from reports such as the IBT study, in which the subjects were not randomly assigned to treatment goals. Nevertheless, despite its correlational basis, the collective findings of several studies (reviewed in Sobell, 1978) allow some hypotheses to be formulated.

First, in terms of pretreatment variables, the findings suggest that persons who have less serious drinking problems on their entry into treatment are more likely to acquire a posttreatment pattern of nonproblem drinking. This relationship is suggested by less pretreatment alcohol intake, less prior symptomatology (especially no signs of physical dependence), and a shorter self-reported history of drinking problems. Also, some recent data suggest that cognitive factors may be related to non-problem-drinking outcomes. Orford, Oppenheimer, and Edwards (1976) reported that subjects who were mainly controlled drinkers at a follow-up assessment had expressed greater pretreatment confidence in their ability to abstain from alcohol.

For within-treatment variables, the use of treatment procedures specifically directed toward nonabstinence appears to be positively related to successful nonabstinent outcomes. Of interest is the fact that individuals who attain non-problem-drinking outcomes following treatment in abstinence-oriented programs also tend to spend relatively less time in treatment. At present, it is not possible to determine whether such individuals have a smaller need for treatment or whether their lessened involvement stems from other sources, such as being alienated from abstinence-oriented treatment programs.

Finally, several posttreatment features of non-problem-drinking outcomes deserve mention. First, successful subjects often experience some drinking problems shortly following treatment and then overcome these problems. Second, as with abstinence, successful drinking outcomes are frequently, but not necessarily, associated with improvement in other areas of life health. Third, it has been suggested that a significant positive change in life circumstances often antedates the onset of a successful nonabstinent pattern. Thus far, the controlled studies that have been done have not provided support for such a relationship; however, those studies have rarely gathered data that could reflect such relationships.

The Contemporary State of Treatment for Alcoholism

In the face of accumulating evidence, non-problem-drinking outcomes are slowly being accepted by traditionalists as part of the alcohol field (e.g., Seixas, 1978). This trend seems likely to continue for several reasons. Primary among these reasons is an increasing recognition that there are a substantial number of individuals who have serious drinking problems, in terms of adverse life consequences, but who have not experienced physical dependence on alcohol. Second, recent evidence on the natural history of alcohol problems suggests that many, and perhaps most, of these individuals will never deteriorate to the point where they do become physically dependent, and that many have episodes of alcohol problems interspersed with episodes of well-controlled drinking. Third, traditional treatment approaches are probably too intense for most of these individuals, because more change is required than is necessary to eliminate the problems. In all likelihood, then, such individuals are less likely to comply with traditional treatment programs.

While arguments will continue to be promulgated by some traditionalists that abstinence must be the only goal of treatment for all individuals with alcohol problems, it appears that the alcohol field is at last coming to grips with more important contemporary issues, the paramount one being determining when, for whom, and by what methods nonproblem drinking might become an appropriate treatment goal. The development of such a multivariate approach is a formidable challenge. Research investigating these differences can be expected to produce substantial gains in our clinical knowledge and skills. For example, perhaps various methods of assessing an individual's capacity to learn greater self-control can be devised. How general is the phenomenon that is called *self-control?* Does learning greater self-control over some behaviors lead to a greater probability of gaining increased self-control over other behaviors? Intuitively, it is an appealing notion that the learning of self-control strategies might have a snowballing effect, so that as an individual is more and more successful, the amount of control attempted increases.

Also, some attention might be given to the question of motivation, a construct frequently used to explain treatment failures. In this regard, the attempt to exercise greater self-control requires an investment of energy and the acceptance of personal responsibility for one's own actions. Perhaps, many persons will be reluctant to become involved in a treatment with such onerous requirements. The topic of motivation, however, can be researched. For example, is shaping of self-control possible, such as having the client initially engage in small, incremental, and low-risk behaviors for which success is nearly assured? Our lack of knowledge is great, but the alcohol field seems to have reached the point where such investigations are being considered worthwhile.

One other indication of the acceptance of non-problem-drinking outcomes comes from the recent development of a new self-help group that currently claims a substantial membership in the United States. That new group is called Drinkwatchers (Winters, 1978), and it advocates the acquisition of greater self-control over drinking for problem drinkers. It is too early to determine the success of this self-help group, but it is significant that it exists at all.

Before closing, a few caveats are necessary. This presentation is not intended to advocate alternatives to abstinence as a panacea for persons with alcohol problems, or even to suggest that many persons can necessarily achieve such an outcome. Obviously, striving toward nonproblem drinking could be highly detrimental, should an individual use this goal to justify continued problem drinking. Like any other therapeutic procedure or goal, and especially because of its experimental nature, it seems best that nonproblem drinking should be advocated to clients only by trained and knowledgeable individuals, aware of the methodology, the benefits, the dangers, and the limitations inherent in such an approach. Since there is a clear and immediate need to develop new, different, and less-intensive and less-demanding treatment services for individuals who have less-chronic alcohol problems, it is reasonable to focus on this population in developing treatment alternatives.

Self-Regulation and the Alcohol Field

Earlier, it was stated that those investigating the self-regulation of other behaviors might benefit from knowing how evidence of the value of control enhancement strategies has been received by the alcohol field, a field where a majority of the constituency have long believed that alcohol abusers lack control over their drinking behavior. In this regard, the experience to be shared by the alcohol field is that research findings change the beliefs that they challenge only after much passage of time and only when the evidence mounts to the point where it can no longer be disputed. From one perspective, this is an obvious demonstration of the ways in which most ideologies change, and Kuhn (1970) has certainly made a strong case that this progression characterizes paradigm change in the physical sciences. We cannot forget that substantial evidence existed in the alcohol literature for a full generation before it was even deemed as being in need of more than cursory explanation. Ideas change gradually. When a conflict exists between ideology and research findings, it can be expected that the ensuing confrontation will be vigorous and not necessarily rational. As evidence of the successful self-regulation of a variety of behaviors continues to accumulate, therefore, researchers may give greater consideration to how their work might impact on a field and how ideological conflicts might be minimized.

References

Alcoholics Anonymous. New York: Works Publishing, 1939.

Caddy, G. R., Addington, H. J., Jr., & Perkins, D. Individualized behavior therapy for alcoholics: A third year independent double-blind follow-up. *Behaviour Research and Therapy*, 1978, *16*, 345–362.

Cohen, M., Liebson, I. A., Faillace, L. A., & Allen, R. P. Moderate drinking by chronic alcoholics: A schedule-dependent phenomenon. *Journal of Nervous and Mental Disease*, 1971, *153*, 434–444.

Cohen, M., Liebson, I. A., Faillace, L. A., & Speers, W. Alcoholism: Controlled drinking and incentives for abstinence. *Psychological Reports*, 1971, *28*, 575–580.

Engle, K. B., & Williams, T. K. Effect of an ounce of vodka on alcoholics' desire for alcohol. *Quarterly Journal of Studies on Alcohol*, 1972, *33*, 1099–1105.

Gross, M. M. (Ed.). *Alcohol intoxication and withdrawal: Experimental studies. Advances in experimental medicine and biology*, Vol. 35. New York: Plenum Press, 1973.

Jellinek, E. M. *The disease concept of alcoholism.* New Brunswick, N.J.: Hillhouse Press, 1960.

Kuhn, T. S. *The structure of scientific revolutions* (2nd ed.). Chicago: University of Chicago Press, 1970.

Lovibond, S. H., & Caddy, G. Discriminated aversive control in the moderation of alcoholics' drinking behavior. *Behavior Therapy*, 1970, *1*, 437–444.

Maisto, S. A., & Adesso, V. J. The effect of instructions and feedback on blood alcohol level discrimination in nonalcoholic drinkers. *Journal of Consulting and Clinical Psychology*, 1977, *45*, 625–636.

Marlatt, G. A., Demming, B., & Reid, J. B. Loss of control drinking in alcoholics: An experimental analogue. *Journal of Abnormal Psychology*, 1973, *81*, 233–241.

Mendelson, J. H. (Ed.). Experimentally induced chronic intoxication and withdrawal in alcoholics. *Quarterly Journal of Studies on Alcohol*, 1964, Supplement No. 2.

Mendelson, J. H., LaDou, J., & Solomon, P. Experimentally induced chronic intoxication and withdrawal in alcoholics, III: Psychiatric findings. *Quarterly Journal of Studies on Alcohol.* 1964, Supplement No. 2, 40–52.

Merry, J. The "loss of control" myth. *Lancet*, 1966, *1*, 1257–1258.

Nathan, P. E. Studies in blood alcohol level discrimination. In P. E. Nathan, G. A. Marlatt, & T. Løberg (Eds.), *Alcoholism: New directions in behavioral research and treatment.* New York: Plenum Press, 1978.

Orford, J. A comparison of alcoholics whose drinking is totally uncontrolled and those whose drinking is mainly controlled. *Behaviour Research and Therapy,* 1973, *11,* 565–576.

Orford, J., Oppenheimer, E., & Edwards, G. Abstinence or control: The outcome for excessive drinkers two years after consultation. *Behaviour Research and Therapy*, 1976, *14*, 409–418.

Paredes, A., Hood, W. R., Seymour, H., & Gollob, M. Loss of control in alcoholism: An investigation of the hypothesis, with experimental findings. *Quarterly Journal of Studies on Alcohol,* 1973, *34*, 1145–1161.

Pattison, E. M., Sobell, M. B., & Sobell, L. C. (Authors/Eds.). *Emerging concepts of alcohol dependence.* New York: Springer, 1977.

Seixas, F. A. Abstinence as a goal in the treatment of alcoholics. *American Journal of Drug and Alcohol Abuse*, 1978, *5*, 293–298.

Sobell, L. C., Sobell, M. B., & Christelman, W. C. The myth of "one drink." *Behaviour Research and Therapy*, 1972, *10*, 119–123.

Sobell, M. B. Alternatives to abstinence: Evidence, issues and some proposals. In P. E. Nathan & G. A. Marlatt (Eds.), *Experimental and behavioral approaches to alcoholism.* New York: Plenum Press, 1978.

Sobell, M. B., & Sobell, L. C. *Behavioral treatment of alcohol problems: Individualized therapy and controlled drinking.* New York: Plenum Press, 1978.

Winters, A. *Alternatives for the problem drinker.* New York: Drake Publishers, 1978.

CHAPTER 8

Teaching Healthy Managers to Control Their Coronary-Prone (Type A) Behavior

Ethel Roskies and Jacqueline Avard

Department of Psychology
University of Montreal
Montreal, Quebec, Canada

After 20 years of intense controversy, the dust of battle is finally settling. The possibility that the aggressive, competitive, time-pressured lifestyle subsumed under the Type A label could significantly and independently increase the risk of coronary heart disease (CHD) initially aroused strong resistance among cardiovascular epidemiologists, but this opposition is now crumbling under the weight of accumulating evidence (Jenkins 1971, 1976). Examples of the growing acceptance of Type A behavior as a risk factor are the two conferences on this topic sponsored by the (U.S.) National Heart, Lung and Blood Institute in June 1977 and December 1978, as well as the inclusion of Type A symposia or papers in the programs of recent annual meetings of the American Psychological Association, the American Public Health Association, the American Psychosomatic Society, and the Association for the Advancement of Behavior Therapy.

Now the issue has become one of whether and how psychological techniques can be used to effectively reduce the risk associated with Type A behavior. Only a few studies reporting the results of intervention attempts have been published to date (Jenni & Wollersheim, 1979; Rosenman & Friedman, 1977; Roskies, Spevack, Surkis, Cohen, & Gilman, 1978; Roskies, Kearney,

The work reported here has been partially supported by grants to the first author from the Conseil de la Recherche en Santé du Québec, Department of Health and Welfare, Ottawa, and CAFIR, University of Montreal.

Spevack, Surkis, Cohen, & Gilman, 1979; Suinn, 1975; Suinn & Bloom, 1978), and it is still far too early to know which, if any, of the current approaches to intervention will eventually prove its effectiveness. Nevertheless, if this newly developing area of research is not to founder in a sea of polemic, investigators involved in it must agree to expose their work to informed criticism by providing detailed descriptions of samples, treatment methods, and dependent measures. Only in this way will it be possible to give meaningful evaluation to claims of success, or even to reports of failure (cf. Roskies, 1980).

In compliance with this guideline, this paper focuses on the rationale and the content of a treatment plan developed for a Type A intervention project currently in progress. A previous paper has already described the theoretical and practical considerations underlying the choice of dependent measures (Roskies, 1979). The sample for this project consists of 66 healthy, middle-aged, middle-level male managers who volunteered for a 13-session stress-management program sponsored by the three large companies in which they work. All volunteers at the designated management level without a history of clinical heart disease were accepted into the program, but, in fact, over 90% of these men have subsequently been classified as Type A by the criteria of the Standard Interview (Rosenman, 1977b).

Of these men 40 met weekly in groups of 10, while the remaining 26 are on a waiting list for treatment following completion of the first series of sessions. Because of the influence of the cultural environment on Type A behavior (Cohen, 1974; Waldron, 1977; Zyzanski, 1977) and the existence of two distinct cultures in Montreal, half of the men in the immediate treatment groups were randomly selected from the French-speaking volunteers, while the other half were randomly chosen from the English-speaking group. The men from the two linguistic communities meet in separate treatment groups with different therapists, but all groups follow the same treatment plan.

Targets for Change in the Type A Pattern

What one seeks to change in the Type A behavior pattern depends on what one considers pathogenic about it in the first instance. However, even though a growing number of studies are attempting to delineate the behavioral and physiological characteristics that distinguish the Type A person from his or her more relaxed, easygoing Type B counterpart (Dembroski, Macdougall, & Shields, 1977; Dembroski & Macdougall, 1978; Glass, 1977; Scherwitz, Berton, & Leventhal, 1977, 1978; Van Egeren, 1979), we are still far from any consensus regarding what specifically must be changed if the risk of CHD associated with the Type A pattern is to be eliminated or reduced. In designing intervention programs, therefore, each researcher is obliged to define his or her individual criteria for evaluating improvement.

For the purposes of our project, we avoided completely the thorny issue of specifying the pathogenic behaviors in the pattern and, instead, focused our interventions directly on the mechanisms through which overt behaviors are transformed into increased atherosclerosis and increased risk of CHD. A number of recent studies have suggested that crucial differences between As and Bs become visible only when both are exposed to challenge. Not only do As have a greater propensity to perceive challenge, but, equally importantly, they also react to it with more intense and longer-lasting rises of autonomic and neuroendocrine levels (Dembroski *et al.*, 1977; Frankenhaeuser, 1977; Friedman, Byers, Diamant, & Rosenman, 1975; Glass, 1977; Williams, Friedman, Glass, Herd, & Schneiderman, 1977). This hyperreactivity is considered particularly important because of the relationship postulated between sympathetic arousal, with its associated endocrine activity, and the development of atherosclerosis (Davis, 1974; Gilmore, 1974; Obrist, 1976, Williams, 1975). The goal of intervention, therefore, became one of reducing the frequency, the intensity, and the duration of episodes of arousal.

In focusing on hyperreactivity as the target for change, we were forced to consider whether Type A behavior causes damage simply by fostering a too-frequent general mobilization or, rather, whether the pattern's pathogenic qualities result from its association with a particular type of emotional response. High levels of hostility, in particular, have been found both to be frequently present in Type A individuals and to be positively associated with the increased spread of coronary atherosclerosis and the increased risk of heart disease. While it is not yet known whether anger does indeed produce a somatic response pattern that is both different from and more harmful than that produced by other emotions, or whether Type A individuals are simply more likely to label any upheaval they experience as anger, we did decide to devote special attention in the treatment program to the handling of intense negative emotions, such as anger.

Treatment Philosophy

In the process of operationalizing a general therapeutic goal—reduction in the frequency, the intensity, and the duration of episodes of arousal—into a detailed treatment protocol, we necessarily had to choose between alternative ways of proceeding. Here, we shall attempt to describe the choices we made and the reasons for making them.

A Limited Intervention Model

Rosenman (1974, 1977a) has repeatedly stressed that Type A behavior is the result of an interaction between an individual who is particularly sensitive to certain environmental cues and an environment that provides these cues. Intervention programs, therefore, can seek either to change the individual's perceptions and behavior, or else to change those elements in the environment that encourage or force the individual to behave in a time-urgent, competitive manner. Our intervention program opts squarely for modification of the individual rather than the environment. We chose individual change as a first approach because, as clinical psychologists, this is our area of specific competence, and also because an individual-based program was likely to be more acceptable to the companies concerned. Nevertheless, we recognize the possibility that certain environments may be sufficiently provocative to make it difficult, if not impossible, for the individual to modify her behavior in the absence of a reduction in environmental pressures.

Another limit on the scope of our intervention was the decision against seeking to modify the general philosophy of life that gives rise to individual Type A behaviors. Although Rosenman and Friedman (1977) have argued strongly that a radical philosophical reorientation is a necessary prerequisite to significant behavioral change, we felt that drastic changes in goals and values were unlikely to be achieved within the time constraints inherent in a program designed for healthy, active managers. Equally importantly, we had strong ethical reservations about the possible adverse consequences that might result from a radical reengineering of lifestyle, not only for the person himself or herself, but also for the family, and perhaps even for society at large. For these reasons, our program explicitly stated that it did not seek to change basic goals, or even customary occupational and recreational pursuits, but simply to help the individual control and modulate his expenditure of energy so that the same activities could be accomplished with less psychological and physiological strain.

Emphasis on Personal Effectiveness

Glass and his associates (Glass, 1977; Glass, Snyder, & Hollis, 1974) have conceptualized the Type A individual as one who is engaged in a perceptual battle for mastery of the environment, furiously increasing his or her pace and aggressiveness whenever he or she experiences the anxiety associated with threatened loss of control. To intervene in this process, therefore, one would either have to lessen the persons's basic need for control or else teach him or her less harmful ways of coping with any threat of diminished control.

Our program chose to capitalize on the individual's need for mastery, rather than seeking to reduce it, on the grounds that appealing to existing deep-seated needs would lessen the resistance to change. Thus, the program presentation placed as much emphasis on the inefficiency of unmodulated Type A behavior as on its relationship to eventual heart disease. As successful managers, the potential participants presumably had already learned how to handle business problems effectively. Now they faced the additional challenge of learning how to control their personal reactions so as to maximize productivity and minimize strain. To emphasize this point further, the treatment plan was presented under the label of "personal effectiveness," rather than the more usual "stress management" rubric.

This emphasis on the use of self-control to increase effectiveness continued throughout the life of the program. Whatever the specific technique being taught, be it rational thinking or communication skills, the therapist repeatedly described the benefits in terms of enhanced effectiveness, as well as reduced physiological wear and tear. Contrary to the men's commonly expressed fear, the modulation of Type A behavior need not diminish performance and might actually enhance it.

A Multimodal Treatment Approach

In classifying an individual as Type A, we are referring not to a single, specific behavior, or even a set of behaviors but to a general way of thinking, feeling, and acting that permeates may aspects of the person's life. This is why we did not think that any single stress-reduction technique, be it anxiety management or stress inoculation, was likely to prove adequate in countering the multiple manifestations of the Type A pattern. Instead, we sought a rationale for combining a number of different techniques. Following Lazarus's categorization of the goals of coping (Lazarus & Launier, 1978), we sought to include strategies that would be helpful both in managing the emotional manifestations of stress and in modifying the stressful situation itself.

The use of a multimodal approach has the added advantage of flexibility in responding to the differences among individuals classified as Type A. As Matthews and Saal (1978) have pointed out, it is possible for one Type A to be very competitive and to be quick in his or her actions, but patient with others, and for another to be very quick in his or her actions and easily annoyed, but relatively noncompetitive. With a broad-spectrum approach, each participant does not have to place equal emphasis on every technique but, instead, can choose to concentrate her or his efforts on those areas where she or he personally experiences the greatest difficulty. There is one disadvantage in using multiple techniques: the inability, should the program prove beneficial, to pinpoint what exactly in the treatment was helpful. At this stage, however, the most urgent priority is to design an effective intervention program. Component analysis to increase efficiency can constitute a subsequent step.

The major consideration governing our choice of specific techniques was the ease with which they could become an integral part of the daily routine. Rather than having the group members set aside a specific time period each day to practice stress reduction, the aim was to have them repeatedly monitor and reduce their physical, emotional, and cognitive tension throughout the course of the day. Following this criterion, we eliminated "nonportable" techniques, such as jogging, yoga, and meditation, and concentrated instead on strategies such as muscular relaxation, rational-emotive thinking, problem solving, and communication skills, all of which can be used unobtrusively during a heated business discussion or a confrontation with an untidy teenage son.

Coping versus Cure

Whatever the advantages for coronary risk reduction in behaving in a Type B manner, it is highly unlikely that any short-term program will completely and permanently transform Type As into Type Bs. To posit this type of "cure" as the goal for treatment, therefore, was to condemn ourselves and our clients to inevitable frustration and failure. Instead, the model presented to the participants emphasized that the control of Type A behavior would require an active effort even after the treatment had been successfully completed, but that the participants could learn to cope with internal and external pressures by continuing their self-observation and practice of stress-reducing techniques.

Treatment Techniques

Underlying the specific methods of reducing tension were some general principles concerning the process of change. These techniques for fostering change were not presented explicitly to the participants, but they directed much of what the therapists said and did.

Awareness as a Preliminary to Intervention

Self-observation is commonly used in behavior therapy to establish baselines for the behavior to be changed. For the Type A individual, this process of self-observation has the additional essential task of alerting her or him to the very existence of the targets for change. Even extreme Type A individuals may either be unaware of their chronic high level of muscular tension, frequent outbursts of anger, and continuous sense of time pressure or may mistakenly consider them essential to maintaining performance levels. Only when they realize how often and in what inappropriate circumstances they engage in these reactions are Type As likely to become motivated to change. For this reason, self-observation constituted an essential element of the program. In the week preceding the introduction of each new technique, the participants were asked to monitor the behaviors that this technique was designed to modify. In the final section of the program, the participants were taught how to develop their own observation schedules, so as to be able to monitor posttreatment regressions in Type A behavior, or even to pinpoint other habit patterns that they would like to change.

Stress Reduction as Skills Training

The process of learning to monitor and reduce tension is similar to the acquisition of any complex skill. Initially, the willing pupil is likely to reproduce the model only awkwardly and imperfectly, whether the instructor is demonstrating a new tennis stroke or muscular relaxation. With regular practice and instructor feedback, however, he or she will gradually increase in ability until the new skill can be executed with ease, and eventually it will become a smoothly functioning part of the total repertoire.

To facilitate this learning process, the various techniques were broken down into small units and were taught as a series of steps. In the case of relaxation, this meant a progression from a 20-minute exercise to a 5-minute one, and still later to the pairing of an immediate relaxation response with specific cues. For other techniques such as rational-emotive thinking, the progression was from *in vitro* to *in vivo*. In the initial practice of this technique, the individual first fantasized a stressful situation and then fantasized the use of the technique to reduce tension, noting carefully the before and after tension levels. The next stage was the practice of rational-emotive thinking "after the fact." Following an upsetting experience, the group members were instructed to mentally replay the scene and imagine how their emotional reactions to these events might have been changed by the application of this technique. The final stage was the use of the technique in the heat of battle itself, beginning with situations that were less upsetting or threatening, and progressing gradually to the use of tension reduction even in the midst of full-scale crisis. A similar step-by-step approach was used for the teaching of communication and problem-solving skills.

Shaping via corrective feedback constituted an essential part of the learning process. Between the weekly sessions, the men were assigned homework of which they were asked to keep written records. This material could then be used by the therapist to provide suggestions for improved performance. There was also actual practice techniques during the sessions under the supervision and correction of the therapist.

Practice between sessions was necessary if proficiency in the use of the technique was to be attained. To make this homework as palatable and as feasible as possible, we asked the participants to take a few minutes at a time, several times a day, rather than concentrating practice in a few massed sessions. The longest single homework session was the 20 minutes required for the long version of the muscular relaxation tape, and this was terminated after four weeks. To further increase adherence, we analyzed the homework records for general trends, such as the most frequently chosen relaxation cues or the variety of situations to which problem-solving skills had been applied, and then fed this information back to participants.

The group format provided considerable therapeutic assistance in the acquisition of these new skills. Many of the stressful situations encountered were common to all the participants, and the discussion of problems was leavened by humor and camaraderie. Other group members, too, were often quick to spot ways in which the effectiveness of the techniques could be improved, or at least the frequency with which they were used increased.

A Hierarchical Presentation of Techniques

From the outset, the aim was to help the participants become problem-oriented, in contrast to technique-oriented. Rather than having them apply individual techniques in a stereotyped fashion, we wanted them to be able to adapt to the demands of specific situations by flexibly combining techniques, or even parts of techniques. The order of presentation of techniques, therefore, was designed to facilitate the construction of an integrated repertoire.

Progressive muscular relaxation was chosen as the first technique taught because it is among the easiest to use and the benefits are almost immediate.

Although the participants were likely to show slightly more resistance to the principles of rational-emotive thinking (RET), practice in the control of negative emotions, such as anger, anxiety, guilt, and depression, also brings an immediate increase in sense of well-being. For this reason, RET was the second technique presented. Communication and problem-solving skills, designed to reduce the stress associated with interpersonal conflict and decision making, followed next in the sequence. Once the participants were proficient in the use of each technique individually, a modified form of stress inoculation was introduced to help them learn how to combine the techniques for maximum impact.

Treatment Content

All of the tension-reducing strategies used in the program constitute part of the standard repertoire of behavior therapy techniques. In addition to combining and presenting them in a novel fashion, however, we also modified some of the techniques themselves, in order to adapt them to the specific needs of our target population.

Progressive Muscular Relaxation

Relaxation was taught in three stages: (1) the long form, (2) the short form, and (3) cue-controlled relaxation. The long form was the 20-minute exercise developed by Bernstein and Borkovec (1973). Following a presentation of the reasons why and the manner in which relaxation techniques are used, the group practiced the exercise directed by the recorded instructions of the therapist. Cassettes of these instructions were then distributed to be used in practice at home. The homework assignment was to practice this 20-minute version twice daily, recording the time of practice and the pre- and post-practice tension levels.

For the next four weeks, this assignment remained unchanged. During the weekly sessions, the therapists discussed problems associated with the twice-daily practice sessions (timing, distracting thoughts), as well as the benefits derived. A group practice was held during each session, emphasizing the importance of frequent repetition and permitting the therapist to correct errors. In order to motivate the men to continue with the required 40 minutes of practice daily, the therapists repeatedly emphasized the short duration of this preliminary training in relaxation. At the end of four weeks, the men were switched to a 5-minute version for a further four weeks. Although recorded instructions were also provided for this shorter form, the participants were encouraged to learn gradually how to induce relaxation without this external aid.

At the end of eight weeks, most of the participants had become sufficiently proficient in the exercise to be able to induce a state of relaxation simply by giving themselves the command "Relax–calm down," taking a deep, slow breath, and/or focusing on a specific muscle group. This process was titled *cue-controlled relaxation.* In the week prior to the introduction of this technique, the participants were furnished with 60 red stars each and asked to paste them in frequently encountered places at work and at home, particularly those places associated with stress. Considerable joking ensued as the men discussed the possibilities of pasting them on the foreheads of wives, supervisors, secretaries, etc. The locations actually chosen were usually more conventional, such as a wristwatch, the steering wheel of the car, the telephone, or an agenda book, but even the elevator buttons of the office buildings concerned soon blossomed with red stars. Each encounter with a red star served as a signal to relax, but in addition, the men soon began reporting the use of internal cues to induce relaxation. We emphasized the importance of taking frequent relaxation breaks in the course of the day, even in the absence of overt feelings of tension.

For the 13 weeks of the program, either the long or short form of the relaxation exercise was practiced at each weekly session. The participants were encouraged to return occasionally to the practice of one of these forms whenever they felt that cue-controlled relaxation was not reducing their tension sufficiently.

Rational-Emotive Thinking

The name associated with this technique is, of course, that of Albert Ellis (Ellis & Grieger, 1977). We introduced this technique specifically to help our participants modulate negative emotions. The justification for seeking to dilute inappropriate negative feelings, such as anger or guilt, is based not only on the physiological wear and tear resulting but also on the premise that emotional upheaval often prevents a person from taking constructive action to improve the situation.

Following Ellis's model, we explained that feelings are produced by the people who experience them, not by external circumstances. The reason why we are likely to experience an inappropriate negative emotion in a given situation, such as anger rather than irritation or disappointment, is our irrational beliefs about ourselves, other people, and the world in general. Believing that we should always be perfect, believing that others should always love us, and believing that the world should always be arranged for our convenience are irrational expectations that lead to inappropriate negative feelings when they are frustrated, as inevitably they are. Abandoning these unrealistic expectations, on the other hand, allows us to encounter unpleasant situations with greater equanimity. Wishing that a surly waiter might be more attentive gives rise to a very different feeling from the one engendered by the belief that every person *ought* to treat one in a considerate manner.

Where we departed from Ellis's standard procedure was in our lessened emphasis on having the therapist debate and disprove irrational beliefs. Because disputing each persons's irrational beliefs individually in a group is a time-consuming procedure, we used an alternative approach, suggested by Maultsby and Ellis (1978), in which each person learns to conduct her or his own internal debate. Following the presentation of the rationale of RET, as well as examples of irrational beliefs, each participant was instructed first to recall a situation in which he had been upset, and then to re-create, as realistically as possible, the feelings he had experienced at that time. The next step was to try to shift the feelings into a lower key. For instance, irritation, annoyance, frustration, disappointment, and so on were suggested as more rational responses than fury. Once the person had modulated his feelings, he was asked to recall what he had said to himself to change his irrational thinking and thereby modify the feelings.

As was usual in the program, the learning of this technique took place in stages. In the week preceding the introduction of the technique, the group members were simply asked to record one or two upsetting situations daily and the negative feelings experienced. In this way, as soon as the procedures for using this technique were explained in the weekly sessions, the participants were able to practice immediately with the material already available. The homework consisted of three practice sessions per day in which the individual imagined two situations with accompanying negative feelings each time, modified them, and then recorded the self-statements used to produce the changes.

The discussion of homework assignments and practices held during the weekly sessions permitted the therapist to point out the irrational nature of many common beliefs, as well as to suggest more rational self-statements. Recording the situations associated with inappropriate negative feelings also helped the men to become more aware of the particular circumstances and people in their lives most likely to induce upset. One of the revelations of the program was that these stressful episodes, particularly in the French-speaking groups, were as likely to occur at home as at work.

The reduction of negative emotions in imagery gradually changed to the modification of feelings on the spot. Rational-emotive thinking was initially most helpful in enabling the participants to shorten the duration of their inappropriate negative feelings once they occurred, but as the weeks progressed, the group members increasingly reported success in short-circuiting even the appearance of these disruptions. There were reports, too, of the combined use of relaxation and RET to prevent or reduce states of arousal.

Communication Skills

The least well known of the techniques used was Richard Stuart's (1974) program for facilitating the discussion of problems in as clear, nonemotional, and constructive a manner as possible. We included this strategy because difficulties in this area constitute one of the major sources of stress for our clients. Moreover, difficulty in communication is not restricted to the work site but was reported equally frequently with wives, children, tradespeople, and so on.

This program posits three levels of discussing differences, the first level focusing on the problem, the second level attacking the person, and the third level questioning the relationship itself. An example of how each of the three levels can be used to deal with the same situation is the supervisor who greets her late-arriving secretary with the message. "I should like you to be in by nine tomorrow" (Level 1), contrasted with "You are always tardy" (Level 2) or, more extremely, "I do not think we can continue to work together if you continue to be late" (Level 3). Clear communication on the level of the problem, in contrast to the person and relationship levels, is most likely to prevent the exchange from escalating into a full-scale battle of words in which much sound and fury hides the absence of any productive problem-solving. It also helps prevent the upset caused by the inability to handle unclear or aggressive messages received from others.

Our first step in teaching communication skills was to have the participants systematically listen to and classify the remarks of others. Gradually, this approach was shifted to self-observation, in which individuals were asked to record two examples daily of what they had said in a given conversation and then to assign the appropriate level to their remarks. Review of the homework during the weekly sessions provided the therapists with the opportunity to furnish additional aids for keeping communications clear and problem-centered. For instance, the participants were instructed to state what they wanted in a positive manner ("I should like to go out more often," rather than "I don't want to stay home all the time"), and to use reformulation to make sure that their messages had been clearly received. It was also suggested that, particularly at first, the discussion of potentially explosive topics should be restricted to short time periods. Issues unresolved at this point could be rescheduled for another short discussion later on.

Problem-Solving Skills

Training in communication skills helps the individuals send and receive messages that are clearer and better-formulated, but it does not provide an automatic solution for conflict. As an aid in resolving interpersonal conflict, as well as in enabling the individual to resolve more efficiently some of the practical problems of daily life, we introduced the problem-solving skills training described by D'Zurilla & Goldfried (1971). In presenting this technique to the participants, we were careful to acknowledge that they, by virtue of the positions they occupied, obviously already possessed considerable skill in making business decisions. Unfortunately, the same systematic approach was not often used in regulating personal problems. Instead, individuals were likely either to remain in a state of indecisiveness or else not to implement the decision taken, in both cases draining their emotional resources. We explained that systematic problem-solving could reduce these stresses by providing an efficient way of making decisions, implementing them, and evaluating the outcome.

Following the presentation of the problem-solving rationale, the steps involved were described. These consisted of defining the problem; brainstorming all possible solutions, including preposterous-appearing ones; appraising the positive and negative features of each alternative; choosing a course of action; making a plan for executing it; and establishing when and how the results of this course of action would be evaluated. The homework assignment for this technique was to go through this procedure for two problems weekly, recording the deliberations in writing. Discussion of these written records during sessions permitted the therapists to point out some of the more common pitfalls in problem solving. Particularly frequent were the failure to consider a wide enough range of alternatives, the failure to be flexible enough to combine a number of alternatives, or parts of them, and, most frequent of all, the failure to plan adequately for how the decision was to be implemented and evaluated.

Stress Inoculation

As developed by Meichenbaum (1977), the stress inoculation procedure is designed to help individuals, such as phobics or test-anxious students, continue to function adequately in the situations that engender stress for them. The emphasis here is on coping with rather than curing completely the feelings of distress. There are four stages to the technique as it is conventionally used: (1) a theoretical explanation for the emotional and physical discomfort experienced in the target situation; (2) training in relaxation as an active coping skill; (3) instructed practice in the emission of self-statements that will reduce the discomfort and allow the individual to continue functioning in spite of residual anxiety; and (4) supervised practice of these new skills in another, unrelated, high-stress situation.

Parts of this procedure, such as the theoretical explanation of distress and relaxation training, had already been covered in previous sections of our program. What was useful for our purposes was the technique of emitting coping self-statements and, even more important, the general emphasis on coping and the introduction of practice sessions to increase coping proficiency. Stress inoculation, as it was adapted for our needs, served both as a specific stress-reduction technique and as a more general "umbrella" technique that integrated previously acquired tension-reduction strategies.

We first taught the group members to become aware of and correctly label physical and cognitive signals of stress. They were then to attempt to defuse these reactions by transforming negative self-statements into positive ones, actively relaxing tense muscles, and employing any other of the previously learned strategies for managing upset that were appropriate to the present situation. As usual, the initial practice sessions were based on the recall of situations already experienced. Gradually, however, the men were encouraged to use this approach to curtail stress reactions as they were happening and, finally, to engage in prophylactic action before tackling situations previously experienced as stressful.

Because time pressure constituted a universal stressor for this group, we used it as an example on which to practice stress inoculation procedures. First, the participants were instructed to monitor their feelings of time pressure in the course of their week, noting the circumstances in which they occurred and the emotional and physical reactions engendered. The next step was to consider procedures for changing the situation and/or the reactions. These could include allowing time for inevitable emergencies and interruptions in drawing up the daily agenda, assigning a priority order to tasks, and discussing unrealistic demands from supervisors or peers in a problem-centered manner. Should the individual find himself pressured by time, in spite of these efforts, he could seek to reduce his distress by actively relaxing and emitting reassuring and positively reinforcing self-statements. The aim here was both to reduce the frequency with which the individual found himself under pressure of time and to teach him to cope with it better when it did occur.

Maintaining and Generalizing Treatment Benefits

As clinicians working in the areas of obesity, smoking, and alcoholism have already discovered to their sorrow, it is much easier to modify these habit patterns temporarily than to maintain the changes once treatment has ended (Bernstein & McAlister, 1976; Marlatt & Gordon, 1980; Stunkard, 1977). In the case of Type A behavior, the potential difficulties of maintenance are intensified by the diffuse nature of the target and the personal and social acceptability of the behaviors involved. An even more important barrier to the generalizability and durability of treatment benefits, however, is the impossibility during treatment of pinpointing all the circumstances under which Type A behavior is likely to occur. To the degree that Type A behavior constitutes a general way of coping with stress, the changing circumstances of the individual's life are likely to create ever-new challenges calling forth this type of response.

It is in the area of maintenance that our program is most tentative. To date, we have developed monthly report sheets that participants are asked to return to us on the dates indicated. In addition, a first booster session has been scheduled for three months following the end of the program. Some of the participants have also made plans to continue meeting informally. But the prime strategy for generalizing and maintaining treatment benefits was to furnish the participants with a model for self-observation and self-induced change that could be applied both to correct regression in the behavior already treated and to tackle new problems. The final sessions of the program were devoted to this blueprint for behavior change.

In this model, we try to be as explicit as possible about how one goes about, first, deciding what has to be changed and, second, instituting procedures likely to achieve the desired goals. The first step, as always, lies in achieving greater precision concerning the target. To operationalize a vague feeling of discomfort into one or more concrete behavioral goals, the procedure is first to localize the general area–intellectual, social, emotional, or physical–in which the discomfort is felt, and then to set up a self-observation schedule designed to provide information on the frequency, the intensity, and the situational determinants. At this point, the individual might decide to seek external help if the changes involved are beyond his skills. For some problems, at least, he would probably be able to use the behavior change strategies already learned to construct his own therapeutic program. The homework assignment of applying this blueprint for change to a current concern led the men to tackle a variety of problems, ranging from the desire to lose weight to that of achieving greater sensitivity in interpersonal relations.

Problems Anticipated and Encountered

In carrying out the program, we did not encounter some of the problems that were anticipated, but we did confront others that were not. Both situations are worth noting.

Personal Disclosure

One anticipated problem was that the men might make personal disclosures during the session that would lead to embarrassment when they next encountered each other at work. Fortunately, this problem did not arise. The emphasis in the program presentation was on problems that anybody might encounter, and in conformity with this orientation, the men's personal examples focused mainly on the minor irritations of daily life. One dramatic exception was a man who arrived at a session obviously in the midst of a deep personal crisis. Interestingly enough, he managed to describe his reactions without going into details concerning the situation itself. It seems that the participants had no particular difficulty in remaining on the skills-training level and did not seek to transform the session into a group therapy process.

Problems of Scheduling

The group format has the double advantage of permitting the economical use of the therapist's time and of providing peer modeling and support for the difficult process of change. What a group meeting on a fixed weekly schedule does not do is to adapt to the changing schedules of men whose jobs require them to travel frequently and at short notice. Irregular attendance caused by business travel was a problem for a fair number of participants, and in a few cases, these men decided to abandon the program completely. To encourage maximum attendance, we permitted the participants to attend either of the two weekly sessions held in their language (French or English). We also tried to maintain continuity via a buddy system and written handouts summarizing the treatment content. Unfortunately, these remedial measures were not always successful. If this type of program is to be generalizable to men who cannot attend regular weekly sessions, then we shall have to develop a format better adapted to their needs.

Homework Records

Although each homework assignment might take only a few minutes to carry out, recording the task in writing was perceived as cumbersome by the participants. Indeed, writing down all the steps involved in solving a problem or debating an irrational belief can be a lengthy process. If one adds to these assignments the written records required for monitoring days every other week (Roskies, 1979), then the participants were justified in their half-joking complaint that the program was generating as much time pressure as it was alleviating.

Because we consider these homework records an essential part of the program, we are seeking ways of obtaining them while reducing strain on the participants. One alternative is to redesign the homework record sheets so as to minimize the amount of writing required. Another alternative is to have the participants tape-record, rather than write, at least some of their homework assignments. A third alternative is to refine the dependent measures so that less writing is required on the monitoring days. Some combination of these alternatives will be used in future programs.

A Cautionary Note

Whatever the theoretical elegance of a particular treatment program, the critical test of its value lies in the results. At the time of writing, the first 40 men have just completed the 13 sessions, and results concerning the effects of the intervention are not yet available. Until then, the program described here must be viewed with caution. We consider it an improvement on previous efforts (cf. Roskies *et al.*, 1978), but it is not necessarily the final version of our therapeutic attempts to modify Type A behavior.

References

Bernstein, D. A., & Borkovec, T. D. *Progressive relaxation training.* Champaign: Research Press, 1973.

Bernstein, D. A., & McAlister, A. L. The modification of smoking behavior: progress and problems. *Addictive Behavior*, 1976, *1*, 89–102.

Cohen, J. B. *Sociocultural change and behavior patterns in disease etiology: An epidemiological study of coronary disease among Japanese-Americans.* Unpublished Ph.D. thesis, University of California, Berkeley, 1974.

Davis, R. Stress and hemostatic mechanisms. In R. S. Eliot(Ed.), *Stress and the heart*. New York: Futura, 1974.

Dembroski, T., & Macdougall, J. Stress effects on affiliation preferences among subjects possessing the Type A coronary-prone behavior pattern. *Journal of Personality and Social Psychology*, 1978, *36*, 23–33.

Dembroski, T., Macdougall, J., & Shields, J. Physiologic reactions to social challenge in persons evidencing the Type A coronary-prone behavior pattern. *Journal of Human Stress*, 1977, *3*, No 3, 2–9.

D'Zurilla, T. J., & Goldfried, M. R. Problem solving and behavior modification. *Journal of Abnormal Psychology*, 1971, *78*, 107–126.
Ellis, A., & Grieger, R. (Eds.). *Handbook of rational-emotive therapy.* New York: Springer, 1977.
Frankenhaeuser, M. Department of Psychology, University of Stockholm. Personal communication, 1977.
Friedman, M., Byers, S., Diamant, J., & Rosenman, R. H. Plasma catecholamine response of coronary-prone subjects (type A) to a specific challenge. *Metabolism*, 1975, *24*, 205–210.
Gilmore, J. P. Physiology of stress. In R. S. Eliot (Ed.), *Stress and the heart.* New York: Futura, 1974.
Glass, D. C. *Behavior patterns, stress and coronary disease.* Hillsdale, N.J.: Lawrence Erlbaum, 1977.
Glass, D. C., Snyder, M. L., & Hollis, J. F. Time urgency and the Type A coronary prone behavior pattern. *Journal of Applied Social Psychology*, 1974, *4*, 125–140.
Jenkins, C. D. Psychologic and social precursors of coronary disease. *New England Journal of Medicine*, 1971, *284*, 244–255, 307–317.
Jenkins, C. D. Recent evidence supporting psychologic and social risk factors for coronary disease. *New England Journal of Medicine*, 1976, *294*, 987–994, 1033–1038.
Jenni, M. A., & Wollersheim, J. P. Cognitive therapy, stress management training and the Type A behavior pattern. *Cognitive Therapy and Research*, 1979, *3*, 61–75.
Lazarus, R.S., & Launier, R. Stress-related transactions between person and environment. In L. A. Peruin & M. Lewis (Eds.), *Perspectives in interpersonal psychology.* New York: Plenum, 1978.
Marlatt, G. A., & Gordon, J. R. Determinants of relapse: Implications for the maintenance of behavior change. In P. Davidson & S. Davidson (Eds.),*Behavior al medicine: Changing health lifestyles.* New York: Brunner/Mazel, 1980.
Matthews, K. A., & Saal, F. E. Relationship of the type A coronary-prone behavior pattern to achievement, power and affiliation motives. *Psychosomatic Medicine*, 1978, *40*, 631–637.
Maultsby, M., & Ellis, A. Techniques for using rational-emotive imagery. In A. Ellis & E. Abraham (Eds.), *Brief psychotherapy in medical and health practice.* New York: Springer, 1978.
Meichenbaum, D. *Cognitive-behavior modification: An integrative approach.* New York: Plenum Press, 1977.
Obrist, P. A. The cardiovascular-behavior interaction—as it appears today. *Psychophysiology*, 1976, *13*, 95–107.
Rosenman, R. H. The role of behavior patterns and neurogenic factors in the pathogenesis of coronary heart disease. In R. S. Eliot (Ed.), *Stress and the heart.* New York: Futura, 1974.
Rosenman, R. H. History and definition of the Type A coronary-prone behavior pattern. In T. Dembroski (Ed.), *Proceedings of the forum on coronary-prone behavior.* Washington, D.C.: Dept. of Health, Education and Welfare Publication, No. (NIH) 78–1451, 1977, pp. 13–18.(a)
Rosenman, R. H. The interview method of assessment of the coronary-prone behavior pattern. In T. Dembroski (Ed.), *Proceedings of the forum on coronary-prone behavior.* Washington, D.C.: Dept. of Health, Education and Welfare Publication No. (NIH) 78–1451,1977, pp. 83–104. (b)
Rosenman, R. H., & Friedman, M. Modifying Type A behaviour pattern. *Journal of Psychosomatic Research*, 1977, *21*, 323–333.
Roskies, E. Evaluating improvement in the coronary-prone (type A) behavior pattern. In D. J. Osborne, M. M. Greeneberg, & J. R. Eisee (Eds.), *Research in psychology and medicine.* New York: Academic Press, 1979.
Roskies, E. Considerations in developing a treatment program for the coronary-prone (type A) behavior pattern. In P. Davidson & S. Davidson (Eds.), *Behavioral medicine: Changing health lifestyles.* New York: Brunner/Mazel, 1980.

Roskies, E., Spevack, M., Surkis, A., Cohen, C., & Gilman, S. Changing the coronary-prone (type A) behavior pattern in a nonclinical population. *Journal of Behavioral Medicine*, 1978, *1*, 201–215.

Roskies, E., Kearney, H., Spevack, M., Surkis, A., Cohen, C., & Gilman, S. Generalizability and durability of treatment effects in an intervention program for coronary-prone (type A) managers. *Journal of Behavioral Medicine*, 1979, *2*, 195–207.

Scherwitz, L., Berton, K., & Leventhal, H. Type A assessment and interaction in the behavior pattern interview. *Psychosomatic Medicine,* 1977, *39,* 229–240.

Scherwitz, L., Berton, K., & Leventhal, H. Type A behavior, self-involvement and cardiovascular response. *Psychosomatic Medicine*, 1978, *40*, 593–609.

Stuart, R. B. *Communication skills training.* Paper presented at the annual meeting of the Association des Spécialistes en Modification du Comportement, Moncton, New Brunswick, Canada, June 1974.

Stunkard, A. J. Behavioral treatment of obesity: Failure to maintain weight loss. In R. B. Stuart (Ed.), *Behavioral self-management: Strategies, techniques and outcome.* New York: Brunner/Mazel, 1977.

Suin, R. M. The cardiac stress management program for Type A patients. *Cardiac Rehabilitation*, 1975, *5*, 13–15.

Suin, R. M., & Bloom, L. J. Anxiety management training for Pattern A behavior. *Journal of Behavioral Medicine,* 1978, *1*, 25–35.

Van Egeren, L. F. Social interaction, communications and the coronary-prone behavior pattern: A psychophysiological study. *Psychosomatic Medicine*, 1979, *41*, 21–19.

Waldron, I. Sex differences in the coronary-prone pattern. In T. Dembroski (Ed.), *Proceedings of the forum on coronary-prone behavior.* Washington, D.C.: Dept. Health, Education and Welfare, Publication No. (NIH) 78–1451, 1977, 253–261.

Williams, R. B. Physiological mechanisms underlying the association between psychosocial factors and coronary disease. In W. D. Gentry & R. B. Williams (Eds.), *Psychological aspects of myocardial infarction and coronary care.* St. Louis: C. V. Mosby, 1975.

Williams, R. B., Friedman, M., Glass, D. C., Herd, J. A., & Schneiderman, N. Summary statement: Mechanisms linking behavioral and psychophysiological processes. In T. Dembroski (Ed.), *Proceedings of the forum on coronary-prone behavior.* Washington, D.C.: Dept. of Health, Education and Welfare, Publication No. (NIH) 78–1451, 1977, 157–169.

Zyzanski, S. J. Associations of the coronary-prone behavior pattern. In T. D. Dembroski (Ed.), *Proceedings of the forum on coronary-prone behavior.* Washington, D.C.: Dept. of Health, Education and Welfare Publication No. (NIH) 78–1451, 1977, 46–67.

CHAPTER 9

Self-Help Approaches to Self-Management

Gerald M. Rosen

Clinical Psychologist
Private Practice
Seattle, Washington

The interest of psychologists in self-management has focused primarily on therapist-assisted programs (see, for example, Stuart, 1977). It is only during the past five years that attention has been directed to self-help approaches to self-management. *Self-help* refers to "self-or-peer-direction of efforts to meet some challenge in daily living" (Stuart & Mitchell, 1978). The combined interest in self-help and self-management follows from a shared educational orientation to problems of living. Furthermore, it has been suggested that self-help approaches to self-management can foster self-attributions of change, thereby increasing generalization and maintenance of treatment effects (Kopel & Arkowitz, 1975).

Self-help and self-management are of recent interest to psychologists, but the concepts and strategies are not new. Consideration of current texts on self-management (e.g., Stuart, 1977) reveals that relaxation, cognitive rehearsal, coping self-statements, and contingency management skills are most commonly taught. These are the same skills that were taught routinely by behavior therapists before "self-management" was in vogue. Self-management techniques were also taught before "behavior therapy" as such existed. Rosen and Orenstein (1976) have reported on the use of thought-stopping techniques in 1875. It is also true that self-help programs have been with us for many years (e.g., Samuel Smiles's 1889 text, *Self-Help).* Katz and Bender (1976) have traced the origins of self-help organizations to nineteenth-century England, while Stuart and Mitchell (1978) feel that the roots of these activities reach still further back in history.

Psychologists who develop today's self-help programs may believe that they have a new idea, but further searching often reveals that this is not the case. As the author of one self-help book on phobias (*Don't Be Afraid*, Prentice-Hall, 1976b), I recently obtained a copy of a related text by Cowles (*Don't Be Afraid*, McGraw-Hill, 1941). It is true that the 1976 program applies a learning framework to anxiety events, while the 1941 text provides an energy nerve-cell theory of fatigue. But often the content of new and old self-help programs is highly similar. Consider, for example, the following passage from one self-help text:

> In all human activities three occurrences follow one another in regular order: (1) the external incident; (2) the thinking which follows the incident; and (3) the bodily action which is caused by the thinking, is governed by it, and consequently takes its character from it.

These words could have been written by Albert Ellis, to whom cognitive behavior therapists owe a tremendous debt. The quotation parallels closely the A-B-C model for cognitions that forms the basis of Ellis's rational-emotive therapy. Yet, the quotation is taken from Aaron Crane's 1905 book on *Right and Wrong Thinking* (p. 177).

Current self-help programs cover the same issues and concerns of earlier programs. With regard to cognitive habits, Wayne Dyer's *Your Erroneous-Zones* (1977) has replaced Norman Vincent Peale's *The Power of Positive Thinking* (1952) and Aaron Crane's 1905 text. For information on social interactions, Eric Berne's *Games People Play* (1964) has substituted for Dale Carnegie's instructions on *How to Win Friends and Influence People* 1936). For the all-purpose, broad-based program, Michael Mahoney's *Self-Change* (1979) takes the place of Samuel Smiles's *Self-Help* (1889).

In addition to broad-based programs, there exist numerous self-help books that have a narrow or specialized function. These are the books that teach the popular, sometimes faddish techniques of the day. At the turn of the century, the "current" approach was "personal magnetism" (Dumont, 1913); in the 1920s, it was *How to Psychoanalyze Yourself* (Ralph, 1921); and now, in the 1980s, the public is deluged with books on personal, do-it-yourself behavior modification.

It has been suggested that today's self-help approaches to self-management are distinguished from earlier programs only to the extent that they have been empirically validated (Rosen, 1976a, 1977). When programs remain untested, then personal magnetism, do-it-yourself psychoanalysis,and self-help behavior therapy have more in common than many would like to think. This issue of empirically validating self-help programs becomes especially important in light of a recent development in the field: today's self-help texts are written frequently by academically based and highly respected clinical psychologists. This involvement of professionally recognized clinicians in the development and marketing of self-help programs is unprecedented. A partial listing of recent authors illustrates the point: Peter Lewinsohn has coauthored a program that relates to his work on depression; Edward Lichtenstein has coauthored a text on smoking; Carl Thoresen has coauthored a book on treating insomnia; Michael Mahoney and Balfour Jeffrey have programs for weight loss; Isaac Marks and others have published on fear reduction; the LoPiccolos have developed a program for female orgasmic dysfunctions; Arnold Lazarus has a cognitive therapy self-help book; Gerald Patterson has a program for child behavior problems; and Phillip Zimbardo has published on shyness.

At first glance, this involvement of psychologists in the development and marketing of self-help programs would appear to be beneficial. Psychologists are in a unique position to contribute to the self-help movement. No other professional group combines the clinical and research experiences that are part of the clinical psychologist's educational background. Clinical psychologists are skilled in current therapeutic techniques, they have clinical experience and sensitivity, and they have the training to assess empirically the efficacy of the programs they develop. Consequently, clinical psychologists are in a position to assess empirically, and thereby distinguish, their self-help programs from previous, untested books of advice. This would represent a most significant and new development in the area of self-help approaches to self-management.[1]

Naturally, the question arises: How well are psychologists applying their professional expertise? From one point of view, the answer to this question is disappointing, and the next section of this paper critiques several areas. At the same time, it is important to provide a context for the critical comments that follow. However disappointed we may be in the quality of self-help materials, psychologists have done more to assess their programs than nonprofessional authors and authors of other professions. The efforts of psychologists have led to an increasingly large literature that now allows us to make statements about the efficacy of self-help approaches to self-management. The work of psychologists has also pointed to future directions for research so that self-help programs may be improved further. So in the following section, the reader is asked to adopt this set: Psychologists are doing more than others to

[1]An additional new development in the area of self-help is that various media exist for delivering the message. In addition to self-help books, there now are available records and audio cassettes. Among the various media, the proliferation and availability of self-help books are unequaled. Accordingly, the present paper focuses on this instructional format in its discussion.

develop adequate self-help programs; our concern is with what more can be done.

The Status of Current Self-Help Programs

Much of the present section is based on two earlier reviews of behavioral bibliotherapies (Glasgow & Rosen, 1978,1979). The first of these reviews was written during 1975 through 1976; the second review was written two years later. In each review, the focus was restricted to treatment programs that (1) consisted primarily of written text; (2) were addressed to prospective clients; and (3) presented behavioral approaches. By means of Goldiamond's guidelines (1975), behavioral approaches were defined to include modeling, aversive conditioning, desensitization, or operant techniques. Even with this restricted focus, a large number of self-help manuals and general texts were located. In the first review, the number of programs was 86; in the second review, conducted two years later, an additional 73 programs were discussed.

The first finding to consider from the above reviews concerns the extent to which behavioral self-help programs have been empirically validated. For the 86 manuals covered in the first review, 74 studies or case reports evaluating the programs were located. For the 73 manuals covered in the second review, only 43 studies or case reports were located. Thus, the overall ratio of studies to books decreased from .86 to .59. This finding is a discouraging one; it suggests that the risks that consumers face when purchasing do-it-yourself therapy books have actually increased from 1976 to 1978. Evidently, the desire among psychologists to publish has been of greater influence than the professional responsibility of psychologists to assess.

Concern about the risks faced by consumers who use untested self-help programs is not unwarranted (Barrera,Rosen, & Glasgow, 1982). First, self-help programs may be applied inappropriately. For example, an individual with thyroid problems might self-administer a stimulus control program for insomnia; an individual with headaches that are caused by a tumor could misapply self-administered relaxation; or an individual in the depressive phase of manic-depressive illness could postpone proper medical treatment while dabbling with pleasant events schedules. The area of self-diagnosis is totally unexplored, and the risks faced by consumers may be legion.

After diagnosis, there is the risk of a consumer failing to understand instructions, misusing instructions, or failing to follow through or comply with therapeutic regimens. In the event of treatment failure, there is the risk of negative self-attributions, of anger toward oneself or others, and of reduced belief in the efficacy of today's therapeutic techniques. As is shown later in this paper, studies have already documented the need for concern in many of these areas.

In addition to a general trend toward untested self-help books, there are specific findings that require consideration. In pointing out these findings, it may be best to start in my own territory: the area of fear reduction. The text mentioned earlier (Rosen, *Don't Be Afraid*, 1976b) is one of over a dozen books currently available to consumers who wish to overcome fears or phobias (see Glasgow & Rosen, 1978, 1979). In comparison with these other texts, *Don't Be Afraid* appears to be adequately assessed. There have been two controlled outcome studies evaluating an earlier draft of the published book (Rosen, Glasgow, & Barrera, 1976; Barrera & Rosen, 1977), and a two-year follow-up was conducted for subjects in the first study (Rosen, Glasgow, & Barrera, 1977). But a careful look at these studies is revealing and can lead to a surprising conclusion.

In the first study (Rosen *et al.*, 1976), highly fearful snake phobics were randomly assigned to receive self-administered desensitization; desensitization with minimal therapist contact; therapist-directed desensitization; a self-administered placebo control manual; or no treatment. The outcome study was well controlled and the prepost measures included self-reports, physiological, and behavioral indexes. As it turned out, the obtained treatment effects were modest; significant group differences were obtained only when combined desensitization groups were compared with combined controls. At the same time, it was observed that 50% of the subjects in self-administered desensitization failed to complete half of their hierarchy items. Furthermore, the correlations between the posttest performance and the progress in treatment were as high in magnitude as .83. Thus, the first study suggested impressive treatment effects for subjects who followed through on a self-administered program.

The purpose of the second study (Barrera & Rosen, 1977) was to improve the subject's compliance with the therapeutic instructions so as to better assess the maximum potential of self-administered desensitization. Highly fearful snake phobics were randomly assigned to receive either self-administered desensitization exactly as in the first study; self-administered desensitization with a pleasant-events self-reward contracting supplement; or the self-administered placebo manual from the first study accompanied by self-reward contracting. The basis for this study came from Mahoney and Thoresen's (1974) suggestion that self-reward strategies can facilitate subjects' implementation of a self-control treatment.

As it turned out, the findings from the Barrera and Rosen study were the opposite of those predicted. Rather than increasing compliance, there was a most significant and dramatic effect toward decreasing compliance. As in the first study, 50% of the regular self-administered subjects completed their program, and all of these subjects showed substantial reductions on measures of fear of snakes. But in the self-administered condition with self-reward contracting, not a single subject finished. In fact, not a single subject progressed beyond relaxation training!

Based on their findings, Barrera and Rosen concluded that self-reward strategies can actually hinder subjects' implementation of a self-control treatment. It has been suggested that the "right" self-reward system would facilitate compliance, and this may be true. Certainly, something was dramatically wrong with the procedures that were adopted by Barrera and Rosen, as no other study has produced such poor compliance. But to argue about procedures is to miss the point of the study. The main point to be drawn from the Barrera and Rosen study is this: for whatever reason(s), well-intentioned changes in instructional materials can have a significant negative effect on treatment outcome. This conclusion should give pause to all responsible authors of self-help books.

What do current findings on self-administered desensitization mean for *Don't Be Afraid* and other do-it-yourself fear-reduction programs? On the one hand, several studies support the finding that 50%–60% of people can use these programs and reduce single phobias. Self-help programs appear to be highly successful *if* an individual takes the time and expends the effort to comply with the instructions and to follow through with the program. But compliance problems have been observed in all reported studies. Furthermore, all published programs for treating fears and phobias either are untested or are "well-intentioned" revisions of tested manuals. If the findings from Barrera and Rosen are to be taken seriously, then consumers may be purchasing instructional materials that they have very little chance of ever using.

It has been argued that it is up to professionals to develop effective programs; it is then up to the consumers to use them. But this is a false argument and a poor defense of professionally developed programs. It is not enough to tell an obese person to stop eating, a smoker to stop smoking, or a phobic to "face the fear." It is the psychologist's responsibility to develop intructional methods that realistically help individuals meet their desired goals. If instructions are presented in such a manner that no one follows them, then the instructions are not useful and should not be marketed.

This discussion has demonstrated that the developers of today's fear-reduction programs have met their responsibilities only halfway. They have demonstrated that self-help programs can be helpful, but they have not satisfactorily dealt with compliance issues. It is also true that additional concerns can be raised with regard to fear reduction programs. One concern is about the application of do-it-yourself materials to the treatment of agoraphobia. Such applications remain untested. Yet, there are two programs

(Frampton, 1974; Weekes, 1977) written specifically for this problem, and some texts include a special chapter on the topic (Fensterheim & Baer, 1977). There is one study on agoraphobia (Matthews, Teasdale, Munby, Johnston, & Shaw, 1977) that provides support for the use of instructional materials under minimal therapist-contact conditions, but these findings cannot be generalized to totally self-administered contexts. Studies on the self-administered treatment of specific phobias also do not apply, as agoraphobia is a complex clinical problem that requires special consideration (Goldstein & Chambless, 1978; Hallam, 1978). Furthermore, Hardy (personal communication, May 1978), who has worked extensively with agoraphobics through an organization called TERRAP, reports that most agoraphobics have difficulty employing self-help materials alone. Sutherland, Amit, and Weiner (1977) similarly cautioned agoraphobics: "in all good conscience we cannot suggest that your best possible option is to try to treat yourself" (p. 145). Thus far, the authors of self-help programs for agoraphobics have not dealt adequately with the clinical risks that self-treatment may entail.

Another significant development in self-help fear programs is a departure from the usual procedures of desensitization and the use of a gradual approach. Recent self-help books explain procedures that are more akin to flooding strategies (e.g., Sutherland *et al.*, 1977; Weekes, 1977). Unfortunately, there is no published report to suggest that people can successfully flood themselves with anxiety-evoking stimuli. Should self-administered attempts at flooding fail, it would seem likely that an individual's fear reactions would be sensitized. Studies should have evaluated the likelihood of this outcome before instructional recommendations on self-administered flooding were made.

While there may be important and unresolved issues in the area of the self-treatment of phobias, the state of affairs in most other areas is no better: at times, the status of self-help programs is significantly worse. For example, in the area of assertiveness, no book has been adequately assessed. The first Glasgow and Rosen review located 11 training books. By the time of the second review, there were 8 additional assertiveness books and 3 new books on shyness. One study (Richey, 1978) assessed a self-help program under conditions including therapist assistance; a second study (Rakos & Schroeder, 1979) evaluated a written program accompanied by tape-recorded instructions; and a third study (Schindler, 1979) assessed a commercially available self-help book based on self-administration. This last study is most relevant to the present discussion, but it has so many problems that the results are rendered meaningless. Most importantly, Schindler's study intended to have 60 subjects, obtained 43, and ended up with only 17 completing the treatment. Clearly, much work remains before self-help assertiveness books will have been assessed adequately. In the meantime, Glasgow and Rosen (1979) have suggested the following for psychologists with gallows humor: Imagine, if you will, the unassertive consumer at a bookstore. There he or she stands, gazing at over 20 untested books of advice, wondering if one book is better than another, but too shy or too anxious to ask! Psychologists who have worked with unassertive clients will appreciate that there is a more serious side to this scenario.

The area of child behavior problems has been thoroughly reviewed by McMahon and Forehand (1979). The present discussion focuses on *Toilet Training in Less Than a Day* by Azrin and Foxx (1974), because this text has been evaluated and the obtained findings are provocative. It should be noted first that the procedures described by Azrin and Foxx were carefully developed and assessed under therapist-directed conditions. However, in an early review of the book, Kimmel (1974) questioned the ability of parents to successfully employ the procedures on their own. Butler (1976) later reported that parents who self-administered the book were not successful, but this information was informal and lacked systematic assessment. It took a small controlled study by Matson and Ollendick (1977) to document earlier concerns. In that study, four of five mothers in a therapist-administered condition were able to successfully toilet-train their children, while only *one* of five mothers in a self-administered group was successful. Moreover, Matson and Ollendick observed negative emotional side effects between mothers and their children; there were increased problem behaviors on the part of the children and uncomfortable feelings on the part of the mothers. The authors noted that the negative reactions were greatest among the nonsupervised mothers. Matson and Ollendick's findings represent the first demonstration that do-it-yourself programs can have negative effects and that these effects are not limited to the person whose behavior is targeted for change. The findings also demonstrate that the success of therapist-assisted programs cannot be generalized to self-administered applications of the same programs without empirical support.

The potential for failure and negative side effects may be greater than psychologists would like to think. Recently, Zeiss (1978) conducted a controlled outcome study on the treatment of premature ejaculation. The subjects were assigned on a random basis to receive either self-administered, minimal-contact, or therapist-directed treatment. As in the earlier reports by Zeiss (1977) and Lowe and Mikulas (1975), the treatment that included minimal contact with a therapist was effective. But of the six couples who were to self-administer the treatment, not a single one successfully completed the program. Zeiss did not follow up on the adjustment of these couples, but if we think of Matson and Ollendick's findings, one can imagine the possible consequences that treatment failures might entail. When a program is not completed, is it the husband's fault or the fault of the wife? We can only hope that the couple would stop to think that it could be the fault of the program.

In general, the area of do-it-yourself sex therapies is highly inadequate, if not professionally embarrassing. Except for studies on premature ejaculation, self-help materials have not been tested. Yet readers are invited to purchase *The Last Sex Manual* (Pion & Hopkins, 1977), whose "revolutionary behavior modification method starts where Masters and Johnson leave off." Or the consumer may want to try *Love Making: You Can Be Your Own Sex Therapist* (Altman, 1977), which has been "proven to work." The claims that accompany self-help sex-therapy books warrant professional concern. Kaplan and Kohl (1972) have noted adverse reactions to therapist-directed treatments of sexual problems. In a recent review of sexual dysfunctions, Wright, Perreault, and Mathieu (1977) noted a "clear danger that some . . . promising techniques are being applied indiscriminately with inadequately selected populations . . . the risk of treatment-provoked deterioration is ever present" (p. 890). If concerns can be raised with regard to therapist-directed treatments, then surely they apply as well to self-administered programs.

In the area of weight reduction and smoking cessation, there has been excellent research on the use of self-help programs. However, studies on smoking cessation strongly suggest that self-help programs are as ineffective as therapist-directed programs (see Glasgow & Rosen, 1978, 1979). To use Lichtenstein's comment from 1971, "Good designs, ineffective treatments." Studies on weight control provide somewhat more support, but they have generally included minimal therapist contact as a part of the treatment. The totally self-administered use of self-help weight-loss books has been inadequately assessed.

As in other areas, the titles and claims that accompany weight loss programs have not kept pace with current findings. Thus, in a 1976 review paper, the Mahoneys observed, "significant poundage losses are still in the minority and long-term maintenance has remained unexamined" (cited in Franks & Wilson, 1978). Yet, as Franks and Wilson noted in their *Annual Review of Behavior Therapy* (1978), the Mahoneys (1976) published in the same year as their review paper a self-help book entitled *Permanent Weight Control.*

Future Directions

Thus far, the present discussion of self-help programs has highlighted areas of concern. It has been shown that well-intentioned instructional materials are useless for all practical purposes, if compliance rates fall to zero. It has been demonstrated that negative side effects can result from participation in a self-help program. It has been seen that results from therapist-assisted programs may not generalize to self-administered contexts. Furthermore, the application of do-it-yourself materials to several complex clinical programs remains unassessed. Finally, the titles and promotional claims that accompany self-help programs far outdistance any available data. Based on these observations, we now consider a number of areas that require further study and a number of professional-ethical issues that deserve attention.

Interpersonal Issues

Research on toilet-training programs for children has demonstrated how important it is that psychologists keep in mind the interpersonal context within which self-help may occur. Recent findings on therapist-directed treatments of agoraphobia serve to highlight further the importance of considering interpersonal contexts. Hafner has shown that the successful treatment of agoraphobic females can lead to deterioration of marriages and symptom development on the part of husbands in 50% of the treated cases (Hafner, 1977; Milton & Hafner, 1979).

One positive approach to interpersonal issues has been taken by Kelly Brownell and his colleagues at the University of Pennsylvania. Brownell developed a self-help weight-loss manual for obese patients *and* a supplemental manual for spouses. In a study that compared treatment with and without the use of the spouse's manual (Brownell, Heckerman, Westlake, Hayes, & Monti, 1979), support was obtained for the supplemental program.These findings should encourage psychologists who develop self-help materials to assess empirically the efficacy of supplemental instructions to family and friends. At the very least, psychologists who conduct outcome studies should include self-report measures to assess the impact of therapy on significant others.

Self-Diagnosis

It is surprising how little attention the area of self-diagnosis has received. Strupp (1977) first raised the issue during a symposium on do-it-yourself therapies. At the present time, there is still no single study addressing this critical issue.

It would appear that two basic errors can be made by those who consider the use of self-help materials (Barrera *et al.*, 1981). First, consumers can treat themselves for conditions that are inappropriate for self-help, either because of the severity of the problem or because nonpsychological treatment methods are needed. When self-help is applied inappropriately in these instances, there is the real danger that it will postpone proper professional care and contribute to the mounting severity of a problem.

The second error is one of commission rather than of omission. While it may be argued that there is always room for improvement and self-development, one can imagine a consumer who uses self-help materials to overdiagnose a problem. If self-help materials do not contain procedures for preventing self-identified false positives, consumers can invest needless time and energy in attempts at self-change. In this way, consumers can also risk the negative consequences of sustained labels of abnormality.

Several self-help books now contain a self-assessment section that attempts to clarify for the reader when it is appropriate to use the materials, but in no case have psychologists assessed these sections. Thus, the rates of false positives and false negatives in the area of self-diagnosis remain unknown.

Noncompliance

As evidenced in the previous discussion, compliance with self-administered instructional materials is a critical problem. This is true not only of the fear reduction area but applies as well to findings on sexual dysfunctions, weight loss, smoking cessation, and other problems (see Glasgow & Rosen, 1978, 1979). It may be that the extensive literature on compliance with medical therapeutic regimens has applicability to the present topic. A major finding from this area (see Sackett & Haynes, 1976) is that the complexity of a treatment regimen is inversely related to compliance. This may explain the Barrera and Rosen study, in which the addition of a self-reward contracting procedure decreased compliance. Put simply, the self-reward contracting system may have been the instructional straw that broke the subject's back. If this is true, then attempts to simplify instructional materials are to be encouraged (Kirsch & Henry, 1979).

A number of factors identified in the medical literature appear to have a positive effect on compliance with therapeutic regimens. These factors include the perceived relationship between the physician and the patient and such convenience factors as the amount of time spent in the waiting room. The possible importance of the doctor-patient relationship in producing compliance does not justify poor follow-through with self-help programs. Readers can often "feel" the concern of an author, and the author of a self-help book can relate in a sensitive manner to the needs of a reader. The question for future research is how to write instructional programs so as to maximize the support and the structure that people appear to need when undergoing behavior change efforts. It may be that compliance is enhanced best when authors begin with general, empathetic discussions of a problem and proceed only gradually to detailed descriptions of step-by-step methods.

Improper Assessment

In general, psychologists have not assessed adequately the self-help materials that they have developed. The figures cited earlier from the reviews by Glasgow and Rosen document this point. In the two-year period from 1976 to 1978, the ratio of studies to manuals declined from .86 to .59. In truth, the picture is considerably worse than these figures indicate. Of all the studies and case reports reviewed by Glasgow and Rosen, only 27% evaluated a self-administered treatment condition. In other words, 73% of all studies on self-help books have evaluated treatment conditions that include some therapist contact. It is hard to understand why psychologists have failed to test self-help programs under the most important condition of intended usage. Findings from Matson and Ollendick (1977) demonstrate clearly that we cannot generalize from therapist-directed programs to self-administered ones. Future work on self-help therapies needs to keep this point in mind.

Nonclinical Applications

The application of self-help programs to daily problems of living, rather than to severe clinical concerns, is beginning to receive attention. Clark and his colleagues have conducted the most systematic work in this area, having written advice manuals for "normal families." The tactic that has been followed is to identify high-frequency nuisance situations that may be disruptive to the family system. Therapist-directed programs are then developed, translated into self-instructional materials, and assessed under self-administered conditions. The best example of this work is a small pamphlet for problems encountered while shopping with children (Clark, Greene, Macrae, McNees, Davis, & Risley, 1977).

The work by Clark and his colleagues suggests the possibility of applying self-help instructional materials on a widespread and preventive basis. In this way, small but high-frequency difficulties could be prevented from becoming major life problems. Nonclinical applications of self-help materials could be developed for couple interaction problems, employment stresses, and a host of parent–child issues.

Ethical Concerns

Concern about the ethical responsibilities faced by psychologists who develop and market do-it-yourself therapies has been expressed in earlier papers (Rosen, 1976a, 1977). In March 1978, the American Psychological Association initiated a Task Force on Self-Help Psychotherapies, co-sponsored by the Board of Professional Affairs and the Committee on Scientific and Professional Ethics and Conduct.[2] An important issue that was considered by this task force was discrepancies between the claims made for self-change programs and empirical evidence regarding the true clinical efficacy of self-help.

One does not have to search deeply to find the reason for the exaggerated claims accompanying self-help programs. As Rosen (1976a) observed in an earlier paper, "At the present time, the only contingencies that need affect the sale of *self-help* materials are monetary ones" (p. 140). And self-help can be big business. "NBC Nightly News" reported that Wayne Dyer was able to take the "two million or so dollars that he made from *Your Erroneous Zones* to quit his practice as a psychologist in New York and move to Florida."[3]

Much of the responsibility for exaggerated claims must fall on the authors of self-help programs, but in some cases, the responsibility may lie with the publishers, or the author's failure to negotiate strongly with the publishers. For example, Arnold Lazarus wrote a book on cognitive strategies for self-management (*In the Mind's Eye*, 1977). The book itself is reasonably well written, but the publisher makes the following claims on the book's back jacket:

> This book will show you how to enhance your creative powers . . . stop smoking, drinking or overeating . . . overcome sadness and despondency . . . build self-confidence and skill . . . overcome fears and anxieties.

The potential purchaser of Lazarus's book is told further that "*In the Mind's Eye* eliminates the need for lengthy psychotherapy or outside help."

Let us consider such exaggerated claims in the context of the *Ethical Standards of Psychologists* (American Psychological Association, 1977). Principle 1 of the *Standards* notes that psychologists are to be alert to personal, financial, or political situations or pressures that might lead to misuse of their influence. The titles and claims of many self-help books show that psychologists have adopted postures that are less than alert.

[2]The members of the Task Force on Self-Help Psychotherapies were Manuel Barrera, Jr., Cyril Franks, Herbert Freudenberger, Russell Glasgow, Susan Gilmore, Edward Lichtenstein, Peter Nathan, and Gerald Rosen (chair).

[3]Appreciation is extended to Sandy Goodman of "NBC Nightly News," who provided a transcript of NBC's story on self-help books, 1978.

Principle 2 of the *Ethical Standards* states that psychologists should provide services, use techniques, or offer opinions only as professionals who meet recognized standards. Publishing a self-help book that is totally untested or, worse yet, publishing a book that has been shown to be ineffective is not fulfilling recognized standards.

Principle 4 of the *Ethical Standards* states that public statements, announcements, and advertisements should be made in a professional, factually informative, and nonsensationalized manner. The previous sections of this paper demonstrate amply how often this code is broken.

In the course of considering the current status of self-help programs, the task force focused on two questions: (1) How can psychologists be encouraged to develop responsible self-help therapies? and (2) How can psychologists help to educate the public in the appropriate use of self-help materials? The following recommendations were made by the task force in response to these questions:

1. Formal guidelines for psychologists should be developed by the American Psychological Association, similar to the standards that guide developers of psychological tests (American Psychological Association, 1966). A set of guidelines could clarify the methodological and assessment issues that are pertinent to the adequate development of self-help therapies.

2. A standard set of information should accompany the instructional materials developed by professionals. For example, books can contain a fact sheet that explains the extent to which the program has been evaluated, the recommended uses of the program, the reading level of the instructions, and realistic expectations regarding treatment outcome.

3. Professionals should participate in developing a short pamphlet to educate the public in the use of self-help therapies. The aim of this pamphlet would be to place the consumer public in a more knowledgeable position with regard to the numerous self-help therapies now available. Realistic expectations in light of sensationalized claims could be discussed. The options of using self-help materials with or without therapist supervision could be considered. Also, reactions to failing at a self-help program and alternative follow-up plans could be considered.

Several additional suggestions were made by the task force. It was noted that the journal *Contemporary Psychology* could develop a special section on self-help books, with editorial guidelines helping to keep published reviews data-based (Rosen, 1978). The task force also recommended the development of sample contract clauses that could help psychologists during their negotiations with publishers.

The task force stressed that its focus on the problems of self-help had a positive intent. Psychologists were encouraged to develop, assess, and promote self-help therapies, for such therapies can be of tremendous benefit to the consumer public. To emphasize this point, the task force referred to a paper that Albert Ellis presented during a 1977 symposium on self-help therapies. In that paper, Ellis invited psychologists to "Imagine what a really great potential for improved human functioning a set of scientifically researched, written and periodically revised do-it-yourself materials would probably have."

It is too early to appraise the response of the American Psychological Association to recommendations made by the task force. Although psychologists have contributed to the development of self-help therapies, much remains to be done before the full potential of these therapies is realized.

References

American Psychological Association. *Standards for educational and psychological tests and manuals.* Washington, D.C.: Author, 1966.

American Psychological Association. *Ethical standards of psychologists.* Washington, D.C.: Author, 1977.

American Psychological Association. *Report of the task force on self-help psychotherapies.* Unpublished manuscript. Washington, D.C., 1978.

Altman, C. *Love making: You can be your own sex therapist.* New York: Berkeley Publishing, 1977.

Azrin, N. H., & Foxx, R. M. *Toilet training in less than a day.* New York: Simon and Schuster, 1974.

Barrera, M., Jr., & Rosen, G. M. Detrimental effects of a self-reward contracting program on subjects' involvement in self-administered desensitization. *Journal of Consulting and Clinical Psychology*, 1977, *45*, 1180–1181.

Barrera, M., Jr., Rosen, G. M., & Glasglow, R. E.Risks and responsibilities in the development and use of self-help psychotherapies. In J. T. Hannah, R. Clark, & P. Christian (Eds.), *Preservation of client rights.* Macmillan, Free Press, 1981.

Berne, E. *Games people play.* New York: Grove Press, Castle Books, 1964.

Brownell, K. D., Heckerman, C. L., Westlake, R. J., Hayes, S. C., & Monti, P. M. The effect of couples training and partner cooperativeness in the behavioral treatment of obesity. *Behavior Research and Therapy*, 1979.

Butler, J. R. The toilet training success of parents after reading *Toilet training in less than a day. Behavior Therapy*, 1976, *7*, 185–191.

Carnegie, D. *How to win friends and influence people.* New York, Simon & Schuster, 1936.

Clark, H. B., Greene, B. F., Macrae, J. W., McNees, M. P., Davis, J. L., & Risley, T. R. A parent advice package for family shoping trips: Development and evaluation. *Journal of Applied Behavior Analysis*, 1977, *10*, 605–624.

Cowles, E. S. *Don't be afraid!* New York: McGraw-Hill, 1941

Crane, A. M. *Right and wrong thinking and their results.* Boston: Lothrop, Lee, & Shepard, 1905.

Dumont, T. Q. *The art and science of personal magnetism.* Chicago: Advanced Thought Publishing, 1913.

Dyer, W. W. *Your erroneous zones.* New York: Avon, 1977.

Ellis, A. *Rational-emotive therapy and self-help therapy.* Paper presented at the 85th Annual Convention of the American Psychological Association, San Francisco, 1977.

Fensterheim, H., & Baer, J. *Stop running scared!* New York: Rawson Associates, 1977.

Frampton, M. *Overcoming agoraphobia: Coping with the world outside.* New York: St. Martin's, 1974.

Franks, C. M., & Wilson, G. T. *Annual Review of behavior therapy: theory and practice*, Volume 5. New York: Brunner/Mazel, 1978.

Glasgow, R. E., & Rosen, G. M. Behavioral bibliography: A review of self-help behavior therapy manuals. *Psychological Bulletin*, 1978, *85*, 1–23.

Glasgow, R. E., & Rosen, G. M. Self-help behavior therapy manuals: Recent developments and clinical usage. *Clinical Behavior Therapy Review*, 1982.

Goldiamond, I. Singling out behavior modification for legal regulation: Some effects on patient care, psychotherapy, and research in general. *Arizona Law Review*, 1975, *17*, 105–126.

Goldstein, A. J., & Chambless, D. L. A re-analysis of agoraphopbia. *Behavior Therapy*, 1978, *9*, 47–59.

Hafner, R. J. The husbands of agoraphobic women and their influence on treatment outcome. *British Journal of Psychiatry*, 1977, *131*, 289–294.

Hallam, R. S. Agoraphobia: A critical review of the concept. *British Journal of Psychiatry*, 1978, *133*, 314–319.

Kaplan, H. S., & Kohl, R. N. Adverse reactions to the treatment of sexual problems. *Psychosomatics*, 1972, *13*, 185–190.

Katz, A. H., & Bender, E. I., (Eds.). *The strength in us: Self-help groups in the modern world.* New York: New Viewpoints, 1976.

Kimmel, H. D. Review of *Toilet training in less than a day: How to do it. Journal of Behavior Therapy and Experimental Psychiatry.* 1974, *15*, 113–114.

Kirsch, I., & Henry, D. Self-desensitization and mediation in the reduction of public speaking anxiety. *Journal of Consulting and Clinical Psychology*, 1979, *47*, 536–541.

Kopel, S., & Arkowitz, H. The role of attribution and self-perception in behavior change: Implications for behavior therapy. *Genetic Psychology Monographs*, 1975, *92*, 175–212.

Lazarus, A. A. *In the mind's eye.* New York: Rawson, 1977.

Lichtenstein, E. Modification of smoking behavior: Good designs–Ineffective treatments. *Journal of Consulting and Clinical Psychology*, 1971, *36*, 163–166.

Lowe, J. C., & Mikulas, W. L. Use of written material in learning self-control of premature ejaculation. *Psychological Reports*, 1975, *37*, 295–298.

Mahoney, M. J. *Self-Change.* New York: W. W. Norton, 1979.

Mahoney, M. J., & Mahoney, K. *Permanent weight control.* New York: W. W. Norton, 1976.

Mahoney, M. J., & Thoresen, C. E. *Self-control: Power to the person.* Monterey, Calif.: Brooks-Cole, 1974.

Mathews, A., Teasdale, J., Munby, M., Johnston, D., & Shaw, P. A home-based treatment program for agoraphobia. *Behavior Therapy*, 1977, *8*, 915– 924.

Matson, J. L., & Ollendick, T. H. Issues in toilet training normal children. *Behavior Therapy*, 1977, *8*, 549–553.

McMahon, R. J., & Forehand, R. Self-help behavior therapies and parent training. In B. B. Lahey & A. E.Kazdin (Eds.), *Advances in clinical child psychology*, Vol. 3. New York: Plenum Press, 1979.

Milton, F., & Hafner, J. The outcome of behavior therapy for agoraphobia in relation to marital adjustment. *Archives of General Psychiatry*, 1979, *36*, 807–811.

Peale, N. V. *The power of positive thinking.* Englewood Cliffs, N.J.: Prentice-Hall, 1952.

Pion, R., & Hopkins, J. *The last sex manual.* New York: Wyden Books, 1977.

Rakos, R. F., & Schroeder, H. E. Development and empirical evaluation of a self-administered assertiveness training program. *Journal of Consulting and Clinical Psychology*, 1979, *47*, 991–993.

Ralph, J. *How to psychoanalyze yourself.* Long Beach, Calif.: Times Mirror Printing and Binding House, 1921.

Richey, C. A. *Relative effectiveness of a group training program to increase social interaction skills among shy women.* Unpublished manuscript, University of Washington, Seattle, 1978.

Rosen, G. M. The development and use of nonprescription behavior therapies. *American Psychologist*, 1976, *31*, 139–141. (a)

Rosen, G. M. *Don't be afraid: A program for overcoming your fears and phobias.* Englewood Cliffs, N.J.: Prentice-Hall, 1976. (b)

Rosen, G. M. Nonprescription behavior therapies and other self-help treatments: A reply to Goldiamond. *American Psychologist*, 1977, *32*, 178–179.

Rosen, G. M. Suggestions for an editorial policy on the review of self-help treatment books. *Behavior Therapy*, 1978, *9*, 960–972.

Rosen, G. M., Glasgow, R. E., & Barrera, M., Jr. A controlled study to assess the clinical efficacy of totally self-administered systematic desensitization. *Journal of Consulting and Clinical Psychology*, 1976, *44*, 208–217.

Rosen, G. M., & Orenstein, H. A historical note on thought-stopping. *Journal of Consulting and Clinical Psychology*, 1976, *44*, 1016–1017.

Rosen, G. M., Glasgow, R. E., & Barrera, M., Jr. A two-year follow-up on systematic desensitization with data pertaining to the external validity of laboratory fear assessment. *Journal of Consulting and Clinical Psychology*, 1977, *45*, 1188–1189.

Sackett, D. L., & Haynes, R. B. (Eds.).*Compliance with therapeutic regimens.* Baltimore: Johns Hopkins Press, 1976.

Schindler, F. *Behavior bibliotherapy: An evaluation of a self-help book.* Paper presented at the Annual Convention of the Western Psychological Association, San Diego, 1979.

Smiles, S. *Self-help.* Pioneer Press, 1889.

Strupp, H. *Nonprescription psychotherapies: Can we dispense with the therapist?* Paper presented at the 85th Annual Convention of the American Psychological Association, San Francisco, 1977.

Stuart, R. B., & Mitchell, C. A professional and a consumer perspective on self-help weight control groups. *Psychiatric Clinics of North America*, 1978, *1*, 697–711.

Stuart, R. S. *Behavioral self-management.* New York: Brunner/Mazel, 1977.

Sutherland, E. A., Amit, Z., & Weiner, A. *Phobia free: How to fight your fears.* New York: Jove Publications, 1977.

Weekes, C. *Simple, effective treatment of agoraphobia.* New York: Hawthorne Books, 1977.

Wright, J., Perreault, R., & Mathieu, M. The treatment of sexual dysfunction: A review. *Archives of General Psychiatry*, 1977, *34*, 881–890.

Zeiss, R. A. Self-directed treatment for premature ejaculation: Preliminary case reports. *Journal of Behavior Therapy and Experimental Psychiatry*, 1977, *8*, 87–91.

Zeiss, R. A. Self-directed treatment for premature ejaculation. *Journal of Consulting and Clinical Psychology*, 1978, *46*, 1234–1241.

Index